Repackaging the Beatles

a fan's look at the compilations, collections and remixes

Terry Wilson

Repackaging the Beatles: a fan's-eye take
on the compilations, box sets and remixes

by Terry Wilson

ISBN: 9798378052349 (print)

First edition, 2023

About the author

Terry Wilson was born in 1968, while Hey Jude was at number 1. He is a freelance writer and journalist, musician, record collector and long-standing Beatles fan. His previous books include the ground-breaking *Four Sides Of The Circle: The Beatles' Second Phase, 1970-1974* (2022) and *Tamla Motown: The Stories Behind The UK Singles* (2009). In addition he occasionally writes for music publications and runs several websites on various musical genres of personal interest. He lives in Sussex, England with his wife and son.

Contents

Introduction

Part One: The Vinyl Age

6

Part Two: The CD Age

Part Three: The Digital Age

Listings

Appendix – Worldwide

Introduction

Repackaging the Beatles. What does that mean?

Generally it means instances when the official labels have marketed, or otherwise made available, tracks recorded years earlier. Every compilation album, for example, gathering up previously released songs, is a work of repackaging, as is the latter-day trend of putting out albums of studio outtakes and hitherto unreleased recordings. These are the records, tapes, discs and downloads you will read about in this book.

What *isn't* covered? We don't discuss re-issues or re-pressings of records already out there. For example on the 50th anniversary of Love Me Do / PS I Love You, EMI released a replica pressing of the original red label single. Similarly on the 30th anniversary of *The White Album*, a CD edition appeared like a little copy of the double LP, complete with serial number on the front. These and countless others are not classed as repackagings, just re-releases, and so we overlook them all – which is just as well for the sake of the size of this volume.

There is an exception: re-issue box sets. Numerous times over the years, EMI has issued out the whole catalogue in a custom boxed edition, sometimes the LPs, sometimes the EPs, and sometimes the singles. (There are some lists towards the back of the book, which show them all in order.) The first was the 1976 *Singles Collection*, the last (at the time of writing) the 2019 equivalent, and in between are self-contained sets of the EPs on CD, the albums on cassette and so on. Provided they came as a single boxed product, which could be bought in one go, they are included here.

We had to make a decision on the so-called 'Super Deluxe' box sets which started with *Sgt Pepper* in 2017. These are really re-issues of specific albums, albeit containing new mixes, so wouldn't automatically qualify. But they also contain a good deal of studio outtake material not heard before, so they could. We decided to include them, but concentrate on the outtakes and extras, not dwelling too much on the albums themselves.

Except for the appendix section, which looks briefly at compilation LPs around the world, we stick to just the official UK and US product released through EMI, and latterly, Universal Music who now control the recordings. Therefore, we do not discuss the Hamburg tapes, nor the Decca tapes, nor Tony Sheridan or whatever other non-canon music is circulating. We don't discuss film or video, and there are no bootlegs either – just officially sanctioned recordings out of EMI.

The book is written informally, from one fan (me) to another (you). It's chatty, as if we were discussing the records over a beer (although I appreciate you can't answer back), but is also meant as a factual survey, with plenty of particulars and details you may not have known. A few times in the text you may notice me having a bit of a tease over how obsessive Beatles fans are, especially where mono vs stereo is concerned. This is meant in good spirit and hopefully will be taken that way. Rest assured, I'm a genuine Beatles fan and include myself in any mention of obsessiveness – as this book itself testifies.

The book is pitched on the assumption that if you bought it, you already know the basics about the group – so I will spare you from revelations like, 'The Beatles were a pop group from Liverpool, England'. For the same reason I don't tell you who Allen Klein is, and I don't need to inform you that Pete Best was sacked from the band and replaced by Ringo. If you don't know this already, you're probably picked up the wrong book, or a distant aunt has given it to you as a present. (But read it anyway!)

Why did we write this? Simply because these releases will all, to various people and for various reasons, bring back memories and connections on a personal level. This commentator, for example, found his 'in' to the world of the Beatles through *Love Songs* and *1962-1966*, and those comps will forever have a special significance. The trouble is, all too often these and other such collections are dismissed, and don't get the attention they deserve. So while this book isn't a love-in for the compilation album, it does shine a light on each and every one of them, noting where they succeed and where they don't – and some do come up short, let's be honest. Others are simply fantastic, and no Beatles fan should be without copies of the *Red* and *Blue Albums*, *Past Masters*, the 2009 mono CDs, and so on. They are landmark releases, and if you don't have at least one of the vinyl box sets in your collection, go and get one!

On this subject, you will note that each entry in this book is given a star rating. This is just for fun, and inevitably subjective – so if you think it daft that I rate *Love* so highly, or are enraged that *Rock 'N' Roll Music* only gets three stars – remember, that's just me. You may see things differently, and in fact probably will.

There seem to be three distinct eras in the world of Beatles repackaging, and so the book is sectioned into three parts, which we call the Vinyl Age, the CD Age and the Digital Age. These periods are so-named not just because of what was going on with the Beatles' catalogue, but also what was happening in the wider world of music. But for us, the story starts in 1966…

Part One – The Vinyl Age

When the Beatles were a current act, vinyl was pretty much the only format which mattered. Sure, their albums also appeared on reel tapes and towards the end of the 60s, cassette, but these were side issues in an era when the LP and 45 were king and queen of the airwaves. Eight-track cartridges also came along (and went again), but vinyl held its own until the second part of the 1980s when CD knocked it off its perch.

The first bit of Beatles repackaging was a 1966 collection of hits, and we end this period in 1986, just before the group made the leap to CD. (Although, ironically, the last compilation of the vinyl age was a cassette!)

A Collection of Beatles Oldies (1966)
Hey Jude (1970)
From Then To You / The Beatles Christmas Album (1970)
The Beatles 1962-1966 (1973)
The Beatles 1967-1970 (1973)
Yesterday / I Should Have Known Better (1976)
The Singles Collection 1962-1970 (1976)
Rock 'N' Roll Music (1976)
Got To Get You Into My Life / Helter Skelter (1976)
Back In The USSR / Twist And Shout (1976)
Ob-La-Di, Ob-La-Da / Julia (1976)
The Best Of George Harrison (1976)
The Beatles At The Hollywood Bowl (1977)
Love Songs (1977)
Girl / You're Going To Lose That Girl (1977, unreleased)
Sgt Pepper's Lonely Hearts Club Band-With A Little
    Help From My Friends / A Day In The Life (1978)
The Beatles Collection (1978)
Rarities [UK album] (1979)
Rarities [US album] (1980)
The Beatles Ballads (1980)
The Beatles Box (1980)

The Beatles EPs Collection (1981)

'The Inner Light' EP (1981)

Reel Music (1982)

The Beatles' Movie Medley / I'm Happy Just To Dance With You (1982)

The Beatles: The Collection (1982)

The Beatles Mono Collection (1982)

20 Greatest Hits (1982)

The Beatles Singles Collection (1982)

Their Greatest Hits (1984)

The History Of Rock Volume Twenty Six (1984)

Sessions (1985, unreleased)

Leave My Kitten Alone / Ob-La-Di, Ob-La-Da (1985, unreleased)

Only The Beatles… (1986)

The doomed album

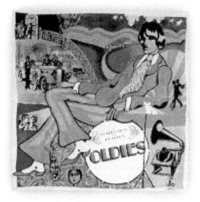

A Collection of Beatles Oldies
★★★★☆

UK release:
10 December 1966

She Loves You	Can't Buy Me Love
From Me To You	Bad Boy
We Can Work It Out	Day Tripper
Help!	A Hard Day's Night
Michelle	Ticket To Ride
Yesterday	Paperback Writer
I Feel Fine	Eleanor Rigby
Yellow Submarine	I Want To Hold Your Hand

Where had the Beatles gone? It was a question on the mind of most fans in the second part of 1966, the group having more or less disappeared since their last public performance on 29 August – and that was in the States; in the UK they hadn't played a gig since May, an extraordinarily long time ago. Scraps of information are trickling out – Paul's gone on safari in Kenya, George is in India somewhere, Ringo's on his holidays. It seemed none of the Beatles were even in the country, much less in the recording studio. They were like a sports team who'd given up arranging any more matches – nowhere to be seen. And the situation was becoming newsworthy. Brian Epstein was called on by the press to deny the Beatles had broken up, while *Beatles Monthly* magazine, a hotline from the group to its most loyal fans, began its December editorial with the observation, "It's quite possible that for the past couple of months you have felt that the Beatles had ceased to exist."

Britain's Independent Television News (ITN) grasped the nettle, turning up at Abbey Road just before Christmas to accost the group members as they reported once again for duty – and they were chasing only one headline:

> **Interviewer**: Are the Beatles going to go their own ways in 1967, do you think?
> **John**: They could be, you know, on our own or together.

> **Interviewer**: Could you ever see a time when, in fact, you weren't working together?
> **John**: I could see us working not together for a period but we'd always get together for one reason or another.

> **Interviewer**: I just want to ask you, do you think that in the New Year you're going to be going your own ways instead of being a group?
> **George**: No. No.

> **Interviewer**: 'No'?
> **George**: Definitely not.

> **Interviewer**: Do you foresee a time when, in fact, The Beatles won't be together and that you'll all be on your own?
> **Ringo**: No.

> **Interviewer**: Have you got tired of each other?
> **Ringo**: No.

> **Interviewer**: Are you getting bored with being The Beatles after all this time?
> **Ringo**: No, I'm having a great time.

The fact was, the group had released nothing since *Revolver* at the start of August. Since their break-through they'd put out two studio albums every calendar year, always having one ready for the lucrative Christmas season – in 1963 it was *With The Beatles* (released 22 November); in 1964, *Beatles For Sale* (4 December); and in 1965, *Rubber Soul* (3 December). These albums took time to prepare, writing and recording to be followed by the usual editing, mixing and packaging ahead of their release date. But by

November 1966 they still had nothing in the pipeline – John had been shooting a movie in Spain since mid-September, and Paul was about to start work on a film soundtrack. They simply didn't have time in their schedules to be Beatles.

The greatest hits package is as old as the hills, but in 1966 the format started gaining serious traction. The Rolling Stones had received the compilers' treatment earlier in the year with their *Big Hits (High Tide And Green Grass)*, about to get its UK release in the festive run-up, while similar collections were starting to stack up in the higher end of the UK album chart – the top 10 listing published on 20 November had *Well Respected Kinks* at number 10, *Best Of Jim Reeves* at 9, the Stones' album at 5 (one place above *Revolver*), *Dusty Springfield Golden Hits* at 4, and just one place off the top, *Best Of The Beach Boys*. For EMI the solution to the Beatles' lack of yuletide product wasn't rocket science.

It was Head of Marketing, Roy Featherstone, who proposed the creation of the Beatles' compilation, believing – not unreasonably – that next to Jim Reeves or Dusty, he could create a product with enough commercial clout to wipe the floor with the competition. The Beatles had more million sellers than they could count, and bringing them together on one glorious package should have resulted in the best-ever best-of. Since Please Please Me back at the start of 1963, the Beatles' next 11 singles had all been UK number 1, two of them as double A-sides, meaning 13 chart-topping recordings. That was almost enough for an album of pure number 1s, to which was added a couple of Paul's ballads in Michelle (number 1 earlier in 1966 in the hands of former folkies, the Overlanders) and Yesterday (not a single in Britain but a month-long number 1 in America, on its way to becoming the most-recorded song in history). One more would make 16 – and it so happened that consequent of Capitol's release jiggery-pokery over the preceding years, there was one Beatles track issued in the States but still unavailable to UK buyers, which would make for an enticing bonus: Bad Boy, a rocking cover version which had so far turned up only on *Beatles VI*. So what could go wrong?

Actually, plenty, and the wheels started to come loose as soon as the project got underway. The first thing to note was that back in the day, singles were only issued in mono, and of the 16 tracks listed for inclusion, seven were as-yet not available in LP-friendly stereo mixes, something which would require the immediate attention of George Martin. His efforts to create stereo mixes kept falling down – it transpired that She Loves You would have to be faked, since the stereo tapes had been recorded over, and further mixing dates were arranged as they kept running out of time. Then as late as 10 November, Geoff Emerick was instructed to make a stereo mix of Bad Boy, only for the message to get lost in translation resulting in a pointless remix of This Boy instead, forcing EMI to use the unfavoured US stereo mix of Bad Boy on the LP.

Further problems would soon arise, perhaps the most damning that the Beatles, once they got wind of the project, declared themselves set against it. And Capitol in America were also unimpressed, announcing they weren't going to release it there, despite being empty-handed themselves when it came to Christmas. Perhaps as a by-product of the Beatles' own resistance to the album, it suffered scant promotion, none of them willing to put in a word for it, even *Beatles Monthly*, which might have trumpeted it on behalf of the group, mentioning it just once in a small notice somewhere in the back half of issue 41 under the deceptively optimistic headline, 'Best collection ever'.

The fact is, the record was doomed before it hit the shops. For one thing it was facing stiff competition from *Revolver* which was still doing healthy business in the top 10 when *A Collection Of Beatles Oldies* was issued. But perhaps its biggest problem was its odd title – a wholly unnecessary characterisation of the album as something past its sell-by date. In 1966, the last thing pop fans wanted was a relic from the olden days, and in point of fact, five of the featured tracks were first released less than a year before. The entirely misleading album name can have done nothing but hammer home the fact that fans had heard it all before (Bad Boy notwithstanding) when they might have bigged up its spectacular contents with something like *The Beatles Number 1s* or *The Beatles' Greatest Hits*. Calling it *Oldies (...But Goldies)* ensured it disappeared up its own existence.

The best-remembered part of the album is its striking cover, a dazzling colourful pop-art painting commissioned by Brian Epstein, which tapped into the current vogue for Edwardian fashion pastiches. (Its cartoon quality has more than a hint of the later *Yellow Submarine* about it, the titular song of which appears here, particularly with the inclusion of a vintage limousine, which reminds us of early scenes from the film. The coincidence may be more than that.) But what of the commissioned artist? The album cover names him as David Christian, but latter-day efforts to track him down have proved fruitless. What else he did, and what became of him, remains frustratingly elusive, even the 2003 auction at Sotheby's of album cover proofs signed by the mysterious Christian shedding no further light.

The back cover too has a little story to tell. Unlike the front, it features a photograph of the group, albeit with their guard down, relaxing at the Tokyo Hilton hotel where they stayed for a few days as June turned into July 1966. Whether by accident or design, Robert Whittaker's image was flipped left-to-right, giving the Beatles' faces a slightly odd appearance but not enough for anyone to really notice. Until, that is, the album made its way to Odeon in Japan, who spotted at once that the design on Paul's Kimono was back-to-front (it shows the Kotobuki symbol of Japanese folklore), prompting them to correct the photo's orientation.

UK   *Japan*

A Collection Of Beatles Oldies was the group's eighth EMI album. Every one of its predecessors had topped the chart, but this cursed release limped only to number 7, despite its mighty track listing. Its fate since has lent to the idea that EMI wished they'd never released it, the record having been more or less disowned since its first appearance. It stayed in print through the 1970s, and when issued on the cassette format in 1972, it even popped back into the top 40 albums for a week, proving that nothing is Beatle-proof. But when *The Beatles 1962-1966* came out in 1973, *Oldies* became obsolete, all of its titles bar Bad Boy appearing on this vastly more successful successor. (Bad Boy itself had further album treatment as the decade went on, making *Oldies* completely dispensable.) In 1983, EMI couldn't bear to delete it, but did the next-best thing and transferred it to its budget Fame label, consigning it to the bargain bins before pimping it out – twice – in 1984 to other companies (see pages 102-105). It got its last rites in 1987 when the Beatles' catalogue made the move to CD, a fresh compilation, *Past Masters*, mopping up everything not in the main album run. *Oldies* was officially redundant and faced the inevitable axe, never to be mentioned again.

Time has been good to the album. Looking back now, it survives as a reminder of the group's halcyon days, its 13 (!) number 1 tracks perfectly summarising the Beatles' touring years, Beatlemania defined on one 12-inch disc. Its cover art too is semi-iconic, ushering in the psychedelic feel of 1967 half a year ahead of *Sgt Pepper*. It's a record which benefits from hindsight; with this album, context is everything.

Capitolizing

Hey Jude
★★★☆☆

**US release:
26 February 1970**

Can't Buy Me Love	Hey Jude
I Should Have Known Better	Old Brown Shoe
Paperback Writer	Don't Let Me Down
Rain	The Ballad Of John And Yoko
Lady Madonna	
Revolution	

In the 1960s the Beatles viewed the relentless recycling of their recordings by Capitol USA with a mixture of curiosity and annoyance. While seven core albums flowed out of the UK between 1963 and 1966, the American market was serviced by 11 (or more, depending how one chooses to count), the trick effected by leaving off tracks which could later be rounded up and put back together with singles and other leftovers. Thus, for example, there was both *Beatles '65* and *Beatles VI* in place of *Beatles For Sale*, Capitol's cutting and pasting eking out the material.

While no-one particularly objected the revenue these creative re-assemblages were generating, there was a sense that Capitol was cheapening the group – something which became more problematic in 1965 when the US released an album sharing its cover and title with a *different* UK LP. (*Rubber Soul* appeared Stateside with four of the tracks held back, and with a couple of older recordings added to stretch over 12 inches.) It's often supposed that the infamous 'Butcher Cover' which adorned original copies of *Yesterday... And Today* (containing the four remaindered *Rubber Soul* cuts alongside a few singles and three advance recordings from *Revolver*), was contrived by the group to protest against Capitol's 'butchering' of their albums.

After *Revolver* appeared in America with only two of John's five songs on, something had to give and so from *Sgt Pepper* onwards, the two release schedules were brought essentially into line – Capitol only deviating from there in issuing *Magical Mystery Tour* as an LP, rounding up the UK double EP tracks plus the group's previous three singles – and so through the pleasantries of the following *White Album*, *Yellow Submarine* and *Abbey Road*, they quietly towed the line.

Then Allen Klein weighed in.

When he first became involved with the Beatles in early 1969, Klein's main sales pitch was that if they let him, he could get them much better royalty deals. Three quarters of the group was convinced and all four signed the paperwork, and so it was with authority that Klein set about getting Capitol to issue an extra Beatles album at the start of 1970. Duties were delegated to Klein's right-hand man, Allan Steckler, whose principle role was to come up with a track listing to include only songs not on existing Capitol albums. But where this new set would differ from previous releases was that it would contain nothing new, nothing not already in the hands of US fans – in other words, while Capitol could always argue its earlier product (including *Magical Mystery Tour*) made for a bona-fide group discography, this was to be a standard compilation album including in the main, non-album singles already in circulation – something unashamedly flagged by its title, *The Beatles Again*.

These are the recent singles Steckler had at his disposal:

> Lady Madonna / The Inner Light
> Hey Jude / Revolution
> Get Back / Don't Let Me Down
> The Ballad Of John And Yoko / Old Brown Shoe

It's curious that of these eight non-album tracks, he entirely ignored The Inner Light. It's also strange that in the case of Get Back, he passed it by while using its B-side instead. (Did he know that Get Back would soon appear on *Let It Be*, while Don't Let Me Down would not?) This meant six songs for his list, one of them (Hey Jude) long enough to count as two. So what else was up for grabs?

These were suitable but were probably never contenders:

> Love Me Do (*rare UK single version featuring Ringo on drums*)
> From Me To You (*previously available only on a Vee-Jay album*)
> Misery (*previously available only on Vee-Jay albums*)
> There's A Place (*previously available only on Vee-Jay albums*)
> Sie Liebt Dich (*probably better left off*)
> A Hard Day's Night (*previously only on a United Artists label LP*)

These were more viable, and all still unavailable on US LPs:

> I'm Down
> Can't Buy Me Love
> I Should Have Known Better
> Paperback Writer
> Rain

Steckler made his choices. Paperback Writer and Rain were in – good decision. Can't Buy Me Love and I Should Have Known Better were in – dubious chronologically, especially in the absence of The Inner Light, but fair enough. I'm Down was out, unloved and unwanted, despite the resultant LP running to a mere ten songs covering 32 and a half minutes. (Why not just throw them all in?)

As with Britain's *A Collection Of Beatles Oldies*, the mono singles would now be appearing in stereo for the first time. The task came back to London of course, and to George Martin and his crew, who prepared mixes of five tracks, sent over to the States along with existing stereo copies of the two oldest selections, Can't Buy Me Love and I Should Have Known Better.

Sequenced in chronological order, *The Beatles Again* was to be housed in a picture cover containing shots from the group's last photo shoot on 22 August 1969. (The front cover was technically a composite of two separate photos, one showing the group hiding among John's weeping atlas cedars, collaged above the door in the main image.) The album was set to retail at the standard $6.98 and all looked set to go, until a late intervention saw the title changed to *Hey Jude* (to plug the inclusion of the spectacularly popular song) and the price dropped to a more attractive $5.98. So late were these decisions that first editions still show *The Beatles Again* printed on the record labels.

When the newly re-christened *Hey Jude* hit the stores on 26 February 1970, *Abbey Road* was still number 2 on *Billboard*, raising the question of whether this collection of already-released material was premature. And for added hindrance in the market place, the next 12 weeks would see the release of new albums by Paul, Ringo and the Beatles (Again) with *Let It Be*, saturating the market. Yet in mid-March it climbed as high as 3 in the listing (ahead of *Abbey Road* which slipped down to 6), and rose from there to number 2 where, for a solid month, it was deprived of top place only by *Bridge Over Troubled Water*.

Hey Jude ended up selling millions all over the world, yet on the British side of the pond, Apple didn't bother with it, despite manufacturing copies for export to various Commonwealth countries. (Tit-for-tat for Capitol's snub of *A Collection Of Beatles Oldies*?) In May 1979 EMI-London quietly gave it a release on the Parlophone label, yet not even the inclusion of four UK number 1 hits in the track listing was enough to get it into the British charts at that late stage, and like *Oldies*, it's been largely forgotten about.

For all its quirks, it remains a strong collection which, for the most part, rounds up the Apple-era 45s. Shame.

The ghost of Christmas past

From Then To You / The Beatles Christmas Album
★★☆☆☆

UK release: 18 December 1970
US release: 14 February 1971

1963: The Beatles Christmas Record
1964: Another Beatles Christmas Record
1965: The Beatles Third Christmas Record
1966: Pantomime: Everywhere It's Christmas
1967: Christmas Time Is Here Again!
1968: The Beatles 1968 Christmas Record
1969: The Beatles Seventh Christmas Record

What was John Lennon's last recording for the Beatles? Overdubs on Oh! Darling? Nope. The final session for I Want You (She's So Heavy)? Nope. It was in fact his contribution to *The Beatles' Seventh Christmas Record*, recorded some weeks after he'd quit the group in the second half of 1969, and taped long after *Abbey Road* was out. That seventh record was the last in an annual series of yuletide freebies distributed to members of the group's official fan club on flexi-disc. They started out in 1963 with relatively simple recorded greetings and thank-yous to the fan-base but over the years morphed into something more abstract, with random chatter, occasional comedy sketches, poems, even bits of otherwise unheard compositions – you name it, the Christmas flexis could accommodate it. And the sleeve designs too, free from EMI's conservative control, were devised by the group themselves and were often strikingly adventurous, way ahead of some of their official record covers. (The seventh one, issued in December 1969, had no text on the front, just an avant-garde photograph of what looked like close-up particles in motion, five months before *Let It Be* with its dull head shots and straight lines.)

By Christmas 1970, the group was no more. The fan club's magazine, *Beatles Monthly*, had folded in December of the previous year but the club itself was still going (it finally closed on 31 March 1972 despite still having 11,000 members) and so in 1970, was able to issue out not just a flexi-disc, but a whole vinyl LP, free and pressed on the Apple label. It didn't contain new recordings, of course, but compiled all seven of the earlier flexis onto a single disc, their combined running time around 44 minutes – perfect. And since it was official Apple product it's fair to assume the individual Beatles still held the fan club close to their hearts, for it was they who must have approved it at their own expense.

As mentioned above, the contents of these seven recordings are erratic and at times bizarre. John's punning story of two balloons name Jock and Yono is memorable, while the 1966 Goons-like 'pantomime' recording is curiously entertaining. But perhaps the most interesting parts of the collection are the musical bits and pieces not otherwise known. Chief among them was the full-on group recording, Christmas Time (Is Here Again), included on the 1967 flexi, where it was presented in several sections. (The whole, uninterrupted song was finally made available on the back of Free As A Bird in 1996, credited to Lennon-McCartney-Harrison-Starr.) But there are a few others too, including:

Please Don't Bring Your Banjo Back (1966)
> Possibly improvised, this 40-second ditty is led by Paul on piano while the others join in. Not much to get excited about.

Plenty Of Jam Jars (1967)

A 37-second group singalong with George at the helm, backed by what sounds like a pub piano.

Happy Christmas, Happy New Year (1968)

Paul on his acoustic, singing a pleasant greeting song, pitched somewhat in the style of Mother Nature's Son. About a minute's worth.

Good Evening To You Gentlemen (1969)

Ringo, on guitar (!). Presumably made up as he went, it lasts all of 20 seconds.

Merry, Merry Christmas (1969)

Paul on acoustic, similar to his previous year's effort. There's more than a minute's worth, with a short interruption in the middle.

Happy Christmas (1969)

This time it's John and Yoko singing along to the guitar. It's bizarre and unpredictable in their usual manner, and endures for a minute before abruptly ending on a tape edit. Then it returns, even stranger than before for another minute or so!

The Christmas recordings were really only for fun but appreciated by British fans, whose original flexis have now become quite valuable. In America things were rather different. Fans there only received the last two flexis, whereas in previous years they'd been sent postcards or similar, a couple of which had audio grooves embossed into them, although in 1965 they got nothing at all. It was particularly pleasing then when Capitol re-issued *From Then To You* and had it sent to US fans in the spring of 1971. This edition boasted superior cover art showing the Beatles' faces changing over the years, and was re-titled *The Beatles Christmas Album* – a much better choice.

Like the original flexis, these two vinyl LPs are much sought after and the number of genuine copies is dwarfed by the quantity of pirate reproductions in circulation, a situation fuelled by the fact that it was never possible to obtain the real deal from shops. A re-issue project in 2017 finally saw the recordings placed on general sale (see relevant entry in this book, page 223).

The Red Album

The Beatles 1962-1966
★★★★★

UK release:
20 April 1973

US release:
2 April 1973

Love Me Do	Help!
Please Please Me	You've Got To Hide Your Love Away
From Me To You	We Can Work It Out
She Loves You	Day Tripper
I Want To Hold Your Hand	Drive My Car
All My Loving	Norwegian Wood (This Bird Has
Can't Buy Me Love	Flown)
A Hard Day's Night	Nowhere Man
And I Love Her	Michelle
Eight Days A Week	In My Life
I Feel Fine	Girl
Ticket To Ride	Paperback Writer
Yesterday	Eleanor Rigby
	Yellow Submarine

"RRP has gathered 60 of their finest songs onto four LP records, cassettes and eight-track tapes for only $13.98! You get such Beatle greats as I Want To Hold Your Hand, A Hard Day's Night, Bangla-Desh… This is an album that you'll want to keep and it will surely grow more and more valuable in years to come! Send $13.98 to Beatles, box 377, Seymour, Connecticut. Specify cartridges, cassettes or records. Money-back guaranteed by Electro Sound Dup Incorporated."

Late in 1972, the above sales pitch blasted frantically out of America's transistor radios and TV sets, imploring the audience to send in their money. In return they were being offered a box of records – four of them – collectively named *Alpha-Omega* and containing a slew of Beatles tracks. And not just that – solo Beatles tracks as well, including a live version of Bangla-Desh, Paul's Uncle Albert-Admiral Halsey, John's Imagine and Paul's Maybe I'm Amazed – intermingled with 56 standard group recordings sequenced in roughly alphabetical order (hence its title – the Greek equivalent of *A To Z*). And who were RRP and Electro Sound Dup when they were at home? Bootleggers, that's who – and advertising on TV! The cheek of it.

Actually, the situation wasn't quite so clear-cut. At the time, American copyright laws varied widely from state to state, and in New Jersey, where the firm Audio Tape Incorporated was based, restrictions were fairly slack. Audio Tape were behind *Alpha-Omega* and reckoned that if they sold their package by mail order out of New Jersey, and were not in direct competition with any official Capitol product, they'd fall just the right side of the law – and so they brazenly promoted *Alpha-Omega* in the broadcast media, attracting any number of sales, a full tally of which was never known.

Allen Klein disagreed with their interpretation of the law and in February 1973, took the matter to court – with the desired effect that *Alpha-Omega* disappeared from the market. A recent law change meant that such shenanigans would certainly be illegal if Capitol-EMI had a similar package of their own on sale, and in order to prevent any such repeat an official four-disc greatest hits collection of hits was swiftly prepared. Cue, *The Beatles 1962-1966* and *1967-1970*.

The package drew directly from the *Alpha-Omega* model, to consist of four full LPs, although without the contentious solo material. Allen Klein had abdicated the job of track selection to one of his ABKCO staffers, the group members showing no interest. The resultant contents ignored cover versions of the calibre of Twist And Shout or Dizzy Miss Lizzy, and presented what was, in the case of instalment 1 (AKA *The Red Album*), purely Lennon-McCartney material with not even a token nod to a certain George Harrison.

Of the 26 tracks, 19 were repeats from *Alpha-Omega*, but the songs largely chose themselves anyway, based on the singles releases and hits achieved in the group's touring years. All 15 of the UK A-sides were selected, 13 of which had topped the charts (and so in the process, *1962-1966* made *A Collection Of Beatles Oldies* virtually redundant). Added to these were the US number 1s, Eight Days A Week and Yesterday, leaving room for just nine album tracks from an available stock of seven UK albums. Not much space to work with.

And here is where things get odd. Whoever was behind the song choices was clearly a fan of *Rubber Soul*, especially it seems, the UK version, since he selected no fewer than six tracks from that album alone! All of which would be fine except for the fact that it left little or no room elsewhere, and almost half the double LP was thereby accounted for by 1965 releases. Thus the group's debut album was shunned – no I Saw Her Standing There or Do You Want To Know A Secret, and even the landmark *Revolver* album had nothing bar its trailer single – no space for Got To Get You Into My Life, for example, or For No One. The selections were, to say the least, lopsided.

Since the package was conceived in the States, its fair to say the Capitol-Apple edition is the definitive one, as compared to the Parlophone-Apple version which came out in the UK. While the London operation assembled the tracks directly from their Abbey Road tapes (with an air of superiority in that they had the 'proper' mixes, don't you know), Capitol did it their way by including the so-called 'Dexterized' versions of tracks like I Feel Fine and Day Tripper – and in the case of Help!, the original US edit with its instrumental 'James Bond intro', pulled straight from the eponymous 1965 album. Differences between the UK and US versions don't end there, and Beatle fans with a penchant for such minutiae will find their curiosity (if not their ears) amply rewarded by some internet searching. For Brits, who absorbed *1962-1966* into their DNA in 1973, a first hearing of the US edition is, to say the least, interesting. (And, one presumes, the converse is true.)

But *1962-1966* is only half the story of course. Read on...

The Blue Album

The Beatles 1967-1970
★★★★★

UK release:
20 April 1973

US release:
2 April 1973

Strawberry Fields Forever
Penny Lane
Sgt Pepper's Lonely Hearts
　　　Club Band
With A Little Help From My
　　　Friends
Lucy In The Sky With Diamonds
A Day In The Life
All You Need Is Love

I Am The Walrus
Hello, Goodbye
The Fool On The Hill
Magical Mystery Tour
Lady Madonna
Hey Jude
Revolution

Back In The USSR
While My Guitar Gently Weeps
Ob-La-Di, Ob-La-Da
Get Back
Don't Let Me Down
The Ballad Of John And Yoko
Old Brown Shoe

Here Comes The Sun
Come Together
Something
Octopus's Garden
Let It Be
Across The Universe
The Long And Winding Road

"Now available, the only authorised collection of the Beatles. The first two-record set encompasses the Beatles 1962 through 1966. The second two-record set continues with the Beatles 1967 through 1970. These incredible collections totalling 54 tunes have been selected by the Beatles, available only on Apple Records and Tapes."

That's better (if factually challenged – the Beatles had nothing to do with the track selections), television ads now trumpeting the arrival of the two double albums. This partner set (released simultaneously but usually thought of as the second of the two) contained another 28 original tracks, and is ultimately a more balanced affair than *1962-1966* with a solid range of album cuts across their later years – although one could still quibble over *Pepper* enjoying five selections from its 13 tracks while *The White Album* had only three from 30 – and wonder why Old Brown Shoe made the album while Blackbird, or Dear Prudence did not. But in the end, fans can only marvel at the sustained quality of the music, four sides here not really enough to contain the best of the Beatles at their peak.

Since the album grew out of the *Alpha-Omega* release, its worth noting that 17 of the selections are repeaters, but again, most of them were automatic choices including all the group's singles during the period, each of which was a major hit in its day. And George now gets his dues with no fewer than four cuts – and even Ringo gets in on the act, with his very own Octopus's Garden. Another point of note is that Dave Dexter Jr hung up his Beatle boots in 1966, so although the UK and US versions of *1967-1970* are different again, there's no 'Dexterization' on the American pressing, variance between the two sets consequently being much less.

The cover art for these two double sets is also striking. Readers may know that when the Beatles were planning their ill-fated *Get Back* album, John Lennon had the idea that they go back to the stairwell at EMI's Manchester Square building and recreate the cover of their very first album, *Please Please Me*, looking down over the edge of the staircase with their beards and extravagant locks. It was a great idea and should have been used for *Let It Be* – but for some reason, wasn't. But *Let It Be*'s loss is this collection's gain, and Capitol were able to find an alternative shot from the 1963 photo shoot for the front of the red collection, and put the 1969 re-creation on the blue. Nice. (Inside the gatefold, although fans knew nothing about it at the time, was a photo from the 'Mad Day Out' in 1968. When further images came to light years later, it emerged Yoko was there too in among the throng, although she's gone from the photo used on the album.)

These two collections, with number 1s coming out of their ears, could hardly fail to sell, and despite the abnormally high retail price for the pair, they were spectacular successes. Chart stats are slightly anomalous – *1962-1966* only made it to 3 on *Billboard*, but ahead of it was *1967-1970* which made the top, before Paul's *Red Rose Speedway* bumped it down again. In Britain they were 3 and 2 respectively, but their wider success is measured by their longevity. Continuing to sell for generations to come, they were re-issued on their appropriate colour of vinyl in 1978 and when CDs rolled around they were re-issued again on the new format, receiving a love from EMI which the group's other compilations never enjoyed. After the Beatles' core catalogue was remastered in 2009 they were issued once again, re-compiled from the new mixes – and affection in the eyes of fans has seldom dimmed. *The Red Album*, and *The Blue Album* – perfect and patriotic after *The White Album*.

In retrospect

Yesterday /
I Should Have Known Better
★★★☆☆

UK release:
6 March 1976

When Allen Klein renegotiated the Beatles' deal with EMI in 1969, one of the concessions he won was that the group would have control of its own output, and not be subject to unwanted commercial exploitation. Thus, only the Klein-sanctioned *Hey Jude* and the *Red* and *Blue Albums* had been released since, EMI having their hands tied for the lifespan of the contract. It expired in January 1976…

With the shackles now off, EMI would waste little time in making '76 a bonanza year for Beatles product, the first fruit of which was this 'new' single consisting of two tracks recorded more than a decade earlier, and issued exclusively now in the UK. The choice of A-side was astute, Yesterday a US number 1 in 1965, and holding the record as the most recorded song in pop history, but amazingly never previously issued on a UK single.

Pulled from *Help!*, it was coupled up with I Should Have Known Better from *A Hard Day's Night* to make a curious film-related double-header, years ahead of *Reel Music*. The selections certainly paid off since the single, the Beatles' first in six years, leaped into the top 10, scoring as high as 8 in the spring. Clearly there was still a market for Beatles singles…

Sea of green

The Singles Collection 1962-1970
★★★★☆

UK release:
6 March 1976

Love Me Do / PS I Love You
Please Please Me / Ask Me Why
From Me To You / Thank You Girl
She Loves You / I'll Get You
I Want To Hold Your Hand / This Boy
Can't Buy Me Love / You Can't Do That
A Hard Day's Night / Things We Said Today
I Feel Fine / She's A Woman
Ticket To Ride / Yes It Is
Help! / I'm Down
We Can Work It Out / Day Tripper
Paperback Writer / Rain
Eleanor Rigby / Yellow Submarine
Strawberry Fields Forever / Penny Lane
All You Need Is Love / Baby, You're A Rich Man
Hello, Goodbye / I Am The Walrus
Lady Madonna / The Inner Light
Hey Jude / Revolution
Get Back / Don't Let Me Down
The Ballad Of John And Yoko / Old Brown Shoe
Something / Come Together
Let It Be / You Know My Name (Look Up The Number)
Yesterday / I Should Have Known Better

Subsequently added to this set:

Back In The USSR / Twist And Shout
Sgt Pepper's Lonely Hearts Club Band-With A Little Help From My
  Friends / A Day In The Life

The wholesale re-issue of the Beatles' singles catalogue was undertaken in March of 1976, and not just in Britain – all corners of the earth were flooded with new editions of the original 45s. Some of the consequent collections are fascinating to look back on from a collector's point of view:

- France had *The Beatles Oldies But Goldies* set, star-lined picture sleeves produced to house some 36 different singles.
- West Germany had its black-fronted set, *Beatles Come Back!*, encompassing 28 different singles releases.
- Italy embarked on its celebrated *The Greatest Story* collection, carrying the *1967-1970* imagery on the front and accounting for 36 discs, pressed variously on Apple and Parlophone.
- USA, which had transferred its singles catalogue onto Apple in 1971, swapped the lot over to Capitol, including the five dating from 1968 to 1970, which had never previously appeared on the label.
- Canada saw the release of *Beatles Forever* – a run of 24 singles with a bizarre collage on the front.
- Spain had *The Singles Collection 1962/1970* comprising 21 re-issues in 21 different picture sleeves.
- Japan (who had to wait until 1977) put out the *15th Anniversary Of Their Debut* series, 33 singles in red and white-lined picture covers.

These re-issue series are all well and good, but it's the UK collection, not least because it was issued as a box-set, which interests us here.

Initially the idea was to just issue out the singles individually, and for this purpose a new set of picture covers was devised consisting of generic bright green card fronts and any one of four colour photos on the back. The set was well-promoted and purchasers of all the discs could get a special cardboard box to keep them in, at least two different designs of which were produced. And along with the basic set of 22 singles was the new one, Yesterday / I Should Have Known Better. EMI's marketing blitz worked, and by April, five of the re-issues joined Yesterday in the UK top 40, Hey Jude rising as high as 12. In fact all 23 made the top 100, and so it was clear that fans wanted them *all*, not just their personal favourites.

All 23 singles appeared in the UK top 100 on 4 April 1976. These weren't necessarily the highest positions they would reach, but the feat of having 23 on chart on a single week was listed in the *Guinness Book Of Records*.

    10 – Yesterday
    45 – Hey Jude
    46 – Paperback Writer
    53 – Strawberry Fields Forever / Penny Lane
    55 – Get Back
    59 – She Loves You
    61 – Help!
    62 – Love Me Do
    63 – Eleanor Rigby / Yellow Submarine
    64 – Let It Be
    66 – A Hard Day's Night
    68 – Can't Buy Me Love
    69 – I Want To Hold Your Hand
    71 – All You Need Is Love
    72 – From Me To You
    74 – Hello, Goodbye
    75 – Please Please Me
    76 – Lady Madonna
    79 – We Can Work It Out / Day Tripper
    81 – I Feel Fine
    83 – Ticket To Ride
    84 – Something / Come Together
    88 – The Ballad Of John And Yoko

And so a proper commercial box set was organised to encompass the full run, issued in a sturdy black case and sold by mail order through EMI's World Records division in 1977. By then, EMI had also issued another 'new' single, namely Back In The USSR / Twist And Shout. And so this was thrown in as well, purchasers of the now incongruously titled *Singles Collection 1962-1970* finding 24 discs inside the box. Sadly, Back In The

USSR had polled 11 places fewer than Yesterday earlier that year, a law of diminishing returns now setting in – confirmed in 1978 when EMI opted to issue Sgt Pepper's Lonely Hearts Club Band-With A Little Help From My Friends which ignominiously scraped to number 63, the worst they'd managed – ever. Nevertheless, that single too was lumped into the box (EMI presumably had plenty of spare copies!) and so editions from 1978 onwards carried 25 records.

Diminishing returns or not, the game was now on – fans could expect an avalanche of Beatles repackages in the coming few years.

The Beatles Singles 1962-1970

Contains extracts from:

Love Me Do
She Loves You
Can't Buy Me Love
A Hard Day's Night
Yesterday

Manufactured in support of the singles box, this flexi-disc runs for three and a half minutes and contains narration giving a superficial overview of the group's career, plus brief excerpts from five songs. Curiously they are all from the period to 1965, despite the fact that the box itself is titled *1962-1970*, as stated on the central 'label' of the flexi-disc.

The swinging fifties

Rock 'N' Roll Music
★★★☆☆

UK release:
11 June 1976

US release:
7 June 1976

Twist And Shout
I Saw Her Standing There
You Can't Do That
I Wanna Be Your Man
I Call Your Name
Boys
Long Tall Sally

Rock And Roll Music
Slow Down
Kansas City
Money (That's What I Want)
Bad Boy
Matchbox
Roll Over Beethoven

Dizzy Miss Lizzy
Any Time At All
Drive My Car
Everybody's Trying To Be My Baby
The Night Before
I'm Down
Revolution

Back In The USSR
Helter Skelter
Taxman
Got To Get You Into My Life
Hey Bulldog
Birthday
Get Back

It's curious looking back, but in the mid-1970s both Britain and America were undergoing some sort of nostalgia trip for the 1950s, resulting in a revival of interest in the rock and roll era. The film, *American Graffiti* came out in 1973, containing, incidentally, the song Only You – paving the way for Ringo to score a hit with his cover version, and it was Ringo again who cashed in with a starring role in *That'll Be The Day* in which he played an archetypal 1950s teddy boy. John too was at it, smitten by rock and roll all his adult life such that in 1975 he issued his album, *Rock 'N' Roll*, featuring a photo of himself from 1961 and containing a raft of celebrated oldies. (On which point, we should mention that album's working title, *Oldies But Mouldies*, playing off an earlier Beatles comp.) And with TV shows like *Happy Days* making a splash, and in Britain, Showaddywaddy returning several rock and roll classics to the pop charts, it's easy to see where the impetus for the Beatles' *Rock 'N' Roll Music* came from. The only hitch was, rock and roll was a phenomenon of the 1950s, while the Beatles were from the 1960s...

It was Bhaskar Menon, head of Capitol Records, who set the project in motion, outlining his plans to the individual Beatles (who weren't much interested) and George Martin, who agreed to have a go at remixing some of the tracks slated for inclusion. And true to his word, Martin duly delivered – only to learn that a legal technicality meant that UK pressings had to retain the original 1960s mixes after all, so while Capitol, and indeed most of the world, got to hear his re-workings, British buyers absurdly didn't – so as with *1962-1966* and *1967-1970*, the UK and US releases ended up sounding different.

Between 1963 and 1965, the Beatles recorded 24 cover versions for EMI, all from the rock and roll era (or, at least, the pre-Beatles years). A few of them were not really suitable for this themed album, but taking out material like A Taste Of Honey and Please Mr Postman, there was still a good dozen or so to pick from, Bhaskar Menon identifying them all. And in fact, there was a little bit of treasure here for UK collectors, although EMI didn't bother pointing it out: one of the rarest Beatles records was the *Long Tall Sally* EP from June 1964, whose four songs (Long Tall Sally; I Call Your Name; Slow Down; Matchbox) were little-known and had to be hunted down by fans, having never been issued in the UK anywhere other than on that little 12-year-old disc – but here they all were.

The real meat of the set, cuts like Dizzy Miss Lizzy and Rock And Roll Music itself would have made for a pretty punchy regular album, but this was business, and if *1962-1966* and *1967-1970* had taught Capitol anything, it was to go for the double album formula for maximum dollar. And that's where things start to go awry. While several early Lennon-McCartney songs could loosely fit the brief (I Wanna Be Your Man or I'm Down, for example) there weren't too many of them, and by the time this double LP gets to side 4, it's as if the thematic basis of the set has been forgotten. Side 4 consisted of three *White Album* tracks, a couple from *Revolver* and one or two others of dubious fit. Got To Get You Into My Life, for example, was a Motown pastiche, while Hey Bulldog was, if anything, a quasi-psychedelic rocker whose natural home was on the *Yellow Submarine* soundtrack. And thus, *Rock 'N' Roll Music* loses its identity, whether or not one likes the individual tracks.

For this reviewer, a more succinct package would have consisted of just a single LP something like this:

Rock And Roll Music	Roll Over Beethoven
Kansas City	Boys
Bad Boy	Money (That's What I Want)
Matchbox	Dizzy Miss Lizzy
Slow Down	Honey Don't
Devil In Her Heart	Everybody's Trying To Be My
Long Tall Sally	Baby
	Twist And Shout

Making it into a double album when there was transparently insufficient material to go around smacks of a good old-fashioned cash-in, something not helped by the album's packaging. The front cover used an early-ish group photo with a couple of life-sized thumbs over the top of the image, presumably to look like someone was holding up the album. In fact it just gave the appearance that the Beatles themselves were a little cardboard cut-out being moved into place beneath the album title. Inside the gatefold was worse, the artwork consisting of a montage of images redolent of 1950s America – a chrome-covered Chevy, hamburgers, jukebox and even a picture of Marilyn Monroe, who'd died before Love Me Do came out. In the US the record labels had glasses of Coca-Cola pictured on them – but what did any of this have to do with the quintessentially 1960s, and London-based, Beatles?

Nothing, opined Ringo who decried the sleeve design as cheap. John echoed the sentiment and when he first saw it, tried to intervene by offering to redesign it himself. For his own *Rock 'N' Roll* LP of a year previous, he'd made use of some vintage Beatles photos shot in Hamburg, which he'd recently found and acquired from Jurgen Vollmer, and he suggested he could use some of those to make a far more effective package. And no doubt he could have, had they let him – images of the leather-clad Beatles playing the dank rock and roll clubs of Hamburg surely more striking and relevant than what Capitol had come up with. Anyway, it never happened. (The US cover did, at least, have something on the UK one, coming out in a shiny metallic finish as opposed to plain paper.)

Were Capitol right? It depends how you look at it. As a business venture, they achieved what they wanted. *Rock 'N' Roll Music* sold a million, and would have topped the *Billboard* album chart in July had a certain Paul McCartney not occupied the number 1 spot with his current album, *Wings At The Speed Of Sound*. So, who are we to say Bhaskar Menon was wrong on any of this? Like several Beatles compilations, *Rock 'N' Roll Music* is remembered fondly by those who grew up with it. .

In 1980 the double LP was split into two for a budget re-issue, the UK editions appearing on Music For Pleasure with redesigned artwork, one cover with a red theme, the other blue (sound familiar?) and with the 1976 remixes finally included. In France and Belgium they went a step further and re-issued the album as a triple set, packaged along with John's own *Rock 'N' Roll!* Like *A Collection Of Beatles Oldies* before it, the album was then quietly laid to rest in the late-1980s, and hasn't been heard of since. Rest in peace, *Rock 'N' Roll Music*.

Rock 'N' Roll Music Medley

Contains extracts from:

Rock And Roll Music
Twist And Shout
Long Tall Sally
I Saw Her Standing There
Money
Bad Boy
Rock And Roll Music
I'm Down
Revolution
Back In The USSR
Get Back

This hard vinyl white label was sent out in promotion of the 1976 *Rock 'N' Roll Music* set. It takes the form of a medley of ten tracks from the album (with Rock And Roll Music appearing twice) and runs for five minutes. The disc is one-sided with just a standard test tone on the B side. It's now a valuable collectors' item.

Taking rides

Got To Get You Into My Life / Helter Skelter
★★☆☆☆

US release: 31 May 1976

Helter Skelter on seven-inch? You bet.

To expand the commercial potential of the *Rock 'N' Roll Music* project, both Capitol in the States and Parlophone in Britain opted to issue their own trailer singles, and in fact this was Capitol's first attempt to wring a hit from the back catalogue. It's perhaps significant that from an LP rooted in the music of '50s, they selected two of the relatively few mid-to-late-era tracks on the album, both pulled from side four and quite a bit removed from the original concept. What linked the two releases, LP and 45, was the image on the front, this new single taking the same illustration and tinting it green, and of course shrinking it so it looked even smaller – and so did those thumbs!

As for the dark and manic Helter Skelter on the flip, the stereo version on *The White Album* ran to 4:30 and could therefore squeeze onto this smaller disc, complete with Ringo's blisters on his fingers. It's easy to sit back and question Capitol's decisions after the fact (and I frequently do!) but for a 45 wedded to the rock and roll concept, it's a wonder they didn't opt for a more relevant choice like Long Tall Sally or Rock 'N' Roll Music – or even the corresponding UK selection, Twist And Shout. (If they wanted it to be a Lennon-McCartney track, why not I Saw Her Standing There? The options were plenty.)

The A-side, though, was a fine choice with plenty of commercial potential to unlock, Cliff Bennett and the Rebel Rousers having taken their version into the UK top 10 a decade before, to be followed in 1978 by Earth, Wind & Fire for another hit version. This Capitol issue proved no exception, climbing to 7 on *Billboard* and returning the Beatles to the singles listing after a gap of six years. So, job done.

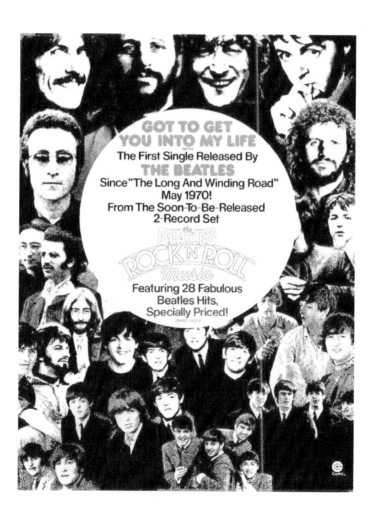

Balalaikas ringing out

**Back In The USSR /
Twist And Shout**
★★☆☆☆

UK release:
25 June 1976

Parlophone's approach to plugging *Rock 'N' Roll Music* was a *little* more conventional than Capitol's but still plundered *The White Album* for its source material. Back In The USSR was, at least, pitched in the rock and roll style, its three-chord structure edging close to Chuck Berry – or would have, had it not been plastered in Beach Boys harmonies. It's an energetic and catchy number which had not previously been a hit, but may have been on the frantic side to win over a general audience. (On the day it was released, the Wurzels were number 1 with Combine Harvester. Go figure.) Nevertheless it dipped its toe into the UK top 20, the Beatles never failing to shift units both to their existing fan base and to a new generation discovering songs like these for the first time.

When Britain or America issued new Beatles records, they tended to be mirrored in other countries too. In this case, with two competing singles to choose from, loyalties were split roughly 50-50, some territories (eg, Canada, Italy, Japan) going for Got To Get You Into My Life, others (eg, Brazil, Ireland, India) preferring Back In The USSR. A few (eg, West Germany, New Zealand) couldn't decide and so issued both!

A fairly routine release in the UK, Back In The USSR made no headlines.

Whitewash

**Ob-La-Di, Ob-La-Da /
Julia**
★★☆☆☆

**US release:
8 November 1976**

The White Album again! There was nothing to prevent Capitol raiding the 1968 set for hits and so six months after their last single, they released another, pinning their hopes on a couple of tracks, one from Paul on the A-side and one from John (in fact a solo performance) on the B. Ob-La-Di had been a British hit in 1969 when Scottish group, Marmalade, took a cover version to number 1. Meanwhile several countries opted to issue the Beatles' original backed with While My Guitar Gently Weeps in early 1969, bridging the seven-month gap between Hey Jude and Get Back – all of which may have been part of the reason why Capitol homed in on the track in 1976. But surely they could have come up with something better from such a rich back-catalogue? (Here Comes The Sun, perhaps? Or something more poppy, like Getting Better?)

Whatever – Ob-La-Di it was, with its B-side completely different in mood and style. It was housed in a rare thing: a picture sleeve with no picture, Capitol using the parent album's concept to issue it out in plain white, on which was printed, 'The Beatles', and the two song titles. Best of all, they marked each copy, in true *White Album* style, with a unique serial number. Unfortunately their efforts didn't translate into a smash hit, Ob-La-Di still charting but only as high as 49, the Beatles' lowest placing since 1963.

Side splitting

The Best Of George Harrison
★★★☆☆

UK release: 20 November 1976
US release: 8 November 1976

Beatles recordings:	*Solo recordings*:
Something	My Sweet Lord
If I Needed Someone	Give Me Love (Give Me Peace On
Here Comes The Sun	Earth)
Taxman	You
Think For Yourself	Bangla-Desh
For You Blue	Dark Horse
While My Guitar Gently Weeps	What Is Life

When the Beatles' EMI contract was coming up to expiry, all four were seen as good commercial bets as individual artists. Ripe for the repackaging game, John's collection, *Shaved Fish*, appeared just ahead of Ringo's *Blast From Your Past*. Paul would have to wait until 1978 for his (*Wings Greatest*), as other blockbuster albums kept his fans sated meantime, but George, unlike Paul, jumped ship from EMI in 1976, so had his career retrospective issued out almost spitefully timed to coincide with his first album on Dark Horse Records, *Thirty Three & 1/3*.

While we're not concerned here with repackaging of the solo recordings, *The Best Of George Harrison* needs discussion because, as fans will know, more than half of it is comprised of Beatles tracks. As to the reasons why EMI opted to go down such a route we can only speculate. (They hadn't with Ringo's set a year earlier, and nor was there any need to in George's case.) Steve Harley had taken a cover version of Here Comes The Sun into the British top 10 over the summer of 1976, so perhaps they felt that needed to be included, and the rest of their scheme followed from there? It could be as simple as that, but even so they had a live 'solo' version at their disposal (from *The Concert For Bangla Desh*) which they could have used instead.

As if to underline their questionable decision, EMI elected to put all the Beatles tracks on side 1, and all the solo material on side 2, despite there being no other chronology to the sequencing. Would it have been better to just mix up the whole thing rather than divide the LP so inflexibly? Or to get back to the main point – why not just include solo George? The usual supposition is that he didn't have 12 or so hits under his belt – but then neither had Ringo. We're getting off track slightly, in a book about the Beatles, but it's worth a short digression into the choice of material, so let's take stock.

George's solo hits to-date included My Sweet Lord (of course) and its flip-side, which let's not forget, was listed jointly at number 1 in the States, Isn't It A Pity. America had also put out What Is Life, and it was covered for chart success in Britain by Olivia Newton-John. Bangla-Desh followed, then Give Me Love (Give Me Peace On Earth), Dark Horse, Ding Dong, You and the non-charting This Guitar (Can't Keep From Crying). I make that nine contenders, just for starters.

The released album, Beatles songs included, contained 13 tracks, so where could we find another four or five solo numbers? Don't Let Me Wait Too Long from *Living In The Material World* was commercial enough and *almost* came out as a single in 1973. George also had a couple of B-sides which might have attracted fans, including the non-album Deep Blue from 1971 and Apple Scruffs, as pulled from the lauded *All Things Must Pass*. Let's throw in Living In The Material World (which also serves to inject some 'Indian' elements into proceedings) and one more – how about the classic song, All Things Must Pass? All told, this is what we could have ended up with:

My Sweet Lord
What Is Life
Don't Let Me Wait
    Too Long
Dark Horse
Give Me Love (Give Me
    Peace On Earth)
Deep Blue
All Things Must Pass

You
This Guitar (Can't Keep From
    Crying)
Bangla-Desh
Living In The Material World
Apple Scruffs
Ding Dong
Isn't It A Pity

Four album cuts and a B-side on a greatest hits package? Sure. EMI's official release contained six album tracks!

Anyhow, back to Beatles. Suppose instead, we were to try and assemble the entire thing just from George's group material? In fairness to EMI they captured the best of it anyway but the Beatles recorded 21 of George's songs in total, and only seven made the cut here. If another seven were added to complete it, the album might have looked something like this:

Something
If I Needed Someone
I Want To Tell You
The Inner Light
I Need You
I, Me, Mine
While My Guitar Gently
    Weeps

Here Comes The Sun
Old Brown Shoe
Think For Yourself
Taxman
Long, Long, Long
For You Blue
It's All Too Much

That's an *extremely* strong collection by any standard, but so much for fantasy albums.

When *The Best Of George Harrison* appeared at the end of 1976 it had different cover art in Britain, where George was pictured sitting on the front of a hot-rod car (eh?), and America where he was portrayed looking mysterious against a paint-spattered backdrop which looked a *bit* like the cosmos, on which was drawn what appeared to be an art-deco wireless. (Obviously!) That it landed within days of *Thirty Three & 1/3* can only have harmed both albums' sales but nonetheless, *Best Of* made 31 on *Billboard*. It didn't chart in the UK, where a Parlophone edition of Capitol's *Magical Mystery Tour* had also just hit the shops, and in both territories, *Thirty Three*

& *1/3* comfortably outsold it. (So much for including popular Beatles recordings; Taxman by the way, had now received two album releases in five months.)

Predictably, given the fate of *A Collection Of Beatles Oldies* and *Rock 'N' Roll Music*, *The Best Of George Harrison* was re-issued in the UK a few years later on EMI's budget label, Music For Pleasure, which further compounded the Beatles association by using George's *White Album* portrait for its revised cover art. (And ditto, the amended cover of *Blast From Your Past*, re-issued on the same morning.) *The Best Of George Harrison* did at least make it to CD in May 1987 – meaning Something, Here Comes The Sun, For You Blue and While My Guitar Gently Weeps actually made their CD debut here, the Beatles' regular back catalogue still mid-way through its sequenced release schedule. (We'll overlook the odd 1983 CD of *Abbey Road*, which was only issued in Japan.)

The Best Of George Harrison has never really become obsolete, since George's only other career retrospective, *Let It Roll: Songs By George Harrison*, omitted three of the solo songs EMI had scooped up, including the non-album single, Bangla-Desh. Thus, it keeps its place in his canon, as well as that of the Beatles.

Rubber boots

The Beatles At The Hollywood Bowl
★★★☆☆

UK release:
6 May 1977

US release:
4 May 1977

Twist And Shout	Boys
She's A Woman	A Hard Day's Night
Dizzy Miss Lizzy	Help!
Ticket To Ride	All My Loving
Can't Buy Me Love	She Loves You
Things We Said Today	Long Tall Sally
Roll Over Beethoven	

Not for the first time, official new Beatles product had the wider collectors' market to thank for its very existence, this first official live album a consequence of the little-noted Lingasong label managing to get hold of a lo-fi recording of the group in Hamburg in 1962. Lingasong packaged it up and announced the imminent release of *The Beatles Live! At the Star-Club in Hamburg, Germany; 1962*, which EMI characteristically tried to block before responding as they had with *Alpha-Omega* and simply bettering it. Their official live release, which landed more or less simultaneously with Lingasong's, predictably sold by the bucket-load, getting to number 1 in Britain and 2 in America – so what, we might ask, had they been waiting for? That it took so long for EMI to get a live Beatles album out is surprising, given their stage act was the biggest draw in pop in the 1960s.

A preliminary concert recording had been made at Carnegie Hall in 1964 but resulted in just a meagre snippet of Twist And Shout being released on the official *The Beatles' Story* later that year. *The Beatles At Shea Stadium* followed, recorded in 1965 but only for a 1967 television broadcast, rather than release on disc. And while Capitol recorded the group's three Hollywood Bowl appearances in 1964-1965, nothing was forthcoming, leading meantime to bootleggers doing the footwork with albums like *Live At Shea* [sic], *Back In 64 At The Hollywood Bowl* and *Hollywood Bowl 1964*, on the celebrated TMOQ label. The demand was there, the recordings were there, but as the 1970s wore on, all remained quiet on the EMI front until Lingasong unwittingly forced the issue.

Actually that's not quite true. Phil Spector was asked to review EMI's recordings in 1971 for a possible release then, but for whatever reason, the project came to nothing, the main obstacles seeming to be that the original tapes had been captured only on basic recording equipment, and that the usual frenzy of female screaming tended to drown out the songs. Come 1977, Capitol went instead to the right man for the job, George Martin, who transferred the three-track tapes onto 16-track and set about improving the soundscape. The Beatles played the Hollywood Bowl three times, first in August 1964 as part of their summer tour of North America, and then twice more in August 1965 where they performed on successive days, and all three were recorded and available. EMI wanted this to be a double album (again), but Martin reasoned he could deliver better product by condensing it to a single disc containing just the very best performances, thereby also getting around the fact that three of the songs (Twist And Shout, Can't Buy Me Love, A Hard Day's Night) were repeated across the 1964 and 1965 set lists.

These are the set lists as originally performed and recorded by Capitol, and tracks marked * were used on the resultant LP:

23 August 1964:	29 August 1965:	30 August 1965:
Twist And Shout	Twist And Shout	Twist And Shout*
You Can't Do That	She's A Woman	She's A Woman*
All My Loving*	I Feel Fine	I Feel Fine
She Loves You*	Dizzy Miss Lizzy*	Dizzy Miss Lizzy*
Things We Said Today*	Ticket To Ride*	Ticket To Ride
Roll Over Beethoven*	Everybody's Trying To Be My Baby	Everybody's Trying To Be My Baby
Can't Buy Me Love	Can't Buy Me Love	Can't Buy Me Love*
If I Fell	Baby's In Black	Baby's In Black
I Want To Hold Your Hand	I Wanna Be Your Man	I Wanna Be Your Man
Boys*	A Hard Day's Night	A Hard Day's Night*
A Hard Day's Night	Help!*	Help!
Long Tall Sally*	I'm Down	I'm Down

(Note that the released version of Dizzy Miss Lizzy was a George Martin mix assembled from parts of both performances.)

While it's possible to commend George Martin for the way the audio was thus presented, the end product has an air of fakery about it, being in essence a make-believe concert set. Further, the LP cover, showing what appear to be concert tickets, is a similar sleight of hand, the items in question being mock-ups (they even got the week day wrong on one), the actual tickets having nothing printed on them but boring text. Of course back in 1977 fans tended to not notice such bending of the truth, but the Beatles did, a typically grumpy George Harrison declaring the album "just like a bootleg".

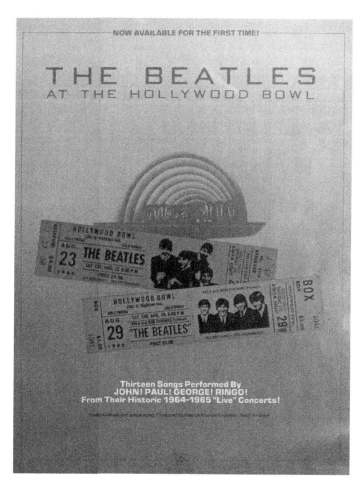

Boosted by an extravagant promotional campaign, *The Beatles At The Hollywood Bowl* topped the UK album chart 12 years after the show, displacing Sinatra and being in turn toppled by the Muppets! Another budget re-issue would follow a few years on, and when the Beatles' catalogue migrated to CD in the late 1980s, the album was ignored and effectively erased from history, which is unfair given its status as the only EMI-sanctioned record of Beatlemania in the flesh. But that's not how it ends – the unused Baby's In Black from 30 August 1965 turned up on the Real Love single of 1996, and parts of I Want To Hold Your Hand from 1964 were included on *Love* in 2006. Inevitably further bootlegs have since landed containing all three shows in their entirety, which is what most fans really want, but the ever-frugal EMI allowed only a couple more of the available tracks out when they finally revamped the album in 2016 (see relevant entry on page 215), the rest kept under lock and key for reasons best known to themselves.

Leather jackets

Love Songs
★★★★★

UK release:
11 November 1977

US release:
21 October 1977

Yesterday	Michelle
I'll Follow The Sun	It's Only Love
I Need You	You're Going To Lose That Girl
Girl	Every Little Thing
In My Life	For No One
Words Of Love	She's Leaving Home
Here, There And Everywhere	
	The Long And Winding Road
Something	This Boy
And I Love Her	Norwegian Wood (This Bird Has
If I Fell	Flown)
I'll Be Back	You've Got To Hide Your Love Away
Tell Me What You See	I Will
Yes It Is	PS I Love You

Beatles product was flooding out come 1977, and without further delay, yet another LP collection was due for assembly. *Love Songs* was, in a way, a complement to *Rock 'N' Roll Music*, another two-record set containing studio recordings but of a consciously opposed style. It included 25 tracks, although as with its predecessor, some of the selections raised eyebrows, given its purported theme – exhibit A, She's Leaving Home which was a potted account of a teenaged runaway – hardly a romantic text. I'll Follow The Sun on the other hand is almost anti-love, while Norwegian Wood is the story of a clandestine affair which never happened (he crawled off to sleep in the bath) – but I guess this is nit-picking.

Love Songs is a quality product, from the endless succession of top-notch material down to its cover, finished in luxurious faux-leather (alright, cardboard, but it looks good) which, in the States, had its main design motif embossed on the front in gold foil, like a valuable book. Not only that, it came with an extravagant set of lyrics stylishly printed on expensive paper, a far cry from the shoddy-looking package chucked together for *Rock 'N' Roll Music* the previous year.

One nice touch was the inclusion inside the gatefold of an arty black and white image of the Beatles, based on photographs by Richard Avedon from 1967. Avedon had originally taken four individual portraits and collaged them together to make the so-called 'Mount Rushmore' image. It's a work of art, but troubling for Capitol in 1977 was that it showed each of the Beatles in different sizes, to give the impression that some were further from the camera, and Paul, the main event when it came to *Love Songs*, was diminished and on the left-hand edge. With Avedon's help, Capitol's Kenneth Anderson took the originals and redesigned the composite so that Paul was now looming largest, with Ringo demoted to the side. And with some further touches to tidy it all up, he'd created a stunning group image worthy of its place on the album.

So what of the contents? There are two Harrisongs on it (I Need You; Something), and one cover version (Buddy Holly's Words Of Love). The rest is all Lennon-McCartney, and curiously it's John who just shades it in terms of coverage, despite the fact that Paul's songs tend to be the more dominant (The Long And Winding Road, for example, dwarfs the following This Boy). And get this – 21 of the songs, that's 84 percent, are from the 1962-1966 era, including PS I Love You from 1962 and six cuts from *Help!*. Surprising.

What's missing is, as ever, a matter for discussion. They might have included more from the group's later albums (the set contains just one track from each of *Sgt Pepper*, *The White Album*, *Abbey Road* and *Let It Be*). There is no Hey Jude or Let It Be, and to balance the chronology they could have gone for numbers like Martha My Dear, Julia, Lovely Rita, Here Comes The Sun, Oh! Darling, Don't Let Me Down, For You Blue, Two Of Us, and so on. OK, these might not all be seen as traditional love songs, but then neither are the goading You're Going To Lose That Girl or the lonely For No One. Perhaps on the back of *Rock 'N' Roll Music* and *The Beatles At The Hollywood Bowl*, EMI reckoned Beatlemania-era songs were what the public most wanted.

So, how to sum up such an object? The quality of the packaging is superb, but the songs themselves are the same ones again and seven of them had turned up on *1962-1966* a few years before. But it would be unfair to say *Love Songs* is all style and no substance. The calibre of the material and the pleasing way it hangs together make this a genuine highlight from this period of intense repackaging, and yet again it performed well on chart, going top 10 UK in the run-up to Christmas.

Lost that girl

Girl /
You're Going To Lose That Girl
★★★☆☆

US release:
14 October 1977 (not issued)

The format of *Love Songs* was based on that of *Rock 'N' Roll Music*, and since the earlier double album had also seen successful trailer singles, it was assumed this one would get the same. It made sense, not much effort needed to pick out two good songs and sit back while the sales rolled in. In making their selections, it's pleasing to see Capitol opt for two John songs back-to-back, all the earlier 'new' singles having been Paul's numbers.

All seemed good to go in the autumn. The single was assigned a Capitol catalogue number (4506, two on from Mull Of Kintyre), promotional copies were sent out, paper labels and commercial sleeves printed up. Then suddenly, and for no obvious reason, the release was cancelled. It's true that *Love Songs* hadn't fared so well on *Billboard*, only making 24, but that was the point of the single – to push it – so why was it withdrawn? The clash with Mull?

The following year a stock of 16,000 of the unused sleeves was purchased by a couple of dealers who started selling them to collectors. These genuine Capitol sleeves, styled like miniatures of the album, could then be coupled up with promotional copies of the single to make novel collectibles, but of course with everything out in the open, the whole saga was a gift to bootleggers and the great majority of copies now in circulation are fakes, including many on coloured vinyl. Nonetheless, if you want to, it's possible to obtain an unofficial facsimile of the cancelled release and put it where it might have been in your collection.

There were never plans to release it in the UK, or indeed any such *Love Songs* 45 – so far as is known – and there are no missing entries in the Parlophone catalogue number sequence at that time. We await an official explanation of what went wrong.

Top of the flops

Sgt Pepper's Lonely Hearts
Club Band-With A Little
Help From My Friends /
A Day In The Life
★★☆☆☆

UK release:
30 September 1978

US release:
14 August 1978

If anyone doubted the popularity of the Beatles in the mid to late 1970s, a quick squizz at what was going on in stage and screen was enough to show the group were still top of many people's pops.

John, Paul, George, Ringo... and Bert was a Willy Russell musical telling the story of the Beatles, for which permission was granted to perform the songs, Barbara Dickson doing the honours. Its 1974 premiere was in Liverpool but when George Harrison saw it, he walked out and withdrew permission for Here Comes The Sun. The play spawned a disappointing LP.

All This And World War II was a film documentary consisting of black and white war footage, over which was played an endless sequence of Beatles songs as performed by the likes of Elton John, Leo Sayer and the Bee Gees. The film spawned a disappointing LP.

Beatlemania was a Broadway show tracing the Beatles' story through song, accompanied by extravagant visuals projected onto screens. Music was performed live by the cast, but Apple Corps sued for infringement. Not before the show spawned a disappointing LP.

Sgt Pepper's Lonely Hearts Club Band On The Road was a poorly received stage musical built around Beatles songs, and featuring a cast of characters including Billy Shears and his girlfriend, Strawberry Fields, fleeing from the evils of Maxwell's Silver Hammermen. Then Robert Stigwood decided to turn it into a film which spawned a disappointing LP.

The fact that *Sgt Pepper's Lonely Hearts Club Band* was in cinemas over the summer of 1978, featuring the then massive Bee Gees in starring roles, drew significant attention – and although reviews were almost uniformly lousy, it put the Beatles' song into the minds of a fresh set of potential record buyers. Consequently Capitol/Parlophone did the predictable thing and issued the original on 45, hoping to bag some piggy-back sales.

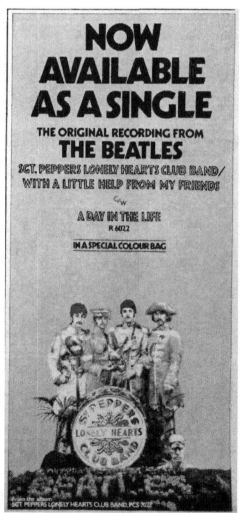

It's a shame the titular song was only a relatively short overture, not likely a hit in its own right. There was a reprise version but running at a different tempo and in a different key – so no chance of editing them together. (And the faster one is also the lower – so no point in trying to pull a Strawberry Fields-style trick on it. Silly idea, anyway.)

The only real option was to use the *Pepper* album's opening segue into With A Little Help From My Friends, making that the predominant track with Ringo on vocals – but was it strong enough?

Apparently not, and the whole thing was too long for radio, and the title too long to read out.

The single flopped all the way to 71 in the US and 63 in Britain, where remaindered stock was thrown into the latest incarnation of *The Singles Collection 1962-1970*, and EMI never again tried to pinch a hit by putting a Beatles oldie out on 45.

Those of a sceptical bent will have enjoyed one other Beatles tie-in released around the same time:

> *All You Need Is Cash* was a superb spoof of the group in the roving documentary style and featured Eric Idle and Neil Innes as two of the Rutles, who released their landmark *Sgt Rutter's Only Darts Club Band* in 1967 under the influence of tea. George Harrison loved the bubble-bursting send-up and made a cameo appearance in the film which has since garnered a cult following. It spawned a fantastic LP.

The Blue Box

The Beatles Collection
★★★★★

UK release:
10 November 1978

Please Please Me	*Sgt Pepper's Lonely Hearts*
With The Beatles	*Club Band*
A Hard Day's Night	*The Beatles*
Beatles For Sale	*Yellow Submarine*
Help!	*Abbey Road*
Rubber Soul	*Let It Be*
Revolver	*Rarities*

Often referred to as *The Blue Box*, or sometimes *The BC13 Box* (its catalogue number), *The Beatles Collection* was a specially compiled set of the group's British stereo studio albums housed, like *The Singles Collection* of 1976, in one sturdy package. There can be little doubt that the corresponding set of 45s, which sold heavily, was the direct factor leading to this LP collection, but it does have a couple of other precedents: in 1974, Capitol had some stylish cases made up for its staff, housing the US album series, and then in 1976, Pathé Marconi boxed up the French album discography in a similar manner for its domestic market.

To be fair it didn't take a genius to think of it, so it was perhaps inevitable that the UK would follow suit in 1978, the idea going international as most countries then issued out their own *Blue Box* collections consisting of albums corresponding as close as possible to the UK set, with just one or two regional variants as appropriate. In the case of USA they were, for the first time, offered the UK albums as the main event, 3000 copies of this collection put on sale, although it's not entirely clear why they didn't go their own way and box up the Capitol albums instead. (It perhaps had something to do with the sheer number of them, which even excluding *The Beatles Story*, and *A Hard Day's Night*, which was on United Artists, ran to 17 long players before the end of 1970.)

What's fascinating with hindsight is the way in which this collection defined the UK discography. There were decisions to be made in compiling it, and they panned out as follows: *A Collection Of Beatles Oldies* wasn't included, and therefore wasn't core. Neither was *Magical Mystery Tour* which had been issued in Britain in 1976, and was made up entirely of non-album tracks. However *Yellow Submarine*, with only four new Beatles songs *was* included, cementing its place in the central discography – while *1962-1966* and *1967-1970*, despite featuring a glut of singles-only recordings, were not rounded up. These choices basically established what counts and what does not count as a proper Beatles album to this day (*Magical Mystery Tour* excepted, whose official status changed in 1987).

The dozen officially defined studio albums contain among them 174 individual cuts. But the Beatles' total output ran to 213 including singles and EPs, and this doesn't count four songs which existed in two different versions (namely, Love Me Do, Across The Universe, Get Back and Let It Be). So, there was an awful lot missing from what at first glance looked like a complete Beatles collection, and that's where *Rarities* comes in (see also next entry), rounding up stragglers, but not all of them – and there's little doubt that at least some fans will have been dismayed to open the box and realise this set was missing essential recordings like We Can Work It Out, I Feel Fine, Hey Jude and others.* What they weren't told was that they needed to add *1962-1966*, *1967-1970* and *Magical Mystery Tour*, then they would indeed have it all (bar the lost Ringo version of Love Me Do, but let's not be pedantic) – but that would add considerably to the expense of course.

Speaking of which, given its high retail price (more than £50, which in its day was a small fortune), this handsome collection was never going to sell in the millions. However it made a decent splash, and the Australian edition sold 25,000, getting it into the top 40, prompting Parlophone / EMI to issue it again there in a limited edition golden outer box. Back in Britain it was also released in a cassette edition, comprising the equivalent albums from the 1973 'gold' cassette series plus *Rarities*. And audiophiles are still willing to praise the vinyl – it contains all the studio albums in pure analogue sound, no digital processing in those days.

* *If you want a full list of what's missing here, subtract the* Rarities *songs from the later* Past Masters *compilation.*

Not what it says on the tin

Rarities [UK album]
★★☆☆☆

UK release:
19 October 1979

Across The Universe	Rain
Yes It Is	She's A Woman
This Boy	Matchbox
The Inner Light	I Call Your Name
I'll Get You	Bad Boy
Thank You Girl	Slow Down
Komm, Gib Mir Deine Hand	I'm Down
You Know My Name (Look Up The Number)	Long Tall Sally
Sie Liebt Dich	

The specially assembled *Rarities* was placed inside *The Blue Box* as an ostensibly free gift, marked 'not for sale' on the back and bound to entice purchasers. However record shop owners soon realised there was a demand for it from fans not willing to pay £50-plus for the privilege, and so reports started coming in that retailers were slipping *Rarities* out of the box and selling it on the side, a sort-of black market trade right under the noses of *Blue Box* purchasers who were therefore being short-changed. Something had to be done, and how fans felt when EMI decided to issue *Rarities* as a stand-alone album likely depended on whether they had already splashed out on the complete box. Many had, and weren't overly pleased to learn that had they waited, they could have bagged this new record for much less.

Rarities is an odd collection of bits and pieces, and is probably the least satisfying Beatles compilation ever issued. That, of course, is because it was assembled to a specific brief which constrained the choices. Re-issues Manager at EMI, Colin Miles, put the track listing together along with Michael Heatley, but shackled as they were by Apple-imposed conditions, which prohibited them from raiding the vaults for unissued tracks and the like, they had to somehow come up with a batch of already-released recordings worthy of the tag, 'rare', which in the case of the best-selling act of all time, was not easy. Most of the selections consisted of non-album B-sides, but the original singles had sold millions. They set some guidelines by only including tracks which hadn't appeared on album before – which meant in practice, dodging the dozen UK studio albums, *1962-1966*, *1967-70* and *Magical Mystery Tour*. But they didn't extend that rule to *Rock 'N' Roll Music* or *Love Songs*, where eight of the tracks had not so long ago appeared, *Rarities* thereby including the songs from the obscure *Long Tall*

Sally EP which had recently surfaced on *Rock 'N' Roll Music* and were easily available, undermining the album's concept. And they put Bad Boy on again, which was once rare but now making its third appearance on a compilation LP. (The B-sides were, at least, warmly welcomed by those who collected the Beatles on cassette, to whom they were not previously available.)

Miles and Heatley did manage to locate three tracks which were unknown to most in Britain, namely the two German-language recordings, Sie Liebt Dich and Komm, Gib Mir Deine Hand, and the 'Wildlife' mix of Across The Universe, previously only available on a 1969 charity record. There is, in addition, an indication that they intended to include rare or new mixes of tracks previously only doing the rounds in mono, the record labels indicating She's A Woman, The Inner Light and You Know My Name (Look Up The Number) were appearing in stereo – although this might have been down to nothing more than sloppy attention to detail when applying the stereo/mono markers to the printed text. Either way, the record played them in mono, as per the existing singles.

In terms of the B-sides, all the eligible ones were included, nine in total from Thank You Girl to You Know My Name (Look Up The Number). These, added to the two German tracks, Bad Boy, the *Long Tall Sally* quartet plus Across The Universe made up 17 in total, but the great majority were from the Beatlemania years meaning some clever sequencing would be required to present them to maximum effect. Sadly the compilers didn't do themselves justice and blundered in sequencing Yes It Is and the similar This Boy back-to-back, not to mention the insertion of the unusual You Know My Name right between Komm, Gib Mir Deine Hand and Sie Liebt Dich. The two Larry Williams covers, Bad Boy and Slow Down, also appeared next to each other – it's genuinely hard to see how it could have been sequenced any worse.

Despite everything, *Rarities* managed a showing on the UK album charts, where it was listed at 71 for a week. And since the track listing was fundamentally attached to the UK album sequence, which other countries also issued in their respective box sets, it went out around the world too. Interestingly, Capitol prepared their own pressing to place inside the box, 3000 copies of which were made, and besides tweaking the layout of the cover, they swapped out the two German-language tracks which were replaced with the much more common English equivalents. But while

Capitol had already issued Komm, Gib Mir Deine Hand on *Something New* in 1964, they hadn't issued Sie Liebt Dich before, making the swap even more difficult to understand.

When the decision was made to put *Rarities* out on its own in 1979, Capitol didn't fancy it and came up with a new and better album of their own…

Capitol's pressing
of the UK album

Mixing things up

Rarities [US album]
★★★☆☆

US release:
24 March 1980

Love Me Do	Penny Lane
Misery	Helter Skelter
There's A Place	Don't Pass Me By
Sie Liebt Dich	The Inner Light
And I Love Her	Across The Universe
Help!	You Know My Name (Look Up
I'm Only Sleeping	The Number)
I Am The Walrus	Sgt Pepper Inner Groove

Although the track listing of the UK-compiled *Rarities* was of less relevance to the US market, the overall concept had merit. Capitol's own version was still constrained by the 'no unreleased material' rule, but they were resourceful enough to cast the net wide and rounded up 15 tracks which US fans either hadn't heard, or which were long-unavailable. In two cases, they even edited up their own 'rarities', something inspired by a recent bootleg which had the cheek to use Capitol branding all over it, tricking buyers into thinking it was a real release.

The story is included in Clinton Heylin's 1994 book, *Bootleg*, in which he recounts events behind the release of *Collectors Items* in 1979. The man behind the boot, who prefers to remain nameless bar the tag, Richard, explained how, disappointed with the cheap and shoddy nature of most bootlegs on the market, he pulled out all the stops to make something worthy of an official album – and using his knowledge of rarer Beatles cuts, assembled a 16-track LP in good sound quality. He succeeded, the record seeming for all the world like a Capitol release and attracting their attention. *Collectors Items* included among its tracks, Richard's own edits of two numbers – a stereo Penny Lane with the trumpet coda from the mono promo version edited on, and a new version of I Am The Walrus in which he took parts from two different releases and sequenced them together to make a new 'mix'. Capitol took note and when they put their own *Rarities* together, they copied the bootleg and made new, matching edits of these two tracks (something Mark Lewisohn politely remarked on in *Beatles Book Monthly*, June 1980: "I'm not totally in agreement with this").

So what else did they consider worthy of inclusion? Having scoured their album catalogue, they realised that both Misery and There's A Place needed a release – they were part of the early material issued by Vee Jay on *Introducing The Beatles*, which, when acquired by Capitol in 1965, were missed off their album, *The Early Beatles* and kept in reserve – but ultimately never used. There was also the Ringo version of Love Me Do, which they had to source from a needle-drop of the 1963 Canadian single, since the original studio tapes were long gone. Other items missing from the back-catalogue included Sie Liebt Dich, and the *Sgt Pepper* run-out groove which had been left off the US pressing – and several others which differed from the originals for varying reasons, all of which is well-documented elsewhere for those who want to know specifics.

In the end, the US *Rarities* was a much better listen than the UK instalment, and was boosted further by its eye-catching artwork, streets ahead of the UK's unimaginative text-based design. Early plans were to use the 'Butcher Cover' on the front, but Capitol baulked at the idea, probably on the grounds of taste but perhaps conscious not to inadvertently fool buyers into thinking they were getting *Yesterday... And Today* inside the package. Nonetheless the full-sized Butcher photo was used inside the gatefold, along with several other rare images and some useful notes. The only disappointment was the front cover itself, which consisted of a miniature snapshot of the group from 1968, plopped into the centre of a large, empty square foot of space.

The album made 21 on *Billboard*, despite being a niche purchase, hanging around for nine weeks. Good effort.

Still they lead me back

The Beatles Ballads
★★☆☆☆

UK release:
13 October 1980

Yesterday	Something
Norwegian Wood (This Bird Has Flown)	The Fool On The Hill
	Till There Was You
Do You Want To Know A Secret	The Long And Winding Road
For No One	Here Comes The Sun
Michelle	Blackbird
Nowhere Man	And I Love Her
You've Got To Hide Your Love Away	She's Leaving Home
	Here, There And Everywhere
Across The Universe	Let It Be
All My Loving	
Hey Jude	

EMI were clearly running short of themes to assemble Beatles compilations by – rumour has it, they were even mulling over a Beatles country album, God forbid. The best they would come up with in 1980 was a collection of the group's finest ballads. But what exactly is a ballad? The Cambridge Dictionary defines it thus:

> "A song or poem that tells a story, or (in popular music) a slow love song."

Well, we're in popular music territory here, so this is to be a collection of 20… love songs. Sound familiar? Of course it does, and a check of the track listing shows that of the selections on this new platter, exactly half are duplicated from the 1977 album.

Which poses something of a quandary. The track listing includes superior options like Hey Jude, Here Comes The Sun, Across The Universe, Let It Be and so on – easily strong enough to stand up by themselves. And given the single-album format and regular retail price, there wasn't any need to cram 20 tracks on, running close to an hour's worth of audio. They could have given the set more of an independent flavour by simply missing out the duplications, proving the axiom that less is sometimes more. If there is a distinction to be made, it's in the average vintage of the songs here, with nine from 1967-1970, and the fact that Paul now predominates, accounting for 13 tracks including nearly all of side 2. As such, a shorter record would have made an effective 'disc 3' to complement the double *Love Songs*, balancing out the earlier album's opposite bias – but it would have been a tough sell that way.

It was, though, heavy on the repetition with absolutely nothing fans didn't already have – except that a few of the songs accidentally had the stereo channels swapped over – but who really took any notice of things like that? The album's most fan-worthy attraction, the 'Wildlife' version of Across The Universe, had already surfaced on *Rarities* a year before, but was still novel enough to catch the ear, particularly as the album packaging didn't even mention this interesting variant.

The record sleeve too was a recycling job, the painting on the front a rejected essay for the 1968 *White Album*, when it was still scheduled as *A Doll's House*. Why did Parlophone purloin it for *Ballads* all these years later? Probably they were inspired by the US *Rarities* collection having featured the Butcher photo in all its glory, and thought they could repeat the trick – but although John Byrne's striking visuals would have worked perfectly for *A Doll's House*, with its sometimes unsettling lyrics about raccoons, piggies, blackbirds and tigers, it had precisely no relevance to the lullaby contents of this 1980 set. (Presumably as a joke, the small print attributes the sleeve design to Shoot That Tiger, a reference to The Continuing Story Of Bungalow Bill.)

And it's the animals theme which predominates on the back as well, the song titles artfully laid out among pencil drawings of all manner of wildlife. It might have been a nice idea to sketch the same animal figures as featured in the painting on the front, but nevertheless it looks good, especially after the disappointing covers of *Rock 'N' Roll Music* and *Rarities*.

Back in the 1960s, Capitol in America had a sometimes fractious relationship with their UK parent company, EMI, as hinted at by their refusal to handle *A Collection Of Beatles Oldies* in 1966. And having largely directed their own repackaging through the 1970s, it wasn't a great surprise that Capitol snubbed this one too, in contrast to much of the rest of the world. Ostensibly they didn't wish to impinge on *Love Songs*, but *Ballads* did spectacular business in some territories, most notably Australia where it topped the album charts for seven straight weeks. That's money in the bank, Capitol.

Suffering the same fate as the rest of the period collections, *Ballads* went out of print and just a few years on, was completely forgotten about. It's never made it to CD and likely never will.

From Liverpool...

The Beatles Box
★★★★★

UK release:
27 October 1980

This extravagant package may have grown out of EMI's struggle to come up with a new angle on Beatles marketing, but if so they clearly had a genius moment. They could have released yet another compilation or another box set, but solved the dilemma by doing both at once: a box set with eight brand new compilation LPs inside. And what a collection it made, with 126 tracks (announced as 124) including several rare mixes, all of it spanning the group's career in chronological sequence. Not only that, there were eight newly designed album sleeves printed in full colour, putting the icing on a Beatles cake which has few parallels.

The Beatles Box is really the 'greatest hits' collection the group's almost limitless creativity deserved. *1962-1966* and *1967-1970* had attempted a career overview some years earlier, but there was a lot left out, mainly popular album tracks like Twist And Shout and Here There And Everywhere, besides anything from the *Abbey Road* medley. This far more expansive set allowed EMI to scoop up loads more, 126 selections constituting more than half of the Beatles' 213 officially released songs. But what makes this box set fascinating to this day is the way the compiler, EMI's Simon Sinclair, put some added spice into things by choosing rare versions of several songs, using his depth of knowledge to get around the 'no unreleased material' rule by scouring overseas pressings for variants, and throwing in some less well-travelled mixes. What's also interesting, for a different reason, is that none of this was particularly brought to buyers' attention, his sterling efforts only hinted at in the advertisements, 'featuring tracks never previously released in stereo in the UK'. But that's only half the story; you'd think they would have made a bigger deal of it all.

The Beatles Box was, like *The Singles Collection 1962-1970*, made available through EMI's sub-division, World Records (although the labels were Parlophone), and sold mail order-only, initially at £29.75 with an option of setting up a monthly payment plan! The sheer weight of the collection was not seen as a barrier to posting, the whole set housed in what, for its day, was luxurious packaging, marked 'From Liverpool' on its crate-style box. The picture covers inside followed a general design pattern of period Beatles photos emerging from half-opened gift wrap, while a lengthy biography of the group served, in eight instalments, as sleeve notes. (Purchasers of the cassette edition got the essay on one large paper insert instead.) Sadly, the piece by Hugh Marshall hasn't aged well and is littered with what we all now know to be errors, caused mostly by the dearth of accurate information available back in the day – for example, he starts by mentioning the meeting between John and Paul on 15 June 1956, when the true date was more than a year later, 6 July 1957 – but to be fair to Marshall, this was written before Mark Lewisohn did the work to establish the correct details.

Anyway, setting aside its quirks, this blazing set is, in size and import, a landmark collection which went around the world – Mexico, Japan, Australia – but once again not to America, who weren't much interested in London product. Fair enough. In Britain the set was heavily advertised in the press, especially in the wake of John Lennon's death which stimulated interest in the group, and was available on vinyl or cassette (eight tapes inside the same outer box). It must have sold out because all went quiet through the middle 1980s until suddenly, in 1987, a fresh round of ads appeared announcing 1500 copies of the cassette box were available in a 'Last Chance Edition'. And it was, for *The Beatles Box* has never been re-issued – another one crying out for a fan-friendly re-appearance on CD, which will never happen.

We'll take a look at the eight individual records and what's on them...

LP 1

On the cover:
The Beatles posing with
instruments, as shot by
Terence Spencer in 1963.

Love Me Do	From Me To You
PS I Love You	Thank You Girl
I Saw Her Standing There	She Loves You
Please Please Me	It Won't Be Long
Misery	Please Mister Postman
Do You Want To Know A Secret	All My Loving
A Taste Of Honey	Roll Over Beethoven
Twist And Shout	Money (That's What I Want)

There
16 tracks from 1962-63, starting with Love Me Do then running through
much of *Please Please Me* and *With The Beatles*, plus contemporary singles.

Rare
Love Me Do with Ringo on drums gets its first UK release since 1962,
having been recovered for the US *Rarities* album earlier in the year. She
Loves You is the faux-stereo mix created for *A Collection Of Beatles Oldies*,
but most notable is All My Loving – with its rare hi-hat intro, as first heard
on the West German stereo pressing of *With The Beatles* in 1963.

Nowhere
No room here for John's great There's A Place, and surely the Lennon-
McCartney original, Ask Me Why would have been better than A Taste Of
Honey. Likewise the *With The Beatles* selections don't really need three
cover versions when originals like I Wanna Be Your Man and Hold Me
Tight might have been chosen.

LP 2

On the cover:
John and Paul, part of the rehearsal
for an appearance on *Shindig!* in
October 1964.

I Want To Hold Your Hand	Things We Said Today
This Boy	I'll Be Back
Can't Buy Me Love	Long Tall Sally
You Can't Do That	I Call Your Name
A Hard Day's Night	Matchbox
I Should Have Known Better	Slow Down
If I Fell	She's A Woman
And I Love Her	I Feel Fine

There
16 tracks from 1963-64, spanning from I Want To Hold Your Hand to I Feel
Fine, encompassing along the way, much of *A Hard Day's Night* and –
again – the whole of the *Long Tall Sally* EP.

Rare
And I Love Her is the novel version with extended coda, taken from the
West German pressing of *Something New* in 1969, then used again on the
US *Rarities* album. The *Long Tall Sally* EP is presented in stereo for the first
time – as is She's A Woman, despite what it said on the labels of the UK
Rarities album in 1978!

Nowhere
A Hard Day's Night is well represented but it's a shame George's vocal, I'm
Happy Just To Dance With You was left off. Ditto John's Tell Me Why.
Also, the compilers decided to overlook Sie Liebt Dich and Komm, Gib Mir
Deine Hand.

LP 3

On the cover:
A snowy shot from the location filming of *Help!* in 1965.

Eight Days A Week	Ticket To Ride
No Reply	I'm Down
I'm A Loser	Help!
I'll Follow The Sun	The Night Before
Mr Moonlight	You've Got To Hide Your Love Away
Every Little Thing	I Need You
I Don't Want To Spoil The Party	Another Girl
Kansas City	You're Going To Lose That Girl

There

16 tracks bridging from 1964 into 1965. Side 1 of the compilation is all *Beatles For Sale*; side 2 contains the whole of side 1 of *Help!*, plus the contemporary B-side, I'm Down.

Rare

Not so much here, just the stereo mix of I'm Down. (It's A-side, Help!, is in mono.)

Nowhere

From *Beatles For Sale*, this reviewer would have liked to have seen Baby's In Black and What You're Doing – and to make way we might have done without Mr Moonlight and I Don't Want To Spoil The Party.

LP 4

On the cover:
This is where the chronology starts to go awry; this cover shows the Beatles on the set of *Thank Your Lucky Stars* in 1963.

Yesterday	Michelle
Act Naturally	Drive My Car
Tell Me What You See	Norwegian Wood (This
It's Only Love	Bird Has Flown)
You Like Me Too Much	You Won't See Me
I've Just Seen A Face	Nowhere Man
Day Tripper	Girl
We Can Work It Out	I'm Looking Through You
	In My Life

There
16 tracks from 1965, continuing the extensive coverage of *Help!*, with six more from that album. Then *Rubber Soul* kicks in and we have eight cuts from that LP, entirely filling side 2.

Rare
Day Tripper comes in the 'Dexterized' mix prepared for *Yesterday... And Today*, which was never released in the UK.

Nowhere
This album rounds up everything from *Help!* bar its final track, Dizzy Miss Lizzy. And while there are rich pickings from *Rubber Soul*, it's surprising that neither of George's Think For Yourself or If I Needed Someone are in.

LP 5

On the cover:
And this one's way out of
time: the group on Granada
Television's *Scene At 6:30*,
filmed November 1963.

Paperback Writer	Eleanor Rigby
Rain	And Your Bird Can Sing
Here, There And Everywhere	For No One
Taxman	Doctor Robert
I'm Only Sleeping	Got To Get You Into My Life
Good Day Sunshine	Penny Lane
Yellow Submarine	Strawberry Fields Forever

There
Only 14 tracks now. but we're into peak territory with 10 of *Revolver*'s
original cuts buttressed by both sides of two hit singles (Paperback Writer /
Rain and Penny Lane / Strawberry Fields Forever), to make for an
'alternate' *Revolver* LP.

Rare
We see a re-appearance of the edited-up 'trumpet ending' version of Penny
Lane, making a UK debut. Its flip-side, Strawberry Fields Forever, is in its
1971 stereo mix. But the real rarity is I'm Only Sleeping which is in a
particularly obscure mix which initially only appeared on US tape format
editions of *Yesterday... And Today,* then certain specific vinyl pressings. It
has the guitar solo fading in, with the first note missing.

Nowhere
Tomorrow Never Knows is a glaring omission, and with two fewer tracks
than the previous LPs, surely they could have squeezed it on. She Said She
Said is also missed.

LP 6

On the cover:
Spot on. The Beatles at an Abbey Road Studios press conference, ahead of the taping of the All You Need Is Love television clip, June 1967.

Sgt Pepper's Lonely Hearts Club Band	When I'm Sixty Four
With A Little Help From My Friends	Lovely Rita
Lucy In The Sky With Diamonds	All You Need Is Love
Fixing A Hole	Baby, You're A Rich Man
She's Leaving Home	Magical Mystery Tour
Being For The Benefit Of Mr Kite!	Your Mother Should Know
A Day In The Life	The Fool On The Hill
	I Am The Walrus

There

15 tracks from 1967, including nine from *Sgt Pepper*, with side 1 almost duplicating that of the original LP. The *Magical Mystery Tour* EP is raided for two thirds of its tracks and both sides of the group's summer 1967 single are included.

Rare

I Am The Walrus comes in the novel US *Rarities* edit, its first appearance on a UK disc. A Day In The Life has a unique clean start rather than the usual cross-fade. And Baby, You're A Rich Man is in its stereo form, as mixed in 1971 for the West German market.

Nowhere

Getting Better is the only track missing from *Sgt Pepper*'s first side. Also, no Sgt Pepper Reprise here.

LP 7

On the cover:
On location, July 1968: 'The Mad Day Out'. (See also the inside of the *Red* and *Blue Album* gatefolds, and the cover of the US *Rarities*.)

Hello, Goodbye	The Continuing Story Of
Lady Madonna	Bungalow Bill
Hey Jude	Happiness Is A Warm Gun
Revolution	Martha My Dear
Back In The USSR	I'm So Tired
Ob-La-Di, Ob-La-Da	Piggies
While My Guitar Gently Weeps	Don't Pass Me By
	Julia
	All Together Now

There

15 tracks, almost all from 1968, with a few current singles then 10 songs from *The White Album*, and just one token track from *Yellow Submarine*.

Rare

Not much… The Continuing Story Of Bungalow Bill has the introductory musical riff edited off, while Don't Pass Me By is in mono.

Nowhere

Did they forget *The White Album* was a double? All ten selections are from the first LP, none from the second. Consequently there is no Sexy Sadie, Long, Long, Long or Mother Nature's Son – and Blackbird or Dear Prudence from the first disc might have been better than, say, Piggies. The final track, All Together Now, is the sole selection from *Yellow Submarine* – but who seriously prefers it to Hey Bulldog?

LP 8

On the cover:
And back to 1967 again,
and that Abbey Road
Studio press conference.

Get Back	Come Together
Don't Let Me Down	Something
The Ballad Of John And Yoko	Maxwell's Silver Hammer
Across The Universe	Octopus's Garden
For You Blue	Here Comes The Sun
Two Of Us	Because
The Long And Winding Road	Golden Slumbers
Let It Be	Carry That Weight / The End / Her Majesty

There

18 tracks recorded 1969, side 1 consisting of songs from the drawn out *Let It Be* era – correctly placed prior to the *Abbey Road* material which takes up all of side 2, to make a miniature version of that album. (The last track is three different songs listed as one – so really there are 18 here, not the 16 numbered on the sleeve.)

Rare

Nothing, except that when Her Majesty follows The End, it's separated by a normal-length pause rather than the 15 seconds of silence on *Abbey Road*.

Nowhere

The *Let It Be* selections are okay but Dig A Pony or I've Got A Feeling would have been nice. *Abbey Road* is well represented but You Never Give Me Your Money would have been a better option that Maxwell.

The Beatles Box Audition Disc

Contains extracts from:

Love Me Do	Eleanor Rigby
A Hard Day's Night	Sgt Pepper's Lonely Hearts
And I Love Her	Club Band
I Call Your Name	Lucy In The Sky With Diamonds
Eight Days A Week	She's Leaving Home
Help!	When I'm Sixty-Four
You've Got To Hide Your	Hello, Goodbye
Love Away	Hey Jude
Yesterday	Get Back
We Can Work It Out	All Together Now
Michelle	The Long And Winding Road

The *From Liverpool* box set also had a promotional flexi-disc produced, the third seven-inch promo issued in the period 1976-1980 in support of the main releases (see also the 1976 *Singles Collection* and *Rock 'N' Roll Music*).

This flexi-disc contains narration, plus segments of 20 different songs, playing for some six and a half minutes. Listen out for a unique piece of editing near the start, where the harmonica in Love Me Do continues after the vocals kick in!

Forgotten format

The Beatles EPs Collection

★★★★☆

UK release:
7 December 1981

Twist And Shout
The Beatles' Hits
The Beatles (No. 1)
All My Loving
Long Tall Sally
Extracts From The Film A Hard Day's Night
Extracts From The Album A Hard Day's Night
Beatles For Sale
Beatles For Sale No. 2
The Beatles' Million Sellers
Yesterday
Nowhere Man
Magical Mystery Tour
'The Inner Light'

The death of John Lennon in December 1980 was a shock to Beatles fans the world over, and in its aftermath, although his solo music was extensively re-issued, all went quiet on the group front. The idea of continuing to exploit the Beatles' back catalogue seemed like bad taste under the circumstances and a year went by before EMI put out anything new. It was initially rumoured that an LP compilation of the group's EP tracks was in the offing, but when it arrived it was in the form of a box set of seven-inch re-issues, styled as per the 1978 *Blue Box* of LPs. (The older *Singles Collection 1962-1970* was also reinvented in 1982 (see entry on page 100) and styled the same again, so all three collections would match.)

When the Beatles were current, it was nearly always the case that UK 45 singles were issued in company paper sleeves, with none of the designed artwork familiar in most of the rest of the world. (In the 60s, the only UK Beatles single to get the picture sleeve treatment was Penny Lane / Strawberry Fields Forever.) This is where the EPs held particular appeal, for not only did each one contain four tracks as opposed to two, they were issued in glossy picture covers typically featuring photographs of the band.

The Beatles released 12 UK EPs between 1963 and 1966, at which point the whole format was falling into a rapid decline, fans clamouring instead for the burgeoning rock albums coming thick and fast. In their time, eight Beatles EPs topped the special EP chart, the rest polling somewhere towards the top end, as the group not surprisingly outsold the rest. (*Twist And Shout* holds the all-time record for UK EP sales, and spent 21 weeks at number 1.) The EP chart was last published on 2 Dec 1967, and so from then on the dwindling number of EPs coming out were simply treated as singles – hence, when the Beatles' final one appeared, the double pack which was *Magical Mystery Tour*, it climbed to number 2 in the *singles* chart. (What held it off the top? The Beatles of course, with Hello, Goodbye / I Am The Walrus. That B-side was also on the EP, so weirdly, the same recording was number 1 and 2 at the same time.)

The EPs are often overlooked these days, but when they first appeared they were pretty central to the group's output. One of them, *Long Tall Sally*, we have already discussed in this book for it contained a quartet of Beatles tracks not available anywhere else in the UK discography, until the second half of the 1970s moved them onto the LP format. Here they are again, restored to seven-inch disc.

While we're on the subject of the Beatles' EPs, we might as well take a brief detour and mention two which were never issued. The first is *The Beatles' Golden Discs* (I Want To Hold Your Hand; This Boy; She Loves You; I'll Get You) which was all set for release in early 1964 when cancelled for reasons not altogether clear. Test pressings and printed labels are known. The second is *Yellow Submarine* (Only A Northern Song; Hey Bulldog; Across The Universe; All Together Now; It's All Too Much), rounding up the new 1968 film music, plus the then unknown Across The Universe – which would have been better value for fans who ended up having to buy the *Yellow Submarine* LP instead.

Tracks on the Beatles' UK EPs:

Twist And Shout
Twist And Shout
A Taste Of Honey
Do You Want To Know A Secret
There's A Place

The Beatles' Hits
From Me To You
Thank You Girl
Please Please Me
Love Me Do

The Beatles (No. 1)
I Saw Her Standing There
Misery
Anna (Go To Him)
Chains

All My Loving
All My Loving
Ask Me Why
Money
PS I Love You

Long Tall Sally
Long Tall Sally
I Call Your Name
Slow Down
Matchbox

Extracts From The Film
A Hard Day's Night
I Should Have Known Better
If I Fell
Tell Me Why
And I Love Her

Extracts From The Album
A Hard Day's Night
Any Time At All
I'll Cry Instead
Things We Said Today
When I Get Home

Beatles For Sale
No Reply
I'm A Loser
Rock And Roll Music
Eight Days A Week

Beatles For Sale No. 2
I'll Follow The Sun
Baby's In Black
Words Of Love
I Don't Want To Spoil The Party

The Beatles' Million Sellers
She Loves You
I Want To Hold Your Hand
Can't Buy Me Love
I Feel Fine

Yesterday
Yesterday
Act Naturally
You Like Me Too Much
It's Only Love

Nowhere Man
Nowhere Man
Drive My Car
Michelle
You Won't See Me

Magical Mystery Tour
Magical Mystery Tour
Your Mother Should Know
I Am The Walrus
The Fool On The Hill
Flying
Blue Jay Way

'The Inner Light'
The Inner Light
Baby, You're A Rich Man
She's A Woman
This Boy

The 1981 EPs collection housed 15 discs inside its royal blue box, encompassing 58 different recordings. The EP format might have been archaic when this re-issue came out but there's no denying the old-fashioned charm of these colourful little things. And with this, the Beatles' complete 1960s discography, LP, EP and single, was available again, in three comprehensive boxes. So of course, EMI would never again need to repackage the Beatles…

Do all without doing

'The Inner Light' EP
★★★☆☆

UK release:
7 December 1981

The Inner Light	She's A Woman
Baby, You're A Rich Man	This Boy

Included in the 1981 *EP Collection* was a mysterious extra disc, untitled and duplicating the cover art of the UK Penny Lane / Strawberry Fields Forever single from back in 1967. But it wasn't a re-press, it was a whole new EP, the Beatles' first in 14 years – a big deal for collectors, you might say, so why didn't they come up with some new artwork too? And why didn't they give it a title? (We'll refer to it as *'The Inner Light'*, but that's not its true name.)

The new EP was put into the set to attract buyers, on the heels of Yesterday in the corresponding singles box, and *Rarities* with the LPs. But it had a supposed purpose – rounding up four tracks which had not been issued in stereo before, or, at least, not where the general public might have heard them. The finer details though tell a dubious tale, so let's see where we're really at:

- **The Inner Light** – issued as a mono B-side in 1968, this was indeed the first time it had appeared in stereo.

- **Baby, You're A Rich Man** – this had been available in stereo for years, but on non-mainstream releases. Its most recent appearance had been on the eight-LP *The Beatles Box* in 1980.

- **She's A Woman** – this had also been issued in stereo before, including on *The Beatles Box*, as the sleeve notes here correctly say. (So why include it?)

- **This Boy** – remember the debacle with *A Collection Of Beatles Oldies*, where Bad Boy was meant to be mixed for stereo, but they accidentally mixed This Boy instead, which wasn't even on the album? That means they had a stereo mix gathering dust but instead of using it here, they turned to the fake stereo version previously heard on *Love Songs*.

I make that one real deal out of four. Not great, is it?

The most interesting aspect of this EP, apart from the genuine stereo debut of The Inner Light, was the fact that She's A Woman suddenly had a count-in, never heard previously. It's Paul counting and it's pretty quiet, but its apparent mis-match with the rhythm of the song has lead to speculation that it was edited on. However the track has a particular rhythm and Paul is actually counting half a bar in accurate time, inserting a number on each off-beat: "one, TWO, three, FOUR". So now you know.

There's no denying '*The Inner Light*' is a lovely little item, its lead-off track sounding great with its Indian instruments sent left and right. It's just a shame that there was no real coherence to the mini-set, and a re-use of what was admittedly an attractive cover image.

Reeling 'em in

Reel Music
★★☆☆☆

UK release:
29 March 1982

US release:
22 March 1982

A Hard Day's Night	I Am The Walrus
I Should Have Known Better	Yellow Submarine
Can't Buy Me Love	All You Need Is Love
And I Love Her	Let It Be
Help!	Get Back
You've Got To Hide Your Love Away	The Long And Winding Road
Ticket To Ride	
Magical Mystery Tour	

First of all, with EMI having returned to the largely dead format of the EP in 1981, it's worth pointing out the obvious: *Reel Music* is *not* a re-issue of the Beatles' albums on reel-to-reel tape. (No such fun.) It is, in fact, yet another themed assemblage of tracks, similar to the ones we've seen before. EMI had tried to put a brave face on their ongoing lack of ideas, but in November 1980 its budget arm, Music For Pleasure, offered up some prizes for readers of the *Beatles Appreciation Society Magazine* in respect of a competition to come up with something new:

> *"Imagine you have been given the job of organising a new Beatles compilation album, and choosing a title for it. Just decide which, of all their numbers, are the ten you'd most like to see put together on one LP. Entering the competition is your chance to actually help influence the decision about which Beatles songs should be included on future compilation albums!"*

Wow. Could they make it any more obvious if they tried?

The *Beatles Appreciation Society Magazine* promised they would publish full details of the outcome of the competition, but never did – bar the name of the winner, Malcolm Weaver. But it wasn't he who thought up the contents of EMI's new Beatles comp, it was Capitol's Randall Davis. The back-story is that Walter Shenson, owner of the film, *A Hard Day's Night*, had been preparing a re-run of the movie with enhanced soundtrack, set to hit US screens in April 1982. Ever-alert to a cash-in, Capitol drew up plans for a collection of the Beatles' film songs, with reference to all five: *A Hard Day's Night*; *Help!*; *Magical Mystery Tour*; *Yellow Submarine*; and *Let It Be.*

Hoping to make something from a none-too-subtle concept, Capitol expended most of their time and effort on the packaging, *Reel Music* including a large, full-colour booklet and an impressive illustration on the sleeve by artist, David McMacken, which ran around both sides to make up an image of multiple Beatles queuing to get into the cinema.

But in truth, the overarching theme was flimsy, there being little to link the group's widely-separated films, much less the music, which consequently ranged from Beatlemania hits to late-period, orchestrated ballads. They simply don't hang together, Capitol's 'solution' of sequencing the tracks into mini-sets, one for each film, merely underlining the paucity of the concept. Even the title was a weak pun, which didn't communicate much to the casual browser.

Ultimately the album received little love from Beatles fans, who too often saw it as a cash-grab – which it was. *Reel Music* suffered a familiar fate, soon deleted and gone for good from EMI's memory. For most, it represents the low-point of Beatles repackaging, and but for a timely 'greatest hits' collection at the end of 1982, it would be the last of its kind. Lesson learned. Perhaps they should have listened to Malcolm Weaver instead!

Movie meddling

The Beatles' Movie Medley /
I'm Happy Just To Dance
With You
★★☆☆☆

UK release:
21 May 1982

US release:
15 March 1982

A bit of a back-story:

In 1979 a couple of Canadian DJs helped splice together a medley of pop songs, using their skills in matching keys and tempos to make a quasi-disco bootleg on the Alto label. It came to the attention of Dutch music publisher, Willem van Kooten, who heard it over the speakers of a record shop and realising he owned the rights to one of the songs, knew it had to be unauthorised. The medley gave him an idea – why not make a legal version by using soundalike recordings, and issue it out legitimately.

That he did, and using a drum loop, he created and released an 11-and-a-half-minute dance medley, in the middle of which were eight successive Beatles songs – and this middle section started getting radio plays, leading to an edited down version, released on seven-inch single and issued under the name Stars On 45. (The anonymous vocalists were in fact Dutch singers,

Bas Muys (John), Hans Vermeulen (Paul) and Okkie Huijsdens (George).)
The single was a major hit, first in the Netherlands then in Britain and
America, and practically everywhere else in the early summer of 1981.

When it came to *Reel Music* and the possibility of issuing a single to
support it, Capitol got their thinking caps on and came up with... a
sequence of song snippets, all edited together. Thank goodness there was
no drum loop, but they did tack together parts of seven songs from the LP,
namely, Magical Mystery Tour, All You Need Is Love, You've Got To Hide
Your Love Away, I Should Have Known Better, A Hard Day's Night,
Ticket To Ride and Get Back. And to satisfy legal requirements, that whole
mouthful had to be printed on the record labels!

The Movie Medley landed in a mini version of the *Reel Music* sleeve, and
was modestly successful on the US charts. In the UK, Parlophone assigned
it a catalogue number but didn't release it, first monitoring the US single to
see how it fared. British Beatles fans soon got wind of it and started
ordering import copies, and given its fairly respectable US sales,
Parlophone capitulated. Issued two months later, the UK edition somehow
scraped into the top 10.

Despite doing well in the market place, The Beatles' Movie Medley was
almost immediately dropped by EMI. They did concede to put copies in
the 1982 singles box (*qv*) for the sake of completeness but its official
deletion occurred on 31 May 1984 – and in true *1984* style, it was
permanently liquidated. It's never been mentioned since, never been re-
issued and never put onto LP or CD – in fact it's the only official Beatles
track unavailable since first release. It's as if EMI/Capitol wished it had
never happened, its gimmicky nature at odds with the revered stature the
Beatles' music is normally accorded.

MFSL: startling quietness

The Beatles: The Collection
★★★★☆

US release:
1 October 1982

Please Please Me
With The Beatles
A Hard Day's Night
Beatles For Sale
Help!
Rubber Soul
Revolver
Sgt Pepper's Lonely Hearts
        Club Band
Magical Mystery Tour
The Beatles
Yellow Submarine
Abbey Road
Let It Be

"Original Master Recordings employ Mobile Fidelity Sound Lab's exclusive half-speed mastering process to capture every nuance of sound from that master tape."

"Original Master Recordings are pressed overseas utilizing Super Vinyl, an exclusive compound far superior to even so-called 100% virgin vinyl for maximum clarity and startling quietness."

"Original Master Recordings are exclusively transferred from the original stereo master tapes that the musicians recorded in the studio."

So reads the hype on the covers of the high-quality records put out by Mobile Fidelity Sound Lab (MFSL) in the late 1970s. (Oh, and did they mention it's all 'exclusive'?) The company started out in the 1950s but in 1977 underwent a reinvention and soon made a mini-splash with its audiophile pressing of *Dark Side Of The Moon*, which got them noticed. And it wasn't long before MFSL struck an unlikely deal with EMI-Capitol, normally fiercely protective of the Beatles' catalogue, to work their stuff on the group's last, and technically most advanced album, *Abbey Road*, which appeared as an Original Master Recording, with its incongruous white labels, in the last days of December 1979.

Abbey Road was a big seller by MFSL's standards and keen to do another one, the US album, *Magical Mystery Tour*, was given the Original Master Recordings treatment in February 1981. Although it sounded fab, there was a compromise in that the master tapes used were third-generation, the true original masters made in London, sent to Capitol for copying and compiling to LP in 1967, then copied back as one for the UK issue of *Magical Mystery Tour* in the 1970s before MFSL duplicated them yet again. They even had artificially created stereo on a couple of the tracks, courtesy of Capitol not having the right stereo sources back in the day. Didn't matter – *MMT* was another biggie for MFSL, and so in January 1982, *The White Album* – and fans could also now get titles like *Band On The Run* and *Double Fantasy* on MFSL.

The success of these releases set MFSL on the inevitable course of doing *all* the Beatles' albums in the same manner, and in October 1982, they issued them out as *The Beatles: The Collection*, so not at all confusing after *The Beatles Collection* (1978). Improbable as it seems, MFSL now managed to get a loan of the original precious Abbey Road master tapes which were sent across the Atlantic, allowing them to fulfil their promise of taking the audio from source.

Necessary this was, but it had an unavoidable knock-on effect, in its way as unlikely as EMI letting them have the tapes in the first place – it meant the contents of this would-be defining collection, pitched primarily at the American market, would comprise the UK LP series – not Capitol titles like *Beatles VI* and *Yesterday… And Today*, feeding a paradigm shift where over the next several years, US collectors began to readjust their understanding of the Beatles' recorded legacy.

It also meant the contents would – exclusive technology aside – be the same as that of *The Beatles Collection*, even down to the UK *Rarities* LP which was set for inclusion until the last minute when it was pulled. However the set did include MFSL's existing *Magical Mystery Tour*, which the 1978 box had not, and there's every reason to think this was a direct trade for the unwanted *Rarities*, which would explain why the album list on the box has it in the wrong sequence, as if it were shoe-horned in.

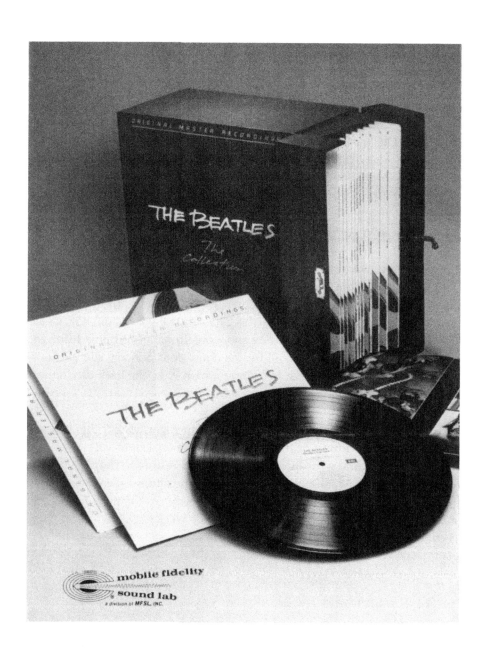

It made sense, providing purchasers with such fare as Penny Lane, I Am The Walrus and All You Need Is Love – rather better than She's A Woman and Slow Down.

The packaging too was well done, the records housed in a sturdy case with metal hinges – but the real curiosity was that MFSL used their own sleeve designs on each LP – yet another improbable concession from EMI, but there they are. What they'd done was replace the usual artwork with images of EMI's master tape boxes, so fans could pore over the hand-written markings telling the story of each tape reel. The actual album covers were instead reproduced in a large book included with the set – but might it have been better to retain them on the sleeves, and put the tape box photos in a book, perhaps with some explanatory notes? Regardless, MFSL's unique covers give this collection a distinctive identity.

The collection made its way around the world in small, but expensive numbers ($325 in the US; £299 in the UK – about 60 times the cost of an ordinary single LP). Japan went its own way and made up a box of old-style LPs, but comprising an astonishing 83 albums in a custom box, called *The Complete Works Of The Beatles* and containing everything from the group and also the solo years, all for the equivalent princely sum of $1400 or £800. The Beatles were fast becoming a cash cow, the back catalogue a gift which never stopped giving.

MFSL continued their standard release pattern regardless of this box set, putting out individual Beatles LPs at occasional intervals over the following few years, with the proper cover art restored. They eventually ran into problems when it became clear the same albums were being lined up for CD in 1987, MFSL realising the game was up for their *passé* vinyl and rush-releasing the last six in a matter of weeks at the close of 1986. They do sound great, though.

One-track mind

The Beatles Mono Collection
★★★★☆

UK release:
3 October 1982

Please Please Me
With The Beatles
A Hard Day's Night
Beatles For Sale
Help!
Rubber Soul
Revolver
Sgt Pepper's Lonely Hearts
           Club Band
The Beatles
Yellow Submarine

Beatles collectors are a difficult crowd to please. Partly that's because they pay extraordinarily close attention to what they're hearing, every drum beat and vocal inflection precisely known and subject to discussion, so it's no surprise they are especially picky when it comes to audio quality. Stereo vs mono is a debate as old as *Please Please Me* itself, and hard-line mono-ists are seldom shy of putting stereo-ites in their place by reminding them that the Beatles personally helped George Martin mix their mono albums, but not stereo, which they therefore can't have been bothered about. Game, set and match.

The fact that by 1969 mono was dead, as buyers abandoned it in droves for the luxurious sound of stereo is merely proof of the mono-ists' superior listening skills. But for the Beatles, their last couple of albums weren't mixed in mono at all, and although the older mono albums weren't deleted, their days were numbered and supply dwindled out in the late 1970s.

By 1981 the market for Beatles product was becoming insatiable, and the fact that here was a product line unfulfilled meant that even if demand for mono was less than overwhelming, there were enough connoisseurs out there to make it a viable sell. So, they had some new mono pressing plates made up and set about rolling brand-new mono Beatles albums off the conveyor belt in June 1981. These were individual LPs, pressed in limited quantities, but they sold well, making their boxing up into a collection, like the stereo albums before them, an obvious move.

The Beatles Mono Collection was designed to match the 1978 stereo *Blue Box* but with a red finish – blue and red counterparts, again. The boxes were limited to 10,000 and arrived in the shops in October 1982. (The US had the same release, but the boxes were black.) This was a niche purchase, given that not only were all the singles and EP tracks missing, as per *The Blue Box*, but there was no *Abbey Road* or *Let It Be*, so this was a long way from being a complete collection. Rather, it was pitched to the group's dedicated fans who respected authenticity and enjoyed hearing their Beatles the old way.

It was 20 years ago today…

20 Greatest Hits
★★★☆☆

UK release: 11 October 1982
US release: 11 October 1982

UK edition:	US edition:
Love Me Do	She Loves You
From Me To You	Love Me Do
She Loves You	I Want To Hold Your Hand
I Want To Hold Your Hand	Can't Buy Me Love
Can't Buy Me Love	A Hard Day's Night
A Hard Day's Night	I Feel Fine
I Feel Fine	Eight Days A Week
Ticket To Ride	Ticket To Ride
Help!	Help!
Day Tripper	Yesterday
We Can Work It Out	We Can Work It Out
	Paperback Writer
Paperback Writer	
Yellow Submarine	Penny Lane
Eleanor Rigby	All You Need Is Love
All You Need Is Love	Hello, Goodbye
Hello, Goodbye	Hey Jude [Short Version]
Lady Madonna	Get Back
Hey Jude	Come Together
Get Back	Let It Be
The Ballad Of John And Yoko	The Long And Winding Road

With the 20th anniversary of Love Me Do on the horizon, speculation and rumour were rife through 1982, word on the street that albums of BBC recordings (all then previously unreleased) were in the offing, bettered only by claims that an album of studio outtakes was imminent – probably coupled with a single release of Leave My Kitten Alone. Prophetic stuff (see pages 106-109) and as summer slipped into autumn, expectations were high as fans waited to see what EMI would come up with.

In truth, they delivered some fine product – the original Ringo version of Love Me Do on vintage red Parlophone, the Beatles' first 12-inch single containing *both* versions, the Beatles' first picture disc single, a new singles box with all the 45s in attractive new picture sleeves (see next entry), and another first – a home video documentary, *The Compleat Beatles*. But were fans happy? Alas no – such was the advance hype about the coming of unheard material that many were disappointed. All they had which was 'new' was the first official release of the Decca audition recordings, and that was a non-EMI LP of tracks already available on bootlegs.

Another key release which arrived among this bounty was the group's next compilation album, *20 Greatest Hits*, a celebration on vinyl of all the Beatles' number 1 singles. This too came with a twinge of anti-climax though. As was widely reported, EMI was planning to assemble all the group's 22 original A-sides on a double album, which seems to have come fairly close to completion since a small number of test pressings are known. But right on the eve of its production, EMI changed their minds and when the LP appeared, it unexpectedly consisted of just a single disc, with a plain front cover, giving grounds for more grumbles. And to add to the let-down, there were no new tracks, and all 20 titles had in any case been featured on *1962-1966* and *1967-1970*.

The official reason for the late change was that other countries were opting for single albums, and so the UK should fall in line – although most overseas releases would have mirrored the UK/US formats anyway, so the argument didn't hold much weight. Time for a theory: in 1979-1980, several European countries had released the new album, *20 Golden Hits*, compiling a score of the group's most popular songs on one LP housed inside a plain white sleeve with just some lettering (see page 277). Meanwhile fearing the double LP format might leave *20 Greatest Hits* looking too much like *1962-1966* and *1967-1970*, Parlophone decided instead to make what was essentially the UK edition of *20 Golden Hits*, which would end up sharing a dozen tracks and a similar cover.

By fluke, the Beatles' UK number 1s numbered 19 (17 singles, two of which were double A-sides). Thus, with Love Me Do thrown on as track 1, they had the requisite tally. For Capitol, watching from the other side of the Pond, the target 20 tracks were even easier: the Beatles had exactly 20 number 1s in America, so the album needed little further planning. (Incidentally, the UK count of 17 number 1 singles, and the US tally of 20, were both all-time records for any artist.) Of course the US number 1s and the UK number 1s were sometimes different, as reflected in the track listing of the two editions of the LP.

Although the UK edition, with its Parlophone anniversary credentials, was the more relevant release, it was the US Capitol version which became the international standard. The inner sleeve carried an interesting montage of Beatles photos down the years, and unremarked on was the fact that the biggest of them, running along the top part of the collage, consisted of photographs from the solo years – an odd thing to see on a group retrospective. The fact is, the solo photos were as irrelevant as the album itself, which ostensibly commemorated that anniversary but didn't really engage the fans, who had it all already. It was a nice, concise package for casual purchasers but there weren't enough of them to make it a big deal. The LP got to 10 in the UK but only 50 on *Billboard*, and would be the last ever compilation while the Capitol-Parlophone dichotomy held sway. When the next one rolled around, six years later, releases were in permanent synchronisation and product was only issued under authority of the Beatles themselves.

UK number 1s not on the US edition:

From Me To You (number 41 in the US)
Day Tripper (number 5 in the US)
Yellow Submarine (number 2 in the US)
Eleanor Rigby (number 11 in the US)
Lady Madonna (number 4 in the US)
The Ballad Of John And Yoko (number 8 in the US)

US number 1s not on the UK edition:

Eight Days A Week (not a single in the UK)
Yesterday (not a single in the UK)
Penny Lane (number 2 in the UK)
Come Together (number 4 in the UK)
Let It Be (number 2 in the UK)
The Long And Winding Road (not a single in the UK)

NB – the US number 1, **Love Me Do***, was not a UK number 1, but was on the UK album.*

A footnote: in May 1983, the Australian Parlophone label issued their own version of this album, consisting of an LP and a bonus single, in order to accommodate 23 chart-topping tracks. Re-titled *The Number Ones*, it preceded the global *1* album by 17 years!

In the picture

The Beatles Singles Collection
★★★★★

UK release:
6 December 1982

Love Me Do / PS I Love You
Please Please Me / Ask Me Why
From Me To You / Thank You Girl
She Loves You / I'll Get You
I Want To Hold Your Hand / This Boy
Can't Buy Me Love / You Can't Do That
A Hard Day's Night / Things We Said Today
I Feel Fine / She's A Woman
Ticket To Ride / Yes It Is
Help! / I'm Down
We Can Work It Out / Day Tripper
Paperback Writer / Rain
Eleanor Rigby / Yellow Submarine
Strawberry Fields Forever / Penny Lane
All You Need Is Love / Baby, You're A Rich Man
Hello, Goodbye / I Am The Walrus
Lady Madonna / The Inner Light
Hey Jude / Revolution
Get Back / Don't Let Me Down
The Ballad Of John And Yoko / Old Brown Shoe
Something / Come Together
Let It Be / You Know My Name (Look Up The Number)
Yesterday / I Should Have Known Better
Back In The USSR / Twist And Shout
Sgt Pepper-With A Little Help From My Friends / A Day In The Life
The Beatles' Movie Medley / I'm Happy Just To Dance With You

The 1976 *Singles Collection* had filled an enormous gap for latter-day collectors, rounding up all the group's 45s and even expanding as new releases came along. There were two small hitches – one was its styling, with the big round logo on the box, which meant it didn't quite match the LP and EP collections. The other was that the 1976 sleeves, generic and not particularly good, were somewhat boring by 1980s standards whereby full picture sleeves were now standard.

And so EMI decided to revamp the collection and issue an updated version, outwardly matching the other box sets and with every one of the singles inside a freshly designed sleeve. (The last 12 months had therefore seen box sets of stereo LPs (MFSL), mono LPs, EPs, and now singles – just about everything anyone could want.)

The contents of the new set were of course what one would expect – the 22 original 45s, plus the three UK singles from 1976-1978, and for completeness, the recent Movie Medley. The new artwork was the big sell, each picture sleeve carrying a period photo of the group, with Penny Lane, Let It Be, Sgt Pepper and the Movie Medley retaining their original cover designs.

Instantly recognisable was the new Love Me Do single, since its contemporary stand-alone release was currently at an all-time high of number 4 on the UK chart. In fact the success of Love Me Do persuaded EMI to go further in their singles marketing, and over the next eight years, every one of the picture sleeve singles from this set was re-issued by itself on the 20th anniversary of the original (or as close as was practical), accompanied each time by a collectable picture disc edition, overhauling the classic 45s for the modern era. Three of them were also issued in new 12-inch editions, but of course none of these novelties were included in the 1982 box.

One point of interest though, this collection was also manufactured in an export edition (catalogue number BSCP1 as opposed to BSC1) and it included along with the 26 picture sleeve editions, the first picture disc, Love Me Do. Nice touch.

Thanks to the regular anniversary releases pulled from this box, the Beatles dipped in and out of the UK singles charts through the 1980s:

> **Love Me Do** – number 4 in 1982
> **Please Please Me** – number 29 in 1983
> **From Me To You** – number 40 in 1983
> **She Loves You** – number 45 in 1983
> **I Want To Hold Your Hand** – number 62 in 1983
> **Can't Buy Me Love** – number 53 in 1984
> **A Hard Day's Night** – number 52 in 1984
> **I Feel Fine** – number 65 in 1984
> **Ticket To Ride** – number 70 in 1985
> **Eleanor Rigby / Yellow Submarine** – number 63 in 1986
> **Strawberry Fields Forever / Penny Lane** – number 65 in 1987
> **All You Need Is Love** – number 47 in 1987
> **Hello, Goodbye** – number 63 in 1987
> **Lady Madonna** – number 67 in 1988
> **Hey Jude** – number 52 in 1988
> **Get Back** – number 74 in 1989

Super-marketing

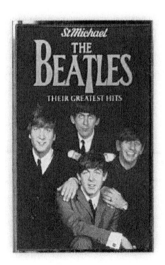

Their Greatest Hits
★☆☆☆☆

**UK release:
November 1984**

She Loves You	Can't Buy Me Love
From Me To You	Bad Boy
We Can Work It Out	Day Tripper
Help!	A Hard Day's Night
Michelle	Ticket To Ride
Yesterday	Paperback Writer
I Feel Fine	Eleanor Rigby
Yellow Submarine	I Want To Hold Your Hand

A familiar fixture of the British high street, the Marks & Spencer department store was probably best known in the 1980s for its clothing line, viewed with a mixture of affection and scorn by the public for its famously frumpy pullovers and notoriously conservative underwear range. It's a little surprising then to find that M&S tried to move in on the music business in the late 1970s, issuing LPs and cassettes by the likes of Twiggy, Brotherhood of Man and even Jimi Hendrix, on its own St Michael label. They must have thought the idea had more legs than their range of men's slacks, since 60 or more LPs were issued in 1978 and 1979 – and then suddenly the St Michael label was history. Until 1984, that is, when a new run of albums appeared on St Michael cassettes, one of them by none other than the Beatles.

The more important thing from Marks & Spencer's point of view was the publication of a large-format paperback book called *The Beatles: The Story And The Music*, copies of which were put on sale in their town-centre shops in November 1984, priced £4.99. The book was nothing much – just a re-working of articles from the 1970s magazine series, *The Story Of Pop*, but what makes it noteworthy here is that inside the packet was this enticing Beatles cassette.

Their Greatest Hits, although it looked like a new compilation, was really a re-issue of *A Collection Of Beatles Oldies*, licensed out by EMI. It had a new cover to match the book, and a new title, but Parlophone had put out cassette editions of the original anyway, so as with the book it was merely a rehash. And while this odd curiosity may have raised one or two interested eyebrows at the time, it signalled the start of a worrying trend towards budget exploitation of the Beatles' catalogue which would reach its low-point in 1986. George's face on the front of the cassette says it all.

Palaeontology

The History Of Rock
Volume Twenty Six
★★☆☆☆

UK release:
18 December 1984

She Loves You	Twist And Shout [live]
From Me To You	She's A Woman [live]
We Can Work It Out	Dizzy Miss Lizzy [live]
Help!	Ticket To Ride [live]
Michelle	Can't Buy Me Love [live]
Yesterday	Things We Said Today [live]
I Feel Fine	Roll Over Beethoven [live]
Yellow Submarine	
Can't Buy Me Love	Boys [live]
Bad Boy	A Hard Day's Night [live]
Day Tripper	Help! [live]
A Hard Day's Night	All My Loving [live]
Ticket To Ride	She Loves You [live]
Paperback Writer	Long Tall Sally [live]
Eleanor Rigby	
I Want To Hold Your Hand	

The History Of Rock was a periodical launched in 1982 by the publisher, Orbis, weekly instalments of which would, by 1984, build into an encyclopaedia of contemporary music. In the end there were 120 magazines produced, forming ten volumes for which matching binders were available, and along the way several Beatles-related editions appeared including, comprehensively, *The Beatles 1956-64* (issue 28) and *The Beatles 1964-70* (issue 58). The magazine's general style and appearance

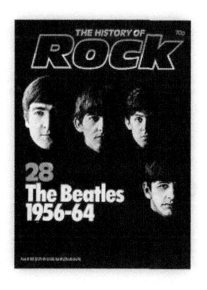

hasn't dated well but the contents included essays by journalistic heavy-weights like Chris Salewicz and Charles Shaar Murray, and many names familiar to Beatles book readers (Barry Miles (*Many Years From Now*), John Tobler (*The Beatles*), Steve Turner (*A Hard Day's Write*) and so on).

Not issued in synch with the magazines, and in fact long out-living them, was a series of 40 double LPs containing original music by many of the artists covered. Elvis was afforded the first volume, the Stones volume 10, Hendrix and Cream number 16 and so on, compiler Bob Fisher really pulling out the stops to make a highly impressive audio catalogue.

The biggest band in the world simply *had* to be included and Fisher and the team managed to do just that, winning permission from EMI to repackage *The Beatles At The Hollywood Bowl* and *A Collection Of Beatles Oldies* as a double album, *The History Of Rock Volume Twenty Six*. (Bear in mind the very recent *Their Greatest Hits* cassette was also a re-issue of *A Collection Of Beatles Oldies*.)

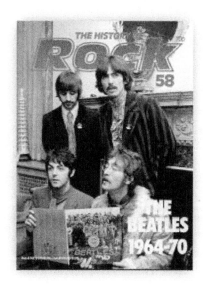

Just getting this album out was some achievement, so it's perhaps unfair to draw attention to its short-comings. However one must note that by its very nature it contained nothing after 1966 (and ironically, the associated magazine series had kicked off with volume 1, *The Year It All Came Together*, making the case that 1967 was popular music's key year). Also, the coupling of a 1964-65 concert recording with a 1966 hits compilation meant inevitable duplication, there being two different versions of A Hard Day's Night, Can't Buy Me Love, Help!, She Loves You and Ticket To Ride.

The album, like the rest of the series, was only available by mail order and is fairly easy to find these days for Beatles completists or those with a penchant for the extravagant *History Of Rock* set.

Unacceptable in the 80s

Sessions
★★★★☆

UK release:
February 1985 (not issued)

US release:
February 1985 (not issued)

Come And Get It	How Do You Do It
Leave My Kitten Alone	Besame Mucho
Not Guilty	One After 909 [1963 version]
I'm Looking Through You [early arrangement]	If You've Got Trouble
What's The New Mary Jane	That Means A Lot
	While My Guitar Gently Weeps [solo acoustic version]
	Mailman, Bring Me No More Blues
	Christmas Time (Is Here Again) [full, uninterrupted version]

The clamour for unreleased Beatles songs took much of its momentum from the very dawn of the bootleg LP, which in 1969 saw two astonishing sets of unofficial releases – namely Dylan and the Band's Basement Tapes (as *Great White Wonder*) and the Beatles' *Get Back* which appeared on albums such as *OPD* and *Kum Back*. These early milestones set fans' imaginations running riot and those who recalled *Kum Back* thought there must be more of the same under EMI's lock and key – although the actual chances of there being unreleased recordings of the calibre of *The Long And Winding Road* or *I've Got A Feeling* were practically nil.

Early on, Beatles fans were treated to several bootlegged concert recordings on albums like *Live Concert At Whiskey Flats* and *Alive At Last In Atlanta*, and various old BBC sessions on titles like *Yellow Matter Custard* and *Soldier Of Love*, but the real interest was in studio recordings. The first EMI outtake to leak was What's The New Mary Jane, which appeared on *Mary Jane (Spicy Beatles Songs)* in 1973. *LS Bumblebee* came out soon after and included the Beatles' Decca recording of Love Of The Loved, but it wasn't until 1976 that the next, How Do You Do It, emerged on a *Strawberry Fields Forever* fanzine single. More *Get Back* boots brought tracks like Suzy Parker and Watching Rainbows to the masses in the late 1970s, while the appearance of the full Decca tapes and the Star-Club tapes kept the conveyor belt rolling.

EMI was watching all this from the sidelines, and are known to have been taking stock. Aware that they had material like If You've Got Trouble, Come And Get It and Christmas Time (Is Here Again), they even started making some speculative compilations to see how they would sit together, one of which (the 'Boardroom Tape') was obtained and played to audiences at a Beatles convention in 1980. That tape soon found its way into the hands of organised bootleggers and so the LP *File Under Beatles* emerged with these and several other tracks.

The wider public of course knew practically none of this and in 1983, *Record Collector* ran an interview with EMI's Mike Heatley, who came out with the deflating news that, "there are only four unreleased tracks [and] a further five unreleased tracks, which for various reasons we can't mention here, which were not ever completed" (issue 80, Oct 1983), which seemed to indicate the coffers were practically empty and there was little prospect of a meaningful release, ever. Meanwhile EMI engineer, John Barrett, was documenting all the group's studio tapes and cataloguing what was there, shedding light on further recordings which EMI were not aware of. Some of John Barrett's finds were heard by select audiences at Abbey Road open days, and thus, the rumour mill cranked up again with speculation that EMI *did* have some unreleased gems up its sleeve after all, which was true.

As we now know, EMI was seriously looking to get some of these recordings out to the public by late 1984, working on the *Sessions* project to the point of having album covers made up with extensive notes explaining the provenance of each track, and a catalogue number allocated. But they characteristically dithered about it until, at the start of 1985, the long-awaited news came out: EMI were set to officially announce the album's arrival, and probably an accompanying single, which were to land in the immediate future.

So whatever happened to it?

The accepted version of events holds that Apple – in other words, the individual Beatles plus Yoko – were in the dark about EMI's plans, and when they found out at the 11th hour they intervened and the release was halted. That's plausible, but again, the record-buying public knew nothing of the behind-the-scenes situation. All they learned was that this would-be historic release was back in indefinite mothballs, the latest in a long series of let-downs.

Soon after, everything leaked and with the original cover art also in the open, bootleggers were able to finish what EMI had started: pressings of *Sessions* could be bought under the counter, an accurate facsimile of what – for some reason – was blocked from the official catalogue. Fast-forward to 1996 and the *Anthology* series captured every last one of these tracks, and so in a sense, Apple did release it after all (make a playlist from the *Anthology* material, and hey-presto!).

Unreleased songs unreleased

**Leave My Kitten Alone /
Ob-La-Di, Ob-La-Da**
★★★☆☆

**US release:
31 January 1985 (not issued)**

As was their way, Capitol decided their proposed new Beatles LP, *Sessions*, would have a single to support it, and for this reason took one of the tracks – Leave My Kitten Alone from 1964 – and paired it up with an alternative version of Ob-La-Di, Ob-La-Da which wasn't going to be on the album, and was therefore a particular attraction to purchasers.

The idea of releasing Leave My Kitten Alone was not new. As far back as 1980, EMI were talking about recordings they might issue and the title of one of them was given as 'Please Leave My Kitten Alone', hot favourite to come out on single. It seems the track was remixed by John Barrett for the *Beatles At Abbey Road* open-days in 1982. It was then remixed properly in 1984, by Geoff Emerick, and so for first time it was ripe for release.

As had been the case with Girl / You're Going To Lose That Girl in 1977, Capitol went ahead and printed up picture sleeves, only to be advised at the last moment that the release was being cancelled, along with its parent album. Signalling the advancement of Beatle knowledge through the 1980s, thanks to the work surrounding John Barrett's vault-digging, these sleeves contained for the first time, take numbers and recording dates – and they confirm the version of Ob-La-Di, Ob-La-Da, take 5, to be the same as featured on *Anthology 3* some years later.

The official release date for this single would have been 31 January 1985, just ahead of the LP. When it was scrapped, the picture sleeves were left behind and can still be found for sale second-hand. Oddly the record itself has never been bootlegged, so unlike with the Girl single, there's nothing to put inside the sleeves. Still, nice to have.

Can of worms

Only The Beatles…
★★☆☆☆

UK release:
June 1986

Love Me Do	Ticket To Ride
Twist And Shout	Yes It Is
She Loves You	Ob-La-Di, Ob-La-Da
This Boy	Lucy In The Sky With Diamonds
Eight Days A Week	And I Love Her
All My Loving	Strawberry Fields Forever

According to their contemporary adverts, Heineken lager refreshed the parts other beers could not reach – but when they tried to refresh their way into EMI's Beatles catalogue things pretty soon went pear shaped. For some 17 months, parent company, Whitbread, had been working on a deal to secure rights to a dozen Beatles tracks, which they intended to compile into a new cassette album, copies of which would be flogged to Heineken drinkers for the knock-down price of £2.99 and some ring-pulls from promotional beer cans. The spanner in the works was that EMI, in true *Sessions* style, had forgotten to consult Apple who only learned of such manoeuvrings when branded cans were spotted in Britain's off-licences accompanied by posters and counter displays plugging the offer.

It's not known how much Whitbread paid EMI for the deal but it was presumably a substantial amount. But if the 1984 Marks & Spencer cassette had threatened to cheapen the Beatles' image, this latest initiative dragged down lower, the group's work being practically given away to boozers for loose change, totally out of keeping with EMI's usual practice of keeping the music off limits to compilers. And it was obvious too, consultancy exec, Paul Watts, trying his best to head off any criticisms by insisting that the Beatles were not being 'ripped off' and adding,

> "The crucial factor behind this deal is ensuring that the integrity of the Beatles' catalogue is maintained".

Yeah, right.

Apple's lawyers intervened at once – but Heineken had already manufactured a reported 100,000 cassettes, and printed up 35 million promotional cans, the costs of which were considerable. Hence they weren't receptive to Apple's insistence just 18 days into the campaign that they pull the plug – but Apple's true argument was not with the beer guys but with EMI itself for agreeing the deal in the first place, which Apple claimed, was done entirely without their consent. The predictable outcome was that *Only The Beatles...* soon disappeared, the lager-swilled episode leaving a bad taste in the mouth for years to come. After this, and Marks & Spencer, and *History of Rock* and *Sessions*, Apple put their collective foot down and from here on, nothing would come out of EMI bearing the Beatles' name without their express agreement, which in practice meant Paul, George, Ringo and Yoko had to be in unanimity. Thus, the decade-long splurge of EMI-led Beatles remarketing came to a sudden end. (Well, up to a point.)

So what of the track selections here? The cassette's listing is odd, maintaining the focus on pre-1967 material as had, for example, *Love Songs*. Whitbread presumably had their pick of a range of tracks but they managed to compile a set of early hits (She Loves You, Twist And Shout) intermingled with lesser-known B-sides (Yes It Is, This Boy), and when it came to what is now regarded as the Beatles' classic era of 1967-1969, there were just three selections, two of them album tracks.

Quirks and quibbles aside, the most enduring part of *Only The Beatles...* is the hangover it left behind. It's now a collector's item but since the number of copies in circulation exceeds the number of collectors who want it, the cassette remains in the proverbial bargain basement, a relic of a time when Beatles repackaging went a tad too far. This release, besides proving pivotal in EMI's treatment of the group's recordings, does have a modest claim to fame however: this was the first time a genuine stereo mix of Yes It Is had been issued, refreshing the parts other compilations couldn't reach.

Part Two – The CD Age

Ah, the compact disc. It really was the future when it burst on the market in the mid-1980s, promising no crackle or hiss, and the ability for listeners to jump from track to track with the minimum of effort. And for record companies, it was party time – they soon realised that if everyone wanted CD, they could sell all their albums again on the new format, and thus, towards the end of the 1980s, practically all major artists had their work re-issued as vinyl rapidly fell out of favour.

When the Beatles' catalogue transitioned, it made the news. It might seem trivial now, but back in the day, it was a big deal. And because CD was suddenly seen as the dominant format, from here we will view each successive release as a CD album primarily (except where no CD edition exists), noting that in most cases a parallel vinyl release also came out. This is the CD age for sure, although just as with the vinyl age, which concluded with a cassette release, irony has seen to it that the last item in this CD era was a box of old-fashioned 45 singles! So be it.

Past Masters Volume One (1988)
Past Masters Volume Two (1988)
Imagine – John Lennon (1988)
The Beatles (1988)
The Beatles CD Singles Collection (1989)
The Beatles Singles Collection On Cassette (1991)
The Beatles Compact Disc EP Collection (1992)
The Beatles CD Singles Collection (1992)
Capitol-CEMA coloured vinyl jukebox singles (1994-1996)
Live At The BBC (1994)
Baby It's You (1995)
Anthology 1 (1995)
Free As A Bird (1995)
Real Love (1996)
Anthology 2 (1996)
Anthology 3 (1996)

Yellow Submarine Songtrack (1999)
1 (2000)
Let It Be... Naked (2003)
The Capitol Albums Volume 1 (2004)
The Capitol Albums Volume 2 (2006)
Love (2006)
The Beatles (The Original Studio Recordings) (2009)
The Beatles In Mono (2009)
Mono Masters (2009)
The Singles (2011)

Note to reader: in Part One of this book, the track listing for each album was given in two columns. The columns signify Side 1 and Side 2 (or if a double album, LP 1 and LP 2). In Part Two and Part Three we are looking primarily at CDs and playlists, which don't have two sides. We sometimes stick to the two-column system so as to fit the track titles conveniently in place, but if so, they should be read now as continuous track listings.

Out with the old...

Past Masters Volume One
★★★★★

UK release:
8 March 1988

US release:
8 March 1988

Love Me Do	Long Tall Sally
From Me To You	I Call Your Name
Thank You Girl	Slow Down
She Loves You	Matchbox
I'll Get You	I Feel Fine
I Want To Hold Your Hand	She's A Woman
This Boy	Bad Boy
Komm, Gib Mir Deine Hand	Yes It Is
Sie Liebt Dich	I'm Down

Past Masters has a long history, really starting in October 1982 – coincidentally the 20th anniversary of Love Me Do – when Philips/Sony unleashed the compact disc upon the world. With several advantages over vinyl, CD quickly gained traction in the pop market, so that by 1985, an individual album could shift a million units on the format. (Dire Straits' *Brothers In Arms* was the first to do just that.) The future was upon us, and many major artists brought their back catalogues to CD, but there was one glaring exception: where were the Beatles?

Abbey Road had been issued on CD as early as 1983 but only in Japan. An expected UK release never materialised and EMI tended to dampen expectations in the following years by claiming the group's early albums would not be suitable for the digital transition, as distortion and background noise would ruin the tracks – an odd claim, but one which shows the extent to which EMI were digging their heels in. But the rise of the CD was unstoppable and so in February 1987, a batch of Beatles CDs was finally issued, their first four albums all appearing (bizarrely) in mono only. Not wanting to overwhelm their disc pressing capacity, EMI proceeded to work its way through the rest of the albums in stages, *Help!*, *Rubber Soul* and *Revolver* coming out in April, then *Pepper* as a special issue in June, followed by the rest in August and October.

So, the complete works available on CD? Not at all – as with the 1978 *Blue Box*, this project provided the original studio albums, but there were some 43 further tracks, including several smash hit singles, which weren't there. And if EMI were now serious about moving the Beatles' catalogue to compact disc they were going to have to round them up – or start re-issuing the old compilations, which was a far from ideal option from a fans' perspective. The obvious move was to assemble another compilation from the remnants, but 43 tracks was some mission, and so just before the final two studio albums, *Abbey Road* and *Let It Be* were due, EMI issued a one-off *Magical Mystery Tour* CD which achieved two things: first, it took care of 10 of the 'missing' songs, leaving a more viable 33 leftovers to deal with; and second it brought Capitol's 1967 comp permanently into the core discography – a dubious development, made in the interests of expediency. And something else was established through these 1987 releases, namely that these discs were now the mainstream standard in America and the world, finally defining the discography as intended by the group in the 1960s.

The 33 waifs and strays were expertly compiled for *Past Masters* by Mark Lewisohn, whose knowledge of what the project required was, of course, faultless. Odd edits and remixes were to be ignored, as were stereo-mono variants, although six songs which existed in two different forms, with different musicianship, were to feature, the appropriate alternates being:

> **Love Me Do** (single version, with Ringo on drums)
> **She Loves You** (German version, as Sie Liebt Dich)
> **I Want To Hold Your Hand** (German version, as Komm,
> Gib Mir Deine Hand)
> **Across The Universe** ('Wildlife' version with its sound effects)
> **Get Back** (single version with proper coda)
> **Let It Be** (single version, shorter and with the original guitar solo)

For once, no-one could argue with the choices made.

Past Masters Volume One contains 18 tracks sequenced chronologically, starting with Love Me Do from 1962 and ending in 1965 with I'm Down. Along the way it visits all the group's non-album singles, B-sides and EP tracks, including in the listing four UK number 1s – something EMI was keen to draw attention to in emphasising this was not just filler material. Nevertheless the album was more of a functional compilation than aesthetic and half a dozen B-sides and several rock and roll EP tracks were really pitched more at collector-completists than the average customer. And it should be pointed out that consistent with the fact that the first four standard CDs had been issued in mono, so were seven of the first nine tracks here.

As for the corresponding singles which came out after I'm Down, volume two appeared on the same day…

…in with the new

Past Masters Volume Two
★★★★★

UK release:
8 March 1988

US release:
8 March 1988

Day Tripper	Get Back
We Can Work It Out	Don't Let Me Down
Paperback Writer	The Ballad Of John And Yoko
Rain	Old Brown Shoe
Lady Madonna	Across The Universe
The Inner Light	Let It Be
Hey Jude	You Know My Name (Look
Revolution	Up The Number)

The second half of the *Past Masters* release was, for most, the more interesting – or, at least, the more satisfying to hear. As mentioned, the 1967 *Magical Mystery Tour* material had been requisitioned for CD when the Capitol album was taken into the main set, meaning there were no leftover EP tracks in this later period. Instead there were the singles and their associated B-sides, many of which were as good as the A-sides, recorded in a period when the Beatles were at their creative summit. It's a curiosity that the *Magical Mystery Tour* album accounted for all the 1967 output not appearing on *Sgt Pepper*, so this collection skips from 1966 straight to 1968, picking up with Lady Madonna / The Inner Light and culminating with Let It Be / You Know My Name (Look Up The Number) – that last track incidentally, appearing in mono whereas the rest is true stereo. In all, volume two is an impressive collection, extensively crossing over with the long-forgotten *Hey Jude*, which it effectively makes redundant.

Past Masters was the first compilation after the difficult Heineken episode and was assembled with direct approval from Apple and the remaining Beatles. It did such a good job that there was simply no need for any more conventional comps and only one other would follow in the next 30-odd years (namely, *1*). This, and the CD campaign generally, also had the effect that all the earlier vinyl compilations were consigned to history, the start of a new era also bringing about the end of another. One more innovation which is worth noting is that this collection carried accurate explanatory notes for each track from Mark Lewisohn, something the earlier collections had been sorely lacking.

None of the previous comps would ever be resurrected for compact disc bar the exceptional *1962-1966* and *1967-1970*, which got their updates in 1993 – a smart move on Apple's part since *Past Masters*, with its pragmatic track selection, was ill-suited to those who may have preferred a greatest hits collection sequencing singles like Please Please Me, Ticket To Ride and Penny Lane, rather than the more obscure tracks presented here.

The two *Past Masters* albums were the first CD-only releases by any act to make the *Billboard* top 200 – another minor milestone. At this point though vinyl was far from dead, and in October 1988, both volumes of *Past Masters* were brought together in a gatefold sleeve and sold as a double LP pack.

Personal best

Imagine – John Lennon
★★★☆☆

UK release:
10 October 1988

US release:
4 October 1988

Real Love	How?
*Twist And Shout	Imagine (Rehearsal)
*Help!	God
*In My Life	Mother (Live, 1972)
*Strawberry Fields Forever	Stand By Me
*A Day In The Life	Jealous Guy
*Revolution	Woman
*The Ballad Of John And Yoko	Beautiful Boy (Darling Boy)
*Julia	(Just Like) Starting Over
*Don't Let Me Down	Imagine
Give Peace A Chance	

Beatles recording marked with asterisk. All others are solo.

After John Lennon's death in 1980 his music saw a significant surge in popularity, while his reputation soared to the point where he was on the verge of sainthood – an idealist who implored everyone to lay down their arms and embrace love and peace. In truth the Liverpudlian dreamer had done most of his political-philosophical work in a narrow window somewhere around the end of the Beatles and the start of his solo career, his other songs just as often full of anger and cynicism, from Give Me Some Truth to Sunday Bloody Sunday and I Found Out – not to mention the nasty How Do You Sleep? – but it was his peace-loving persona, carefully cultivated by Yoko through the 1980s, which appealed most to the general public.

Yoko committed herself to releasing something new for John's fans at regular intervals through the decade, and she did, from standard repackagings (*John Lennon*, a nine-LP box set of albums issued in 1981; *The John Lennon Collection* greatest hits compilation issued 1982) to previously unreleased studio material (*Milk And Honey*, 1980 outtakes released 1984; *Menlove Avenue*, mid-1970s outtakes released 1986) and video (*Imagine: The Film*, recorded 1971 and issued 1985; *Live In New York City*, recorded 1972 and issued in 1986). And fans lapped it up, most of these and other projects warmly received and sometimes making a notable commercial splash.

In the spring of 1987 it was announced that Yoko was helping with a documentary-style film charting John's story, provisionally titled *In My Life* and for which she gave producer, David Wolper, mountains of privately held footage never before seen. It took a year and a half for the film to emerge and when it did, it had been renamed *Imagine*, not the best choice since John already had a movie and album of that name, but nonetheless offering a treat for his fans. And it was accompanied by a compilation, split between Beatles and solo recordings – and it's the first half, covering 1963-1969 which of course interests us here.

The premise of the album was to tell John's life through his songs, a tricky task but one which was achieved surprisingly well, thanks partly to the fact that his lyrics were often introspective and self-referential. Each of the tracks therefore had a place in his life story, and where the Beatles recordings are concerned, it's worth considering their individual significance, which also explains why they were selected:

> **Twist And Shout** – the early cover version from *Please Please Me* which captured John in his primitive, rock and rolling prime

> **Help!** – Lennon 1965, undergoing something of an identity crisis and singing out his woes, not Please Please Me, but please please *help* me

> **In My Life** – the gentle ballad in which John recalls friends and faces from days gone by, through the prism of his Liverpool past (first-draft lyrics included mention of Penny Lane, well ahead of Paul)

Strawberry Fields Forever – another trip into his infancy, commemorating the children's home not far from where he grew up, shaped through LSD into one of his best songs

A Day In The Life – possibly *the* greatest song he wrote, and a cornerstone of the landmark *Sgt Pepper* album

Revolution – a shout-out to the New Left in the turbulent year of 1968 in which he – for the first time – sounds off about politics and the state of things

The Ballad Of John And Yoko – uniquely personal, a sort-of diary in song documenting his romance and marriage to Yoko through 1969

Julia – a plaintive love song revealing its true subject through its title – John's mother, whom he lost when he was 17

Don't Let Me Down – this is the immediate John, shouting his obsession for Yoko from the London rooftops

All-told this is an impressive set of meaningful moments in song, fulfilling the album's brief and giving a glimpse of the many sides of John Lennon. But we must also mention the opening cut, Real Love at this stage nothing more than a solo guitar demo made in 1979. The appearance of such a relic happened to coincide with Yoko's decision to let out hours and hours of John's outtakes (including a high number of Beatles recordings) for broadcast on the *Lost Lennon Tapes*, contemporary with this album, making Real Love just one of countless revelatory tracks in the air at the time. But history tells us this song was to be transformed into a bona-fide Beatles track in 1995 – no-one could have known that in 1988, but it's as if fate lent a helping hand to put this particular recording at the start of the Beatles sequence.

Imagine – John Lennon was typically appreciated by fans and although it didn't burn up the album charts in Britain or America, it did serve to bring some of his most poignant music, group and solo, together in a succinct retrospective – more effectively than *The Best Of George Harrison* had for that particular Beatle.

Disc drive

The Beatles

★★★★★

**UK release:
31 October 1988**

*Please Please Me
With The Beatles
A Hard Day's Night
Beatles For Sale
Help!
Rubber Soul
Revolver
Sgt Pepper's Lonely Hearts
        Club Band
Magical Mystery Tour
The Beatles
Yellow Submarine
Abbey Road
Let It Be
Past Masters Volume 1
Past Masters Volume 2*

This uninspiringly named collection was advertised as the 'Connoisseur's Cabinet', which was 'presented in designer black ash', 'exclusive', 'beautifully crafted' and so on. Beatles fans took one look at it, with its roll-top lid, and dubbed it the *Bread Box*, a name which has stuck.

It is, simply, the group's CD catalogue as released through 1987, all brought together in one place along with both volumes of *Past Masters* – so here, finally, was a comprehensive set of the Beatles' official EMI recordings. Of course many Beatles collectors had been following the CD re-issue campaign through '87 and buying the discs as they came out, and were hardly likely to shell out another £214.99 for the privilege of having the outer case. So EMI did what was right and sold the box as a separate item, along with the Mark Lewisohn-penned booklet, for the much more manageable sum of £29.99 – and they were shrewd because the average collector who had, say, 10 of the CDs plus the box, would now be itching to fill up the gaps – hence a fresh trip to the local record shop.

The 1987 re-issue campaign wasn't just CDs, although that was the headline story. It also meant the UK albums were to be standardised, but of course in the States, they weren't available on vinyl and so through 1987, as the CDs were landing, so too were their LP equivalents, branded as 'Digitally remastered from the original British catalogue'. And the cassette versions didn't escape a long-overdue revamp either, the original UK albums (the so-called 'gold' cassettes, because of the colour of the inserts) being a source of frustration for the fact that in practically all cases, the track sequencing had been shuffled around. Thus, cassette buyers had gotten to know *Revolver* as starting off with Good Day Sunshine, *Please Please Me* with Misery, and so on, apparently a legacy of the fact that the sequencing was originally tailored for 8-track, where the length of each 'programme' was crucial. Why the 8-track versions had to also be used on the cassettes is unclear, but suggests EMI simply weren't bothered. Anyway, as part of the 1987 overhaul, the cassette series was corrected, with the new editions using the digital files as a source, and also featuring XDR technology for improved sound, with better printed inserts. And so the *Bread Box* also came along for vinyl and cassette, both for the much lower price of £124.99. And with *Past Masters* especially prepared for these formats as well, and included in their respective boxes, this really was everything anyone could ask for, whichever version was preferred.

There was one snag: the new digital source used for the vinyl box and the cassette box meant everyone ended up with the first four albums in mono, as per the CDs. Less of an issue at first, the absence for 20-odd years of *Please Please Me, With The Beatles, A Hard Day's Night* and *Beatles For Sale* in stereo meant once again that fans were being pushed towards bootleggers, who had the MFSL albums at their disposal for high-quality source material – which they of course took advantage of. Apple's decisions defy belief, sometimes. (George Martin had also remixed the stereo *Help!* and *Rubber Soul* for the CD campaign, overcoming the sometimes quirky 1960s mixes, and so these too were now standard across the board.)

There was, in fact, another CD box set in 1988, and it came out before EMI's *Bread Box*. It was issued by retailer, HMV, seemingly with EMI's co-operation since it was the culmination of a series of individual box sets which they had put out through 1987. HMV had presented their own special LP-sized box editions every time the new CDs were issued, typically including the discs plus a book, sometimes a reprint of an existing title, and sometimes a freshly written volume, or in some cases, photos, badges and the like. So on 22 June 1988, HMV unveiled their own comprehensive box set, named *The Beatles' Complete Compact Disc Collection*, housing all 15 of the new CDs together, with a hologram image on the lid, priced at £215 – the same as the EMI box which followed. These HMV sets – whose place in the official discography is a bit of a grey area – are highly collectable today, and although they look superior and have a better title than their EMI equivalent, given the choice few would prefer one over the definitely official *The Beatles*.

Compact sized

The Beatles CD Singles Collection
★★★★☆

UK release:
27 November 1989

Love Me Do / PS I Love You
Please Please Me / Ask Me Why
From Me To You / Thank You Girl
She Loves You / I'll Get You
I Want To Hold Your Hand / This Boy
Can't Buy Me Love / You Can't Do That
A Hard Day's Night / Things We Said Today
I Feel Fine / She's A Woman
Ticket To Ride / Yes It Is
Help! / I'm Down
We Can Work It Out / Day Tripper
Paperback Writer / Rain
Eleanor Rigby / Yellow Submarine
Strawberry Fields Forever / Penny Lane
All You Need Is Love / Baby, You're A Rich Man
Hello, Goodbye / I Am The Walrus
Lady Madonna / The Inner Light
Hey Jude / Revolution
Get Back / Don't Let Me Down
The Ballad Of John And Yoko / Old Brown Shoe
Something / Come Together
Let It Be / You Know My Name (Look Up The Number)

The issuing of the Beatles' albums on compact disc had been a success from the start, each batch of releases selling well and earning positive reviews. And knowing the fun (and revenue) would come to an end in October 1987, EMI had more up their sleeve: once the album releases ended, a similar run of CD singles would immediately follow.

There was an historical expectation that a single had to be smaller in size than an album, and so was the case here. Two inches narrower than a standard CD, and typically containing two tracks, most CD players could handle these three-inch discs, and for those which couldn't, an adaptor could be used, essentially a plastic ring fitted around the disc to make it the correct diameter. It seems a lot of trouble when they could have just used a standard five-inch CD in the first place, but that's how it was.

Two three-inch Beatles CD singles were issued each month, starting in November 1987 with Love Me Do / PS I Love You and Please Please Me / Ask Me Why, running over 11 months until Something / Come Together and Let It Be / You Know My Name (Look Up The Number) completed the set in September 1989, the 'new' singles of 1976-1982 being completely ignored. (This series, incidentally, was appearing concurrently with the ongoing 20th anniversary vinyl singles, with their picture sleeves and picture disc editions, which wouldn't come to a conclusion until the anniversary of Let It Be in 1990.)

It's worth noting that in the interests of authenticity, all the first 19 CDs were issued in mono, stereo having been introduced for the first time with The Ballad Of John And Yoko back in 1969. And they were nicely packaged, each three-inch disc housed in a little gatefold cover, carrying the 1982 artwork on the front.

In an echo of the CD albums before them, the rub was that fans who had bought the discs as they came out only learned at the very end that EMI was planning a box set containing the lot, priced at £59.95 – and this time, the box was *not* for sale on its own, so the choice was – do without it, or buy all 22 CD singles again. It was a bit of a cheek, and public pressure was brought to bear on EMI – the disgruntled customers after all, being the most loyal, having purchased the singles all along. EMI eventually relented and agreed to sell the box and its printed insert as a stand-alone item, £11.99 all-in. (In the US, there was no such box available, all the individual singles having appeared in the popular 'long box' style.)

Taped up

The Beatles Singles
Collection On Cassette
★★★★☆

UK release:
12 August 1991

Love Me Do / PS I Love You
Please Please Me / Ask Me Why
From Me To You / Thank You Girl
She Loves You / I'll Get You
I Want To Hold Your Hand / This Boy
Can't Buy Me Love / You Can't Do That
A Hard Day's Night / Things We Said Today
I Feel Fine / She's A Woman
Ticket To Ride / Yes It Is
Help! / I'm Down
We Can Work It Out / Day Tripper
Paperback Writer / Rain
Eleanor Rigby / Yellow Submarine
Strawberry Fields Forever / Penny Lane
All You Need Is Love / Baby, You're A Rich Man
Hello, Goodbye / I Am The Walrus
Lady Madonna / The Inner Light
Hey Jude / Revolution
Get Back / Don't Let Me Down
The Ballad Of John And Yoko / Old Brown Shoe
Something / Come Together
Let It Be / You Know My Name (Look Up The Number)

Surprising as it may seem today, in the late 1980s the dominant format for bought music was not vinyl or CD, but cassette, sales fuelled in no small measure by the ubiquitous Sony Walkman. In 1991 CD caught up, but the cassettes retained a significant market share for many years, and for a while, cassette editions of current hit singles were being issued by most major artists, in parallel with the vinyl and often carrying both songs on both sides.

So far as the Beatles were concerned, by the end of the 1980s fans could get just one cassette single: All You Need Is Love, which was issued in a hard plastic case concurrent with its 20th anniversary vinyl counterpart. Why that one in particular was selected is anyone's guess. Maybe they were planning to start issuing them all that way, but sales were too low so they scrapped it? Whatever the case, by the time the run of anniversary singles came to a conclusion in 1990, this remained the only cassette release.

A gap in the market then, in this period of prolific repackaging, leading Capitol to come up with this new collection. Each cassette played one track on the A-side, the other on the B-. Each was packaged in an outer card slip cover with a miniature of the corresponding single sleeve, and in the UK, the whole lot appeared the same morning – 12 August. Not so in America though, where they were released in periodical batches, but in adopting again the UK discography they stuck to the authentic UK mono mixes up to and including Get Back / Don't Let Me Down.

For British retailers, the full set came housed in a printed display box for the shop counter, only flimsy cardboard but looking good. And those who decided to buy all 22 were often allowed to take the box as well, making this a ready-packaged collection to carry home. In truth the outer box wasn't sturdy enough to contain 22 heavy cassettes for the long term, and consideration was given to the production of a proper hard box like the others before it, but nothing ever appeared. With the slow decline of the cassette through the following decade, this item now has the feel of an obsolete relic, the bulky size of each cassette out of proportion to the few minutes of audio it contained.

Extended but compact

*The Beatles Compact Disc
EP Collection*
★★★☆☆

UK release:
15 June 1992

US release:
30 June 1992

Twist And Shout
The Beatles' Hits
The Beatles (No. 1)
All My Loving
Long Tall Sally
Extracts From The Film A Hard Day's Night
Extracts From The Album A Hard Day's Night
Beatles For Sale
Beatles For Sale No. 2
The Beatles' Million Sellers
Yesterday
Nowhere Man
Magical Mystery Tour
' The Inner Light'

CD albums, CD singles – what would they think of next? Blindingly obviously, they completed the trilogy by re-issuing the 1981 vinyl EP box in compact equivalents – the antiquated seven-inch discs making the move to (then) cutting-edge digital.

True to the originals, these CDs were presented in mono, and as such, several tracks were receiving their mono CD debuts (Nowhere Man, Yesterday, Drive My Car…) – and *Magical Mystery Tour* was in both mono *and* stereo in this collection, as it had been in 1967, although here the two formats shared the same disc. Each EP came inside a miniature replica of the original picture sleeve – and in deference to the 1981 vinyl, the *'Inner Light'* disc was also included. With its outer box styled to match the others, this was an impressively designed product, priced between £59.99 and £69.99 depending where it was stocked.

There's not much more to add, except to note the box set went on sale in America too, a couple of weeks after its UK release.

Size is everything

The Beatles CD Singles Collection
★★★☆☆

UK release:
2 November 1992

US release:
11 November 1992

Love Me Do / PS I Love You
Please Please Me / Ask Me Why
From Me To You / Thank You Girl
She Loves You / I'll Get You
I Want To Hold Your Hand / This Boy
Can't Buy Me Love / You Can't Do That
A Hard Day's Night / Things We Said Today
I Feel Fine / She's A Woman
Ticket To Ride / Yes It Is
Help! / I'm Down
We Can Work It Out / Day Tripper
Paperback Writer / Rain
Eleanor Rigby / Yellow Submarine
Strawberry Fields Forever / Penny Lane
All You Need Is Love / Baby, You're A Rich Man
Hello, Goodbye / I Am The Walrus
Lady Madonna / The Inner Light
Hey Jude / Revolution
Get Back / Don't Let Me Down
The Ballad Of John And Yoko / Old Brown Shoe
Something / Come Together
Let It Be / You Know My Name (Look Up The Number)

Beatles collectors are always hungry for new items, but there was sometimes a sense that EMI knew this all too well and tended to exploit the fan base with unnecessary new editions. The Beatles' singles had originally made the transition to CD only via the miniature three-inch format, although the five-inch disc was generally more popular.

EMI dipped its first tentative toe into the world of standard-sized CD singles with the Love Me Do 30th anniversary in October 1992, when, making the most of the opportunity, they re-issued it in two editions, each with different outer packaging. And then they issued it again here, part of the roughly concurrent new *CD Singles Collection*, which included the whole run from Love Me Do to Let It Be once more. Whether this latest singles box set fell into the oft-touted 'cash-grab' category is a matter of opinion, but the collection landed just three years after the last lot of CD singles, the only real difference being an extra two inches of nothing around the edges of the discs.

It should be said that this new box set had a better look than the first, mirroring the recent EP collection by housing the discs in a square box with a flip-top opening. Another advance was that the discs themselves had illustrated designs printed on them, in contrast to the earlier ones which were basic silver. (EMI advertised them as having full-colour labels, but of course there are no labels on a CD.) One other change – Hey Jude / Revolution had a newly designed sleeve for some reason.

So, were fans delighted with this updated package? Not really. At another £53.90, many felt there was too much product coming out, too many expensive box sets and an underlying sense that they were being taken advantage of. Of course they didn't have to buy it – they could just have a nagging hole in their collection instead, if they preferred. On the other hand, if EMI hadn't released this and the earlier CD sets, they would have stood accused of not servicing the market properly, and not giving fans what they wanted – so they couldn't really win.

At least, for the foreseeable, this was the end of the boxed re-issues. The CD debuts of the *Red* and *Blue Albums* would happen in 1993 to much publicity but by now Apple had more exciting projects in the pipeline.

Listen to the colour…

Capitol-CEMA coloured
vinyl jukebox singles
★★★★★

US release:
28 January 1994 - 24 January 1996

Birthday / Taxman
A Hard Day's Night / Things We Said Today
She Loves You / I'll Get You
Here Comes The Sun / Octopus's Garden
I Want To Hold Your Hand / This Boy
Norwegian Wood (This Bird Has Flown) / If I Needed Someone
Across The Universe / Two Of Us
Here, There And Everywhere / Good Day Sunshine
It's All Too Much / Only A Northern Song
Lucy In The Sky With Diamonds / When I'm Sixty-Four
Magical Mystery Tour / The Fool On The Hill
While My Guitar Gently Weeps / Blackbird
You've Got To Hide Your Love Away / I've Just Seen A Face

For this entry, we are bending the rules of the book slightly, since these vinyl singles – 13 of them – did not come as a package, but as individual discs issued over a few years. The reason we're including them is because they consist either of brand new couplings, or in some cases, new issues for Capitol consisting of singles only previously available on other labels. In this sense, all 13 could be included in this book individually, but that would be silly. Anyway, rules were made for breaking. Ask John Lennon.

First, some background info: these singles were pressed for jukeboxes, and although not technically released to the general market, could be readily bought by mail order, or from dealer stocks. The discs were put out by CEMA Special Markets, a section of Capitol which managed supply lines and had their logo on the labels. The first one we might consider part of the run was in fact an accident, Capitol intending to put out a standard 30th anniversary re-issue of Love Me Do / PS I Love You on normal black vinyl – but somehow a few hundred copies ended up on red, looking exactly like all the ones which would follow.

It wasn't until the end of 1993 that Capitol announced it was planning to (intentionally) re-release many of the group's old 45 as coloured vinyl jukebox editions, and five appeared in January 1994. Three of them were re-issues: Hey Jude / Revolution (blue vinyl); Sgt Pepper-With A Little Help From My Friends / A Day In The Life (clear vinyl); Something / Come Together (blue vinyl), but one was a previously unseen pairing, and another one was a single not previously available on Capitol:

28/01/1994 – **Birthday / Taxman** (green vinyl)
- Two tracks from the 1976 *Rock 'N' Roll Music* album.

28/01/1994 – **A Hard Day's Night / Things We Said Today** (white vinyl)
- This coupling reflects the UK release of 1964. Capitol had originally put I Should Have Known Better on the flip-side of A Hard Day's Night.

Four more appeared in February: All You Need Is Love / Baby, You're A Rich Man (pink vinyl); Can't Buy Me Love / You Can't Do That (green vinyl); Yellow Submarine / Eleanor Rigby (yellow vinyl), plus another pairing not previously issued by Capitol:

21/02/1994 – **She Loves You / I'll Get You** (red vinyl)
- This single was originally issued by Swan in 1963.

In March there were another six, four of them re-issues: Help! / I'm Down (white vinyl); Let It Be / You Know My Name (Look Up The Number) (yellow vinyl); Strawberry Fields Forever / Penny Lane (red vinyl); Twist And Shout / There's A Place (pink vinyl), plus another new pairing and one more new to Capitol:

22/03/1994 – **Here Comes The Sun / Octopus's Garden** (orange vinyl)
- New pairing of two tracks from *Abbey Road*.

22/03/1994 – **I Want To Hold Your Hand / This Boy** (clear vinyl)

- This coupling reflects the UK release of 1963. Capitol had originally put I Saw Her Standing There on the back of I Want To Hold Your Hand.

After this, all went quiet and it seemed the series had run its course – until the end of 1995 that is, when a special new release kick-started the project again:

20/11/1995 – **Norwegian Wood (This Bird Has Flown) /**
If I Needed Someone (green vinyl)

- Very rare, this single was issued as a promotional disc given away when buyers purchased a full set of Beatles albums currently being promoted in support of the *Anthology* project. Both tracks from *Rubber Soul*.

Then on 24 January 1996 no fewer than 14 singles were issued out, bringing the overall total to 31, counting Love Me Do. Those which merely re-issued existing Capitol discs are as follows: Got To Get You Into My Life / Helter Skelter (orange vinyl); Nowhere Man / What Goes On (green vinyl); Ob-La-Di, Ob-La-Da / Julia (clear vinyl); Paperback Writer / Rain (red vinyl); The Long And Winding Road / For You Blue (blue vinyl); We Can Work It Out / Day Tripper (pink vinyl); Yesterday / Act Naturally (pink vinyl). But there are seven brand new ones which continue the policy of taking either side from the same original source (essentially there's now one newly created single from each studio album released after 1964):

24/01/1996 – **Across The Universe / Two Of Us** (clear vinyl)

- New pairing of two tracks from *Let It Be*.

24/01/1996 – **Here, There And Everywhere /**
Good Day Sunshine (yellow vinyl)

- New pairing of two tracks from *Revolver*.

24/01/1996 – **It's All Too Much / Only A Northern Song** (blue vinyl)

- New pairing of two tracks from *Yellow Submarine*, both George songs.

24/01/1996 – **Lucy In The Sky With Diamonds /**
When I'm Sixty-Four (red vinyl)

- New pairing of two tracks from *Sgt Pepper*.

24/01/1996 – **Magical Mystery Tour /**
The Fool On The Hill (yellow vinyl)

- New pairing of two tracks from *Magical Mystery Tour*.

24/01/1996 – **While My Guitar Gently Weeps / Blackbird** (blue vinyl)

- New pairing of two tracks from *The White Album*.

24/01/1996 – **You've Got To Hide Your Love Away /**
I've Just Seen A Face (orange vinyl)

- New pairing of two tracks from *Help!*.

These colourful singles are great to look at, all carrying the deep red Capitol label, and pressed in vinyl colours which are translucent, giving them an extra sheen. The selections, while ostensibly random, seem to indicate a slight preference for George, bringing six of his Beatles songs to seven-inch. Of course none of these were for sale in the conventional way, but typically they could be snapped up for $6 or $7 a piece, and are still fairly plentiful, excepting the 'accidental' Love Me Do and the promotional Norwegian Wood – but market price for them all edge higher and higher.

Together on the wireless machine

Live At The BBC
★★★★☆

UK release:
30 November 1994

US release:
30 November 1994

From Us To You	A Hard Day's Night
I Got A Woman	I Wanna Be Your Man
Too Much Monkey Business	Roll Over Beethoven
Keep Your Hands Off My Baby	All My Loving
I'll Be On My Way	Things We Said Today
Young Blood	She's A Woman
A Shot Of Rhythm And Blues	Sweet Little Sixteen
Sure To Fall (In Love With You)	Lonesome Tears In My Eyes
Some Other Guy	Nothin' Shakin'
Thank You Girl	The Hippy Hippy Shake
Baby It's You	Glad All Over
That's All Right (Mama)	I Just Don't Understand
Carol	So How Come (No-One Loves Me)
Soldier Of Love	I Feel Fine
Clarabella	I'm A Loser
I'm Gonna Sit Right Down	Everybody's Trying To Be My Baby
And Cry (Over You)	Rock And Roll Music
Crying, Waiting, Hoping	Ticket To Ride
You Really Got A Hold On Me	Dizzy Miss Lizzy
To Know Her Is To Love Her	Kansas City
A Taste Of Honey	Matchbox
Long Tall Sally	I Forgot To Remember To Forget
I Saw Her Standing There	I Got To Find My Baby
The Honeymoon Song	Ooh! My Soul
Johnny B Goode	Don't Ever Change
Memphis, Tennessee	Slow Down
Lucille	Honey Don't
Can't Buy Me Love	Love Me Do
Till There Was You	

The story of *Live At The BBC* is long and winding, and begins at the dawn of the Beatles, who headed off to Hamburg in 1960 as a raw five-piece with hundreds of stage hours ahead of them, needing to be filled with *something*. As a result the fledgling band soon learned a vast range of songs, many of them drawn from the hits and B-sides of acts like Buddy Holly, Elvis, Little Richard and so on, which gave them an extraordinarily rich catalogue. (Playing long, gruelling sessions every night, the Beatles resolved not to perform the same song twice in any one evening, forcing them to develop their extensive repertoire.)

It's a curiosity that until they signed to EMI in mid-1962, they tended not to play original compositions on stage, 90 percent of their act consisting of cover versions. An impression of their live sets can be had from the two substantial pre-fame tapes in existence, the Decca audition from the start of 1962 and the Star-Club tapes from the very end, which between them, include 34 different cover versions, 10 of which they would also record in their BBC radio sessions, bringing their Liverpool and Hamburg material to the airwaves.

Whole books have been written about the BBC sessions, and here's not the place to go over the history again (instead, see *The Beatles: The BBC Archives: 1962-1970* by Kevin Howlett). Suffice to say, the Beatles' BBC radio slots which ran between 8 March 1962 (while Pete Best was still a Beatle) and 7 June 1965, make a fascinating archive of material which despite the appearance of *Live At The BBC* and its later sequel album (see entry on page 203) tends to be under-valued in the group's history. It says something that there's *too much* music among the BBC tapes to be able to sift through it all here, and in particular, the Beatles had not one but two regular radio shows all their own: *Pop Go The Beatles* and *From Us To You*, which if Universal Music, Calderstone Productions, Paul, Ringo, Yoko, Dhani, the ghost of Michael Jackson, or whoever decides these things nowadays are reading this – us fans might like a box set of a few of these historic shows in full.

The lack of official releases until now had the inevitable effect of feeding bootleggers with a stream of material ripe for picking. Probably the first such record to appear was *Yellow Matter Custard* in 1971, which rounded up 14 songs sourced from old home recordings of the radio broadcasts. *Mary Jane* would follow, and *Soldier Of Love*, and *Rare Beatles, Youngblood, Beatles Broadcasts* and so on. EMI were missing out and in 1980 they started negotiations with the BBC to see if some of the tracks could be assembled for an official LP. Nothing happened until 1982 when rumours started to circulate that an agreement had finally been reached and a double LP could be in the offing to coincide with the 20th anniversary of Love Me Do. Again fans were let down but to make up for it, a new radio show called *The Beatles At The Beeb* was prepared, containing 40 or so songs plucked from the vaults, broadcast in pretty clear AM sound – a fresh present for the bootleggers.

1988 and BBC radio were busy again, putting together a 14-part series of 30-minute shows named *The Beeb's Lost Beatles Tapes*, which hit the airwaves in October (this time in glorious FM) and included material never before heard. The show was sent out to broadcasters around the world including in America, and many fans simply pressed 'record' and helped themselves to the treasures within. Still absent any official releases, it provided yet more hours of audio for the illicit market, now transitioning to CD, and while EMI continued twiddling their thumbs, Great Dane issued the impressive nine-CD *The Complete BBC Sessions* containing 247 tracks!

The slow and arduous route to EMI's *Live At The BBC* took a decisive turn in late 1991 when Neil Aspinall, in his capacity as head of Apple, asked George Martin to go through and evaluate the BBC tapes, then draw up a proposed track listing ahead of a new release. You would think it relatively easy to achieve, once the songs were decided, but a further two years of radio silence followed, before EMI started speculating on a release date – proving at long last that the project was indeed happening. And so in November 1994, roughly a third of a century after the group walked into Manchester's Playhouse Theatre to record the first of their 52 BBC sessions, we were finally allowed to hear some on disc. What on earth had they been waiting for?

The earliest recording here is the January 1963 version of Keep Your Hands Off My Baby, the last one Dizzy Miss Lizzy from May 1965. In between are Beatles hits and album tracks familiar from the EMI discography – 25 of them, including Love Me Do, A Hard Day's Night, I Feel Fine, Roll Over Beethoven and so on. Added to these are 29 of those old stage songs, never recorded for EMI but drawing on the material which had established the Beatles as the greatest live band in the world before they were famous. And their formative influences are there to see, including:

> **Chuck Berry**: Carol; I Got To Find My Baby; Johnny B Goode; Memphis, Tennessee; Sweet Little Sixteen; Too Much Monkey Business
>
> **Elvis Presley**: I Forgot To Remember To Forget; I Got A Woman; I'm Gonna Sit Right Down And Cry (Over You); That's All Right (Mama)
>
> **Little Richard**: Lucille; Ooh! My Soul
>
> **Carl Perkins**: Glad All Over; Sure To Fall (In Love With You)

And curiously, only one from the great **Buddy Holly**: Crying, Waiting, Hoping

If only these had been available for selection when Bhaskar Menon was sketching out plans for *Rock 'N' Roll Music* back in 1976, what a set it could have been.

There was one other track buried in the long list of songs making up *Live At The BBC*, which was easy to miss: I'll Be On My Way. This was of course, a Lennon-McCartney original, written in 1959 and which, in 1963, they gave away to Billy J Kramer with the Dakotas, never returning to it themselves. Consequently this near-studio standard recording is the only place the Beatles can be heard playing the song, as taped on 4 April 1963, three weeks before Billy J released it.

Several other tracks catch the ear too:

> **From Us To You** is a brief re-working of the hit single, serving as a theme tune to four episodes.

> **Some Other Guy** was a semi-legendary early Beatles favourite which for no obvious reason, wasn't recorded for either *Please Please Me* or *With The Beatles*.

> **Honey Don't** appears here with John on lead vocals, recorded August 1963. It was subsequently included on *Beatles For Sale* but with Ringo singing lead, and later BBC versions were also taped that way.

> **Matchbox**, **Long Tall Sally** and **Slow Down** were all recorded here in July 1963 but not re-done for EMI until June 1964. (They would make up three quarters of the *Long Tall Sally* EP.)

And a few more of these old favourites will be familiar to latter-day followers of the Beatles' solo careers:

> A version of **Sure To Fall** would be recorded by Ringo on his own *Stop And Smell The Roses*.

A version of The Phil Spector classic, **To Know Her Is To Love Her** would be made by John in sessions for his 1975 *Rock 'N' Roll* LP and issued on the outtakes album, *Menlove Avenue*, in 1986.

New versions of **That's All Right (Mama)** and **Lucille** were recorded by Paul and released in 1988 on *Choba B CCCP*.

There's so much music on this double album that it's difficult to digest. In truth, it's a sprawling set with a disorganised chronology, but despite everything, it makes a valuable addition to the discography. It's easy to forget in these post-*Anthology* days, that *Live At The BBC* was the first time previously unreleased Beatles recordings had been officially marketed (discounting *The Beatles At The Hollywood Bowl*), and there was a mountain of them. The album is, therefore, something of a landmark, and like the radio shows themselves, is deserving of more note.

Fans appreciated it, sending it to the top of the UK album charts, and to number 3 in America, with a reported five million units sold in the first five months. And having released it, there was more than enough material in the can for a second volume, which would come to pass 18 years later, more than *fifty* years after the Beatles' first BBC session. Weren't in any hurry, were they?

Tuned in

Baby It's You
★★★☆☆

UK release:
20 March 1995

US release:
20 March 1995

Baby It's You	Devil In Her Heart
I'll Follow The Sun	Boys

The arrival of *Live At The BBC* put the Beatles back in the news and the anticipated strong sales meant an obvious second step: a single to support it. This would be the first 'new' Beatles single in Britain since the Movie Medley almost 13 years earlier, so had the potential to be a big deal. The main question was, which of the dozens of BBC tracks would be selected?

There was a possibility they could issue a familiar song which hadn't been an A-side before, like I Saw Her Standing There, or All My Loving. Conversely they could go for something outside the usual repertoire – one of the cover versions from the album, like Memphis, Tennessee or The Hippy Hippy Shake. There was a political angle to deal with as well – this was the first single proposed since Apple and the Beatles commanded a say in release plans, so would this be a Paul song, or a John song, or even a George or Ringo lead?

EMI in London stepped forward with a proposal that they issue Soldier Of Love / I'll Be On My Way. Soldier Of Love was a strong choice, and the B-side was a good idea too, but Capitol in the States countered with Baby It's You for the A-side, with a double selection on the flip consisting of tracks not included on *Live At The BBC*. Cue debate, objections, compromise, and with the Christmas market missed, delays, delays, delays. EMI then wanted something out for Valentine's Day, which was also missed, and their alternative proposals for A-sides were rejected. In the end, Baby It's You was settled on, per Capitol's original wishes, but instead of a single this was to be a four-track EP, with each of the ex-Beatles getting one lead vocal each, and in the correct sequence – John, Paul, George then Ringo, so everyone was happy. What a lot of fuss over a harmless little EP.

Here's the anatomy of what was finally released:

Baby It's You
Recorded: 1 June 1963
Broadcast: *Pop Go The Beatles*, 11 June 1963
> The second of three BBC versions the group performed. This recording had appeared as the 11th song on *Live At The BBC*.

I'll Follow The Sun

Recorded: 17 November 1964

Broadcast: *Top Gear*, 26 November 1964

> The only BBC version ever taped, and the only Lennon-McCartney song on this EP. Not on *Live At The BBC* so previously unreleased.

Devil In Her Heart

Recorded: 16 July 1963

Broadcast: *Pop Go The Beatles*, 20 August 1963

> The first of two BBC recordings of this song. Not on *Live At The BBC* and so previously unreleased.

Boys

Recorded: 17 June 1963

Broadcast: *Pop Go The Beatles*, 25 June 1963

> Ringo's star turn, this was the fourth of seven BBC tapings. Not on *Live At The BBC* and so previously unreleased.

Baby It's You was an attractive package, its cover similar to that of *Live At The BBC* but showing the group in higher spirits. It was also issued on the now reactivated Apple label, the first such 'single' since 1976. It didn't set the world alight but made the top 10 in the UK. The path was clear for the big project now on the drawing board: *The Beatles Anthology*.

From caverns to kings

Anthology 1
★★★★★

UK release:
21 November 1995

US release:
21 November 1995

Free As A Bird
That'll Be The Day
In Spite Of All The Danger
Hallelujah, I Love Her So
You'll Be Mine
Cayenne
My Bonnie
Ain't She Sweet
Cry For A Shadow
Searchin'
Three Cool Cats
The Sheik Of Araby
Like Dreamers Do
Hello Little Girl
Besame Mucho
Love Me Do
How Do You Do It
Please Please Me
One After 909 (Sequence)
One After 909
Lend Me Your Comb
I'll Get You
I Saw Her Standing There
From Me To You
Money (That's What I Want)
You Really Got A Hold On Me
Roll Over Beethoven

She Loves You
Till There Was You
Twist And Shout
This Boy
I Want To Hold Your Hand
Moonlight Bay
Can't Buy Me Love
All My Loving
You Can't Do That
And I Love Her
A Hard Day's Night
I Wanna Be Your Man
Long Tall Sally
Boys
Shout
I'll Be Back (Take 2)
I'll Be Back (Take 3)
You Know What To Do
No Reply (Demo)
Mr Moonlight
Leave My Kitten Alone
No Reply
Eight Days A Week (Sequence)
Eight Days A Week (Complete)
Kansas City

This double CD or triple vinyl LP finally achieved what many thought would never happen: it delivered longing Beatles fans a stock of previously unreleased material, and there was a great deal of it too, this being only the first instalment in a series. The context is well-known. When the Beatles split in 1970, there was a plan to create a documentary telling the group's story 'from the inside', with the working title, *The Long And Winding Road*. The project kept surfacing then disappearing again, getting close to completion at one point when a provisional edit was done (a copy of which, incidentally, was handed by George to Neil Innes and Eric Idle to help them shape up their Rutles spoof) – but nothing ever came out and it remained the stuff of legend.

In May 1992, Apple suddenly announced the project was back on and was being reinvented as a series of 90-minute television shows which, they hoped, would be out in 1993. That proved vastly optimistic and by August of '93, Apple were still collecting together every scrap of footage they could find, using their legal clout to block others from putting anything out until they had the rights to just about all of it. (In reference to the extended timescale, Derek Taylor offered, "There's an absence of desperation about it, because they're working to their own timetable" – not much of an explanation.)

The documentary was officially announced in the summer of 1995, after a bidding war from broadcasters. (ABC got the American rights, ITV the UK.) The name *Anthology* didn't sit right, and for a while there was speculation it might be re-christened *The Beatles Story* or *The Beatles By The Beatles* (George's favourite) but when it finally aired in November and December, they stuck with plan A.

The whole story of the *Anthology* deserves to be told in full, but not here. (And if there are any budding Beatles researchers/authors stuck for ideas, you can have that one for free.) What we are interested in is the associated audio – the albums and singles which came out as part of a long, drawn-out multi-media *Anthology* package. It wasn't in the original plan, but by the end of 1993 all parties were in agreement that it was time for EMI to prise open their safes and let some of the Beatles' tapes out for all time. The idea was that if the documentary was to arrive in instalments, so would the music, with one CD matched to each episode. But it soon became apparent that the needs of a fast-paced video and the historical-archival nature of the available audio meant they would have to work to different agendas, and so the *Anthology* albums shifted from being effectively a soundtrack to the documentary, to something in their own right, associated but independent, tied together mostly just by the title.

It's interesting at this early stage to note that six CDs were in the pipeline, long before George Martin and the team had even been through the stockpiles to see how much audio was there. Nonetheless, certain tracks were almost guaranteed a show, Martin immediately nominating take 1 of Strawberry Fields Forever plus How Do You Do It, to which the knowledgeable fan could easily have added a dozen or two more. In fact the real problem wasn't going to be finding songs to include, but deciding what to leave out, the constraints of the two-CD format for volume 1 insufficient to house it all. While the BBC recordings had been adequately covered with *Live At The BBC*, there was still, for example, a whole album's worth of Decca recordings to choose from, while the archived *Please Please Me* session from 11 February 1963 could have taken up another disc. The Star-Club recordings of 1962 contained enough to cover a double album by themselves, and then there was the Tony Sheridan stuff, and the 1960 home tapes of a primitive Quarry Men, with Stu on bass, running through such titles as I'll Follow The Sun, One After 909, Hello Little Girl and others – and also live recordings from the Beatlemania years, plus the Ed Sullivan shows, and the rest of the EMI studio outtakes including unheard original compositions. In short, unless this was to be a multi-CD box set, which was never on the cards, a lot would have to give.

One of the key decisions was whether to include the recording of the Quarry Men playing at the Woolton Church Fete on 6 July 1957 – the very day John met Paul – which by a million-to-one chance happened to have been captured on an amateur reel-to-reel tape. This was a genuine piece of history, but after much deliberation it was decided to leave it off, since the fidelity was so poor. And this, in a sense, highlights the tension lurking beneath the *Anthology* collection, more pressing on volume 1 than on the others, Apple finding themselves caught inescapably between hardcore Beatles fanatics, who craved this kind of stuff, and the general listener (including, incidentally, most mainstream reviewers) who definitely did not. Impossible to please everyone, they ended up satisfying too few, with a set which tried to straddle both camps.

When *Anthology 1* appeared in November 1995, it featured 60 tracks, but some of them were snippets of speech to guide the listener through the story – an idea which didn't go down well and was dropped for volume 2. But there was some real treasure among it, top 10 highlights comprising:

- **In Spite Of All The Danger** – written by Paul in his teens, the Quarry Men recorded it in a little home studio in Liverpool, in July 1958. By rights it should have been the first of the archive tracks on *Anthology*, but that honour went to:

- **That'll Be The Day** – Buddy Holly's song which the Quarry Men recorded on the same day as In Spite Of All the Danger, both ending up on opposite sides of a shellac 78, now the most valuable record in the world.

- **Cayenne** – from the 1960 Forthlin Road tapes, this instrumental was written by Paul and was hitherto unknown. The recording is said to feature just John, Paul and Stu on bass.

- **Love Me Do** – this is the 6 June 1962 recording, made while Pete Best was in the band – his performance on the day contributing to his imminent ejection from the group. It was meant to be lost forever until George Martin's wife found a copy buried in the bottom of one of their cupboards.

- **How Do You Do It** – this Mitch Murray song was forced on the Beatles in 1962 with a view to it becoming their first single. It had been doing the rounds for years on bootleg, but here it was officially at last.

- **One After 909** – the song from the *Let It Be* album was a golden oldie, having been taped twice by the Quarry Men before being attempted formally at EMI in March 1963 in this version, which almost came out as the group's third single.

- **And I Love Her** – short, early arrangement, with Ringo's rumbling drums and an electric lead guitar solo. Evidently this was taped before George came up with the song's memorable riff.

- **Shout** – performed in front of television cameras on 28 April 1964 for the show, *Around The Beatles*, the only time the group ever played it. The Isley Brothers had done it first, and Lulu was about to have a UK hit with it.

- **You Know What To Do** – George's second composition for the Beatles which never came out and was unheard until *Anthology*. It was recorded 3 June 1964 at the end of the *A Hard Day's Night* sessions.

- **Leave My Kitten Alone** – taped on 14 August 1964 for *Beatles For Sale*, it's a mystery why this cover of a Little Willie John single was left off the album, while Mr Moonlight went on. It was earmarked for release more than once in subsequent years, including as a 45 in 1985 (page 109), but here was its first official outing.

Given treats like these, it seems churlish to pick through and grumble about omissions – but there are some. Perhaps the most mystifying is Love Of The Loved from the Decca tapes. This is the group's only known recording of the Lennon-McCartney original, which was one of three performed on the day. The other two, Like Dreamers Do and Hello Little Girl, were both on *Anthology*, but instead of Love Of The Loved, the less notable Searchin', Three Cool Cats and The Sheik Of Araby were selected from the same session.

Other 'missing' tracks included early demos of more of the songs Lennon and McCartney gave away – Bad To Me, I'm In Love, and One And One Is Two, as well as a live performance of Paul's Catswalk taped at the Cavern Club. The Cavern performance of Some Other Guy would also have been nice, although a different version had been included on *Live At The BBC*, and another pleasing selection might have been the unique medley of hits which the Beatles taped for *Around The Beatles* in April 1964 – the same show they played Shout.

But when it comes to musical selection, the elephant in the room is the decision to include Free As A Bird as the first track. One imagines the debates were fierce, there being strong arguments for and against. On the plus side, it meant the album would include something special, considering the single release was still two weeks away, and that would attract sales. It also had the benefit of preventing the chronologically-based album starting with the scratchy That'll Be The Day, which wasn't much of an opener to an important new set. On the other hand, Free As A Bird was entirely at odds with the concept of gathering up relics from the group's early period, and although it might boost album sales in the short term, it inevitably harmed the 45 when it did come out, part of the reason it didn't make number 1.

One of the striking things about the *Anthology* album series was the extravagant cover art by Klaus Voormann, which eventually made an impressive three-part panorama of posters torn from posters, plastered over a wall and showing glimpses of the Beatles through the years. (On one, poor Pete Best had his head ripped off, with Ringo's filling the space. He got revenge by releasing his own album, with just the missing piece on its cover!) We must also comment the long, detailed notes by Mark Lewisohn, without which, the albums wouldn't have made much sense.

For all the debate about what went in and what did not, *Anthology* is a landmark in the Beatles' history and sold in vast quantities – reportedly by the end of 1996 it had gone eight times platinum in the US, outdoing every previous Beatles album bar *Pepper* and *Abbey Road*. Fans didn't have long to digest it before the next disc in the series hit the shelves.

The life that we once knew

Free As A Bird
★★★★★

UK release:
4 December 1995

US release:
12 December 1995

Free As A Bird	This Boy
I Saw Her Standing There	Christmas Time (Is Here Again)

When the *Anthology* project was first decided on, there was a natural tendency on the part of Paul, George and Ringo to think about preparing some music for the soundtrack. All of them had repeated their position over the years that there could never be a Beatles reunion in the absence of John, but Paul had an idea.

As early as December 1992 he asked the others if they would help write some incidental music for the documentaries, which was agreed. And they did – probably through 1993, since the 'first phase' of recording is said to have come to an end in February 1994 – although what they came up with, and where it might have been used in the documentary remains unknown. But somewhere, probably in the secure possession of Paul, are tapes of this unheard stuff.

Then came an even better idea – if the Threetles couldn't make Beatles music without John, then why not do it *with* him – or at least with tapes of him. From 1988 until 1992, US radio network, Westwood One, had been broadcasting hours of John's outtakes provided to them by Yoko in the *Lost Lennon Tapes* series, so there was no shortage of compositional drafts and demos doing the rounds, any number of which were ripe for overdubs. And that was the proposal put to Yoko, who in January 1994, handed Paul a few select tracks to bring back to England and work on with George and Ringo to create some new Beatles songs, chief among them, Free As A Bird, a provisional John demo committed to cassette in 1977. (The song had been included in *Lost Lennon Tapes* and so was already known to many of John's fans.) By all accounts the Threetles wasted little time, collectively writing some new sections and wrapping up the recording, produced by Jeff Lynne, at Paul's home studio by the end of March.

It's interesting to take a digression here and consider the extent to which Paul was the driving force behind all this, George in particular said to have been dragged along reluctantly. Their true enthusiasm levels can be known only to themselves and their immediate circle, but from the outside it looks as if Paul was leading the project almost single-handedly, and even tried to get George to agree to a new version of The Long And Winding Road to close the video series – which admittedly would have been great. Press reports in June 1994 also stated a version of Let It Be was in the frame – but either way, the song selections reveal how insensitive Paul could be to George's feelings, each of these titles having been dominated by Paul in 1969, the very era which caused so much difficulty between them.

More examples were on display in the *Anthology* film itself, where one scene shows Paul, George, Ringo and George Martin playing back original Beatles studio tapes and commenting on the music – and it's Golden Slumbers which is heard, written by Paul, sung by Paul and with Paul on piano and, so George assumes, Paul on bass too, leading George to remark pointedly, "It doesn't sound like *anyone* [else] is on it!". Similarly, when the three of them are playing ukuleles on George's lawn, Paul opts to slip in a Beatles song, and he chooses I Will (not included in the final video edit) – which he wrote alone and overdubbed himself in 1968 in George's absence, George quite possibly never having played it before. It seems doubtful Paul realised any of this, but these examples show both his natural tendency to take the lead, and his seemingly oblivious slights to George who was still festering at being marginalised all the time.

Anyway, back to Free As A Bird. This historic recording was wrapped up in early 1994 but remained unissued, awaiting the *Anthology* project for its chance to shine. A year after it was done, the Threetles pulled a similar trick on John's Real Love, which was intended as the B-side, even as late as autumn 1995. In the event, Apple decided to make them into separate releases, and so not one but two alternative B-sides would need to be found, and quick. In fact, six were required – since each single was to be issued in a four-song CD edition, technically an EP. So what to do?

The obvious move was to pull a few tracks from *Anthology*, but Apple went a step further and raided the stockpiles for further outtakes not featuring on the album. Thus, when the CD of Free As A Bird came out, it did so with the following additional material:

> **I Saw Her Standing There** – take 9, a late (failed) attempt to improve on the released *Please Please Me* version, which wasn't needed. A curiosity is that the count-in heard on the LP version was in fact edited on from this performance.

> **This Boy** – actually two takes (12 and 13) as the group struggle to get it right. John's chronic problem remembering whether to sing 'this boy' or 'that boy' causes a humorous break-down.

> **Christmas Time (Is Here Again)** – the song recorded for the 1967 Christmas flexi, where it was only heard in small sections. Here it was in its entirety for the first time.

The vinyl edition of course only had room for one B-side, and given the release date, 4 December, Christmas Time (Is Here Again) was the one. It seemed a good idea to grab some radio airtime over the festive season, even though it fell out of the timeframe of *Anthology 1* and was therefore a bit of an anomaly. The other two tracks were only available on the CD and as such, turned *Anthology 1* into a three-CD event – if one wanted to get everything, of course, which many did.

Free As A Bird suffered the fate of not getting to number 1, disappointing everyone associated with the project. (In the UK its expected place at the top was denied by Earth Song from a certain Michael Jackson, whose record company reportedly celebrated their victory by sending Apple a 'present' of a Christmas turkey with a copy of the Free As A Bird CD stuffed up its jacksy!) Sour-faced reviews didn't help either, the *Sunday Mirror* taking the prize for the nastiest piece of journalism. Speaking of John: "As a rock god, he was all washed up. If only Mark Chapman had hung about on the steps of the Dakota a few years earlier. That way we'd have been spared some of the worst records of all time: Imagine, Woman and Free As A Bird." The season of good will, eh?

Like some forgotten dream

Real Love
★★★★★

UK release:
4 March 1996

US release:
5 March 1996

| Real Love | Yellow Submarine |
| Baby's In Black | Here, There And Everywhere |

Written and demoed by John, Real Love was overdubbed by the Threetles at Paul's home studio in February 1995. As mentioned previously, the song had already been included on *Imagine – John Lennon*, but whereas that was a 1979 guitar demo, the one used here was a piano version from 1980. Real Love differed from Free As A Bird in one significant way: it was essentially complete as John left it, not requiring any additional writing (and as such, it's copyrighted to Lennon alone). All it needed was a clean up, the original tape suffering from hiss and mains hum. Jeff Lynne did his best, but after the offending frequencies were stripped out, John's voice was left sounding thin and wiry, masked to an extent by the overdubbing process which gave the whole thing an unconvincing sheen.

The process of working on these tapes, given personally by Yoko to Paul, had the effect of bringing them closer together after some up-and-down years, and a few weeks later, she paid a visit to Paul's Hog Hill Mill home where Real Love had just been attended. The two of them made another little bit of history on 11 March 1995 when, along with Sean Lennon, they recorded together. Noting that 1995 was the 50th anniversary of the Hiroshima bombing, they taped one of Yoko's songs, Hiroshima Sky Is Always Blue, which was never released but reinforced the sense of reconciliation which the *Anthology* project had engendered.

It took much of 1995 for the Threetles to decide what to do with Real Love, which wasn't, then was, then wasn't the B-side of Free As A Bird. Its first public airing was as early as 23 November, more than three months before release, when it was broadcast on ITV to coincide with the television debut of the *Anthology* documentaries. But why the rush? Officially it was to counter the possibility of bootleggers getting hold of it, but this didn't make a great deal of sense since putting it on television could only *increase* the chances of illicit copies being distributed. When Real Love did hit the shops, it stuck to the template set by Free As A Bird, appearing on two-track seven-inch as well as a four-track CD which contained the following:

> **Baby's In Black** – live recording from the Hollywood Bowl concert of 29 August 1965, which had not been released on *The Beatles At The Hollywood Bowl*, and was, therefore, new. (This was the track selected as the B-side of the vinyl edition.)

> **Yellow Submarine** – not a 'new' version but a remix of the existing, featuring a curious introductory part which had been dropped when the song first came out in 1966. This re-working also had enhanced sound effects.

> **Here, There And Everywhere** – take 7 with guide vocal, on which was added newly remixed harmonies from the finished *Revolver* track. This, incidentally, flagged Apple's interest in making up versions of songs from different pieces, which often served to present the material well, but annoyed many fans when more of the same appeared on *Anthology 2*, the most disgruntled flagging them as 'outfakes'.

Issued with a video of the Threetles in the studio, it was hoped Real Love would do what Free As A Bird had not, and top the singles chart. Yet it turned out to be a relative flop, not even making the top 10 on *Billboard*. As for the UK, its chances were effectively sabotaged by the BBC, who more or less banned it from their key Radio 1 station. The corporation claimed it was because of their current drive to keep Radio 1 'modern' for the sake of retaining younger listeners. However the episode smelled of revenge for *Anthology* having been sold to the rival ITV network, and understandably infuriated many associated with the single. The effect was that it missed out on crucial exposure and limped only to number 4, which was lapped up by the same press reviewers who seemed to have an axe to grind: "If you hear any background noise on the 'new' Beatles record, it is likely to be the sound of Lennon – turning in his grave," mocked the *Daily Mirror*.

A footnote: 24 years after Real Love didn't appear as the B-side of Free As A Bird, the two tracks were finally pressed up together on the same disc and inserted into the 2019 *Singles Collection*, as noted elsewhere in this book. (See page 237 for further details.)

Inside the studio

Anthology 2
★★★★★

UK release:
18 March 1996

US release:
18 March 1996

Real Love
Yes It Is
I'm Down
You've Got To Hide Your
    Love Away
If You've Got Trouble
That Means A Lot
Yesterday
It's Only Love
I Feel Fine
Ticket To Ride
Yesterday
Help!
Everybody's Trying To Be My Baby
Norwegian Wood (This Bird
    Has Flown)
I'm Looking Through You
12-Bar Original
Tomorrow Never Knows
Got To Get You Into My Life
And Your Bird Can Sing
Taxman
Eleanor Rigby (Strings Only)
I'm Only Sleeping (Rehearsal)
I'm Only Sleeping (Take 1)
Rock And Roll Music
She's A Woman

Strawberry Fields Forever
    (Demo Sequence)
Strawberry Fields Forever (Take 1)
Strawberry Fields Forever
    (Take 7 And Edit Piece)
Penny Lane
A Day In The Life
Good Morning, Good Morning
Only A Northern Song
Being For The Benefit Of Mr Kite!
    (Takes 1 And 2)
Being For The Benefit Of Mr Kite!
    (Take 7)
Lucy In The Sky With Diamonds
Within You Without You
    (Instrumental)
Sgt Pepper's Lonely Hearts Club
    Band (Reprise)
You Know My Name (Look Up
    The Number)
I Am The Walrus
The Fool On The Hill (Demo)
Your Mother Should Know
The Fool On The Hill (Take 4)
Hello, Goodbye
Lady Madonna
Across The Universe

Whereas *Anthology 1* had appeared a couple of weeks before the headline-grabbing Free As A Bird, this second round of releases saw the schedule reversed, *Anthology 2* coming out a fortnight *after* Real Love, which also served as the album opener. Probably this was the better way to do it, fans willing to snap up the cheaper 45 first then await the album, rather than conversely, but it was now springtime and the documentaries ushering in this batch of recordings hadn't been seen since the Christmas period, and were starting to recede into memory.

Anthology 2 covered a pivotal period in the Beatles' history, straddling the last 18 months of performing-flea Beatlemania, across the apex of their studio work, *Sgt Pepper*. As such it has a set of contents ranging from live recordings from Shea Stadium, Hollywood Bowl and the Far East tour, to intricate workings concocted in the seclusion of EMI. But whereas the various live and studio recordings on *Anthology 1* had tended to mesh fairly successfully, here there is an increasing sense that the Beatles were living parallel lives through 1965 and 1966, switching between mop-tops and serious artists until they gave up touring altogether. And as their recording craft had become so much more sophisticated through 1966, it made little musical sense to lurch here from the fascinating studio development of I'm Only Sleeping to the screaming mayhem of Rock And Roll Music, live at Nippon Budokan Hall in Tokyo.

The mix of styles was unavoidable since Apple were bent on a chronological format. On which note, the arrival of *Anthology 2* was delayed by a few weeks when someone noticed the album therefore started with three successive John numbers. Despite the fact that a reported 2.5 million CD booklets had already been printed, Apple shuffled the pack and plucked Paul's I'm Down to insert it as track 3, then reprinted all the booklets with the correct details, at a considerable cost. Was it really necessary? (One wonders if it was done at Paul's insistence.)

Probably the most impressive of the two discs is the second one, consisting entirely of studio material. From the three instalments of Strawberry Fields Forever, which succinctly trace its growth from John's solo demo to a full hearing of Take 7, to a preliminary version of Across The Universe, the collection here is full of interest, giving the feel of a behind-the-curtains peek at the group at work.

If there's a downside to the coverage of the studio years, it's in the jiggery-pokery which went on in the preparation of the album, several songs edited, re-assembled and otherwise tinkered with to make them flow nicely. The process raises again the tension between trying to provide devout fans with authentic outtakes and catering for the more casual buyer who just wanted something pleasant to listen to. There's merit in either approach of course, but inclusions like A Day In The Life opened Apple up to charges of making Frankenstein's Monsters, Mark Lewisohn's excellent sleeve notes describing it thus: "Assembled expressly for the *Anthology*, this composite mix embraces the best of the unreleased outtakes of A Day In The Life", and a composite it was, consisting of five different leftover scraps recorded at different times, all bolted together in 1995 to make a complete song.

Notable album omissions included the much-longed-for Carnival Of Light, which according to those who have heard it, is a lot less impressive than one might hope. (Fancying his own *Anthology*-like 'photofilm', re-telling the Beatles' story through stills and music, Paul soon after expressed a wish to use Carnival Of Light there instead.) There were one or two other little gems which might have been included on *Anthology 2*, such as the acoustic demo of Love You To (which eventually came out in 2022), and although the 'laughing' version of And Your Bird Can Sing was a revelation with its alternative arrangement, little did we know then that Apple had the same, but with a regular vocal track, still in storage.

No matter; this new release had more than enough valuable inclusions to delight any fan. Here again are our top 10 highlights:

- **If You've Got Trouble** – recorded for *Help!*, this Lennon-McCartney original was supposed to be Ringo's feature spot, but fell by the wayside. Described by Ian MacDonald as an unmitigated disaster, it's not bad and deserves preservation here.

- **That Means A Lot** – another Lennon-McCartney track which never made it onto *Help!*, this song was offloaded to PJ Proby, but here it is performed in its original state by John, Paul, George and Ringo.

- **Norwegian Wood (This Bird Has Flown)** – take 1, this exploratory recording is more basic than the *Rubber Soul* cut but also has more 'Indian' moments, and tells us something about the way the Beatles initially pictured it.

- **12-Bar Original** – this Lennon-McCartney-Harrison-Starr instrumental was likely based on Green Onions by Booker T & The MGs. It was cut to half-length for *Anthology* and remains a novel curio.

- **Tomorrow Never Knows** – AKA 'Mark 1' – which is what it was – this is one of the more fascinating *Anthology* selections, taped while John was still trying to work out how to turn it into something cosmic.

- **And Your Bird Can Sing** – the laughing take, whose hysterics were probably assisted by various chemical compounds. A superb Byrds-like guitar arrangement, it was good enough to have been issued like this on *Revolver* (once they'd managed to stop laughing through it).

- **I'm Only Sleeping** – this somnambulistic attempt at the song, although called take 1, was actually an attempted re-make, after the *Revolver* version was already nailed. It suggests John wasn't happy with the track and thought he could do it better.

- **Strawberry Fields Forever** – take 7, the first part of this was used in the finished 1967 release, George Martin splicing it part-way through to a second, different version. Here it is complete, as originally taped on 29 November 1966.

- **I Am The Walrus** – the simple basic arrangement, lacking any of the adventurous overdubs which later adorned the song, this version was used by George Martin as a template to score the orchestral parts.

- **Across The Universe** – simpler than the later overdubbed versions, this is take 2, with 'Indian' musical elements and a gentler, more natural sound.

Anthology 2 was an exceptionally strong release, worthy of more praise than it got. In stereotypical style, the media was cool about it but sales were strong. It sold 78,000 in the UK in its first week and 440,000 in the US, thereby entering at number 1 on both sides of the Atlantic. Although sales subsequently trailed off, the feat of crashing both charts at once was exactly what it, and the Beatles, deserved.

Anthology live

One of the many things the *Anthology* did was to expand the amount of live performance available. Until now, all that had been released was the 1977 *Hollywood Bowl* LP, and then some scattered performances which fell under the BBC broadcasting banner and were included on the 1994 album. But *Anthology* brought many more – most of them in front of television audiences, although some were bona-fide concert recordings. In addition to *The Beatles At The Hollywood Bowl* and a few BBC cuts (see page 210 for details of those) we now had the following on *Anthology 1* and *2*:

13 October 1963: The London Palladium
(*Sunday Night At The London Palladium* television show):

- **I'll Get You**

24 October 1963: The Karlaplansstudion, Stockholm, Sweden
(*The Beatles, Pop Group From Liverpool Visiting Stockholm* on Swedish television)

- **I Saw Her Standing There / From Me To You / Money / You Really Got A Hold On Me / Roll Over Beethoven**

4 November 1963: Prince of Wales Theatre, London
(Royal Variety Performance, televised)

- **She Loves You / Till There Was You / Twist And Shout**

2 December 1963: Elstree Studios, Hertfordshire
(*Two Of A Kind*, the Morecambe and Wise television show)

- **This Boy / I Want To Hold Your Hand**

9 February 1964: CBS-TV Studio 50, New York
(the *Ed Sullivan Show*)

- **All My Loving**

19 April 1964: IBC Studios, London
(*Around The Beatles* television show)

- **I Wanna Be Your Man / Long Tall Sally / Boys / Shout**

1 August 1965: ABC Theatre, Blackpool
(*Blackpool Night Out* television feature)

- **I Feel Fine / Ticket To Ride / Yesterday / Help!**

15 August 1965: Shea Stadium, New York

- **Everybody's Trying To Be My Baby**

30 August 1965: Hollywood Bowl, Los Angeles

- **Baby's In Black** [also included on the B-side of Real Love]

30 June 1966: Nippon Budokan Hall, Tokyo

- **Rock And Roll Music / She's A Woman**

Fallen apples

Anthology 3
★★★★★

**UK release:
28 October 1996**

**US release:
28 October 1996**

A Beginning
Happiness Is A Warm Gun
Helter Skelter
Mean Mr Mustard
Polythene Pam
Glass Onion
Junk
Piggies
Honey Pie
Don't Pass Me By
Ob-La-Di, Ob-La-Da
Good Night
Cry Baby Cry
Blackbird
Sexy Sadie
While My Guitar Gently Weeps
Hey Jude
Not Guilty
Mother Nature's Son
Glass Onion
Rocky Raccoon
What's The New Mary Jane
Step Inside Love / Los Paranoias
I'm So Tired
I Will
Why Don't We Do It In The Road
Julia

I've Got A Feeling
She Came In Through The
   Bathroom Window
Dig A Pony
Two Of Us
For You Blue
Teddy Boy
Medley: Rip It Up / Shake, Rattle
   And Roll / Blue Suede Shoes
The Long And Winding Road
Oh! Darling
All Things Must Pass
Mailman, Bring Me No More Blues
Get Back
Old Brown Shoe
Octopus's Garden
Maxwell's Silver Hammer
Something
Come Together
Come And Get It
Ain't She Sweet
Because
Let It Be
I Me Mine
The End

The time span of *Anthology 3* covers the group's last few albums, and its layout better suits the CD format than the triple vinyl, with a convenient break between disc 1, covering the *White Album* period, and disc 2, which takes care of *Abbey Road* and *Let It Be*. As a whole the set encompasses the group's Apple years and since there's no reunion single, it starts at the correct place – summer 1968.

This third instalment of the series had a similar problem to the first – too much source material to select from. The 1968 Esher tapes alone were enough to fill a whole CD (and would in fact do so in 2018 – see entry on page 225), but there's only room for seven of the 27 demos here, although they include the then surprising Mean Mr Mustard and Polythene Pam, which no-one knew existed from so early. (On the other hand, the rumoured arrival of the Esher Child Of Nature and Circles proved not to be.) There are quite a few others which for reasons of space just wouldn't have been viable, including the legendary long version of Helter Skelter, all 12 minutes of it, which appears here in a self-defeating five-minute edit. The similarly vaunted take 20 of Revolution is also absent – it's basically Revolution 1 from *The White Album*, with an extravagant extended coda onto which was plastered all the mayhem and sound effects which were then purloined and turned into Revolution #9, to make it into two separate tracks. Then there was also a mooted recreation of the *Abbey Road* medley said to be under consideration, made up from alternative takes of each song. Again, too excessive for the *Anthology* format.

Before we get onto the joys of what *was* included, we should also consider further material which was suitable for use, but overlooked. There was Paul's demo of Goodbye, for instance, and the longer performance of Dig It from the *Get Back* sessions. Speaking of which, there were absolute mountains of outtakes from January 1969, ranging from work-in-progress rehearsals to unreleased originals and all manner of rock and roll oldies. Apple was forced to cherry pick just a few, and their conservative approach meant that more often than not, the versions on the album were pretty similar to the well-known recordings. Case in point: Two Of Us, which was rehearsed every which way, including full band arrangements and lush harmony versions, but which on *Anthology* is presented as an alternative take much like the *Let It Be* release.

The treasure lies in the songs which were inserted into the gaps between album outtakes – three superb George Harrison demos sprinkled in among unlikely fare such as Come And Get It – which was reported to have been vetoed on the grounds that it was never meant for the Beatles, yet made the final cut anyway – and Step Inside Love, a Beatle version of the Cilla Black hit. These and others make *Anthology 3* another wonderful trove for Beatles collectors, in an era when studio outtakes like these were as rare as hen's teeth. So here is a top 10 of what was in:

- **While My Guitar Gently Weeps** – this was famous before its release, consisting of George playing the song alone on his guitar, and with some different lyrics here and there.

- **Not Guilty** – more George, a song which took up a vast amount of working time, this being take 102! Still the Beatles couldn't nail it, and so George kept it to one side and re-made it in 1979 for his *George Harrison* album.

- **What's The New Mary Jane** – another of John's crazed avant-garde creations, well-known to bootleggers but new to most of the public. (John tried to release it as a Plastic Ono Band track in 1969!)

- **Step Inside Love** – one of the many songs John and Paul gave away, this was donated to Cilla but re-recorded here in a supposedly ad-libbed version by John, Paul and Ringo.

- **She Came In Through The Bathroom Window** – an interesting run-through of the *Abbey Road* song, recorded during *Get Back*, slower and dominated by wah-wahed electric guitar.

- **The Long And Winding Road** – 26 years after Phil Spector had controversially overdubbed it, here was the original group take, as nature intended. (Curiously, in the 1980s Paul had re-recorded the song in the studio twice, and retained the orchestral decorations both times – so he can't have disliked them that much!)

- **All Things Must Pass** – George on his own, demoing what would become the title track of his first proper solo album. A gem which slipped through the group's fingers.

- **Something** – the third of George's solo guitar demos, captured at EMI on his birthday in 1969. He'd been taped writing it during *Get Back* but this is the earliest full recording.

- **Come And Get It** – Paul on his own, but you wouldn't know it. He plays piano, drums and bass himself and gave this recording to Badfinger with instructions that they copy it exactly, and they'd have a hit single. He was right.

- **I Me Mine** – the very last Beatles recording, made on 3 January 1970. Like The Long And Winding Road, this was 'Spectorized' for *Let It Be*, but this is the original, unadorned take, running less than two minutes.

- Special mention: the seven Esher demos.

As with *Anthology 2*, the arrival of this new collection was delayed, and quite considerably so. It was at first intended for a pre-summer release but actually landed at the end of October 1996, partly because of arguments over the allocation of copyrights on some of the previously unreleased tracks. Likely one of the sticking points was Los Paranoias, a brief thing spontaneously created by Paul, but accompanied by John and Ringo. When it appeared on *Anthology*, it had a four-way copyright assigned, despite the fact that George wasn't there and had absolutely nothing to do with it – so what went on behind the scenes in 1996 is intriguing.

And speaking of delays, there was also meant to be an *Anthology* book available, assembling bits of their interview transcripts, and a copy was even shown off at a book fair in October 1995 so was presumed ready to go in tandem with *Anthology 1*. But as 1995 turned into 1996 there was not a sniff of it, and so it remained until October 2000! What on earth was the problem there? And there was the expected arrival of a box set containing all three *Anthology* albums, along with an extra disc of leftover outtakes, which at the time of writing, we are still awaiting.

Fans enjoyed scrutinising Klaus Voormann's cover art, this album's timeline coinciding with the absurd Paul Is Dead legend, and unsurprisingly more clues were found, including the fact that 1969 Paul was ripped away in favour of his 1965 version – whose head had a fracture through it – and so on… all good fun of course. Reviews? Mixed, from *Melody Maker*'s 'pure genius' to the *Glasgow Herald*, 'one for the completist saddo'. (That's us!)

Who cared? The album shifted 279,000 in America and 52,000 in the UK in just a week. It crashed into the US album charts at number 1, emulating *Anthology 1* and *2*. Not bad for a *double* album (triple, on vinyl!), especially one made up of leftover scraps recorded decades earlier.

The missing third reunion single

It's an anomaly that only two 'reunion' songs were released, one on *Anthology 1* and one on *Anthology 2* but nothing on *Anthology 3*. What happened to the plans is something we can never be entirely sure of, but there's enough reliable information out there that we can have a go at sketching out the likely sequence of events.

Grow Old With Me

Back in early 1994, it was generally understood that when Yoko handed over John's demo tapes to Paul, they included three songs: Free As A Bird, Real Love and Grow Old With Me. This was in print long before the *Anthology* series was scheduled with its three main instalments, and so it's fair to assume not a back-engineered theory. Possibly Paul and the others, knowing what was coming, specifically asked Yoko for three songs at the outset.

But in late 1995, Paul remarked to Allan Kozinn that Grow Old With Me was barely looked at because when they played it back, it was clear it would have needed too much doing to it before overdubs could be applied, and so the Threetles abandoned it and turned their attention to another, different song instead. So what was it?

Now And Then

While no-one in the inner circle spelled it out, several interview comments painted the picture. In the same interview with Allan Kozinn, Paul confirmed a song had been worked on but not completed, yet couldn't put a name to it. Ringo also stated an unfinished song had been worked on, and Geoff Emerick described it a piano-based home demo. Jeff Lynne meanwhile said the song in question had no formal title (hence, why Paul couldn't name it) and described it as a bluesy ballad in A minor, suggesting it could likely be christened either Now And Then or Miss You – which is the clincher.

John's 1978 piano demo is in the correct style and key, and is now universally known as Now And Then (it also contains the line cited by Jeff Lynne, 'I miss you'). If it's true that Yoko only gave Paul three of John's demos in the first place, this begs the question of how and when this fourth tape was obtained. In any case, it's now understood that although preliminary work was done, George took a dislike to it and called proceedings to a halt.

All For Love

The abandonment of both Grow Old With Me and Now And Then caused a bit of a problem. By 1995 it was clear that the *Anthology* records were due to come out in three phases, and so the plan to release a new track each time had hit a snag, likely why, in the months leading up to *Anthology 1*, Free As A Bird and Real Love were intermittently considered for one double-sided 45 release.

But the story doesn't end. After Free As A Bird had appeared without Real Love on the B-side, and the release of Real Love came closer, rumours started circulating that another new track was in the offing after all, by the mysterious title, All For Love. The song's name was revealed by Peter Hodgson, an old pal of the group who happened to have possession of one of the 1960 rehearsal tape reels made by the Quarry Men at Paul's home on Forthlin Road. Agreeing in 1995 to sell the tape to Paul, he visited him at home and was treated to a hearing of a song identified to him by Paul as All For Love. The story was that Paul, George and Ringo had been working on it the week before – but by then (27 March), Real Love was long-finished – so this new track could not have been that one by a different name.

In the March 1996 edition of *Beatles Monthly*, Andy Davis went further: "Recording of the third new Beatles 'reunion' song, 'All For Love', is now complete. It's understood that the song isn't one of the John Lennon demo tapes handed to Paul by Yoko Ono, but is in fact a brand new song written by Paul McCartney and George Harrison."

Davis went on to question how such a song could be called a Beatles track if John wasn't on it. But many Beatles songs from the 1960s didn't feature John, and are no less group work than the others – Yesterday, for example, was just Paul, Within You Without You just George, and Goodnight was just Ringo – and anyway the George-Paul-Ringo trio had featured on Maxwell's Silver Hammer, I Me Mine and others – so this would certainly have met the same standard.

Hear Them (or not...)

- As with Paul, George and Ringo's incidental music, you won't hear **All For Love** anywhere. It's securely locked away as if a priceless heirloom.

- John's original demo of **Now And Then** has leaked on bootlegs, along with a substantial amount of home-taped material from his so-called house-husband years. Anything resulting from the 1995 sessions has never been heard, however.

- **Grow Old With Me** has a happier story. John's recording was released on the 1984 album, *Milk And Honey*, and then re-released on *John Lennon Anthology* with a new orchestral score by none other than George Martin, giving a hint of how he might have worked Free As A Bird and Real Love, had he taken them on. Paul later mentioned he was tempted to go and finish a 'Beatles' version as originally intended, and his wish came partly true in 2019 when Ringo selected the song for his album, *What's My Name*. This new version had Paul on bass and backing vocals, and a little musical quote from Here Comes The Sun, indirectly summoning the foursome one last time. Those wanting to complete the reunion triptych therefore have this to fall back on, job sort-of done.

Newer and bluer

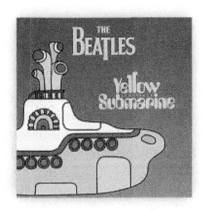

Yellow Submarine Songtrack
★★★★☆

UK release:
13 September 1999

US release:
13 September 1999

Yellow Submarine	Sgt Pepper's Lonely Hearts
Hey Bulldog	Club Band
Eleanor Rigby	With A Little Help From My Friends
Love You To	Baby, You're A Rich Man
All Together Now	Only A Northern Song
Lucy In The Sky With Diamonds	All You Need Is Love
Think For Yourself	When I'm Sixty Four
	Nowhere Man
	It's All Too Much

After the *Anthology* was done and dusted, word from Paul was that the Beatles were now finished, the story complete, and there would be no more work on group projects ever. While that might well have been his personal agenda, and, one supposes, that of George and Ringo, the money men saw things differently and following spectacular sales, EMI and Capitol set up a new business purely to handle the Beatles' back catalogue: EMI-Capitol Entertainment Properties, which described itself as an 'exclusive, worldwide marketing entity', who would 'oversee all existing Beatles catalogue and any new initiatives involving the group's repertoire'. (It also took charge of John Lennon's 'entertainment properties' while, we must assume, imagining no possessions.)

Possibly the first thing to cross EMI-Capitol Entertainment Properties' desk was a proposed 30th anniversary edition of *Sgt Pepper*, due in November 1997. A box set was drawn up, enclosing a CD designed as a mini-LP edition (then a fairly new idea), inserts and a drum skin badge – but although it got as far as prototype stages, it didn't happen. (Perhaps in part because at the same time, sleeve designer Peter Blake was in legal dispute with EMI for royalties on CD sales, which, he argued, his original 1967 contract did not preclude, since it only specified no royalty on *records*.)

Interestingly, the new *Sgt Pepper* CD was set to be remastered to enhance the sound quality, an innovation which indirectly fed into the next proposal: *Yellow Submarine Songtrack*, a newly compiled album of Beatle music from the film, all in remastered sound. Work on the project started in October 1997, and the main event was not an album, but a restored edition of the film for cinema and DVD. The challenge was that issuing the movie for home cinema would require a 5.1 surround-sound audio track, and that would mean returning to the original studio tapes and mixing from multi-track sources. The only problem was, some of the songs had been recorded as early as 1965, on EMI's four-track technology, not suited to a six-channel remix.

The movie itself was a massive and arduous undertaking, and apart from revamping the sound, the original film negatives had deteriorated over the last couple of decades, requiring every individual frame to be re-touched by hand. They managed it, and when *Yellow Submarine* was finally re-launched, it came with blaze of merchandising from a Yellow Submarine festival to Blue Meanies on the pitch at Liverpool football matches, and all manner of toys, novelties and figurines on sale. The film and DVD were a commercial and critical hit, but beyond the scope of this book where we focus instead on the associated record and CD.

This new collection was dubbed a 'songtrack', differentiating it from the 1969 soundtrack album which had included all the original songs, but overlooked all but two of the other Beatles recordings which turn up in full or in part during the film. This reinvention captured them all, bar A Day In The Life, whose orchestra crescendo appears in the movie, just as the submarine departs Liverpool for Pepperland. To make the songs into multi-channel events, EMI traced back through their studio tapes and found more than was previously known. In the mid-1960s, the Beatles used four-track tapes exclusively but when the tracks were full, they'd mix two or more together onto a fresh track, freeing up space again, a technique they called bouncing down. EMI found they had recordings left on their original tape reels from before the bounce downs, so whereas only four-track tapes were used to generate the 1960s album mixes, EMI now had several additional tracks to work from, with separate instruments and various bits of sound effects in each, which could be polished up individually and the songs remixed again from scratch.

This, and a few other tricks, such as using stereo mikes to obtain quasi-stereo recordings of old mono tapes, enabled the compilers to achieve a sound stage ahead of anything done previously, including the MFSL albums of 1982. The results were greeted with delight across the board, the album impressing everyone who heard it, bringing sonic depth to tracks taken from studio albums which now sounded dull by comparison. Understandably there was clamour among Beatles fans for the whole catalogue to be given the same treatment, an inevitability in the long term, given the possibilities now obvious.

The newly compiled songs

The original *Yellow Submarine* album contained half a dozen Beatles songs: Yellow Submarine; Only A Northern Song; All Together Now; Hey Bulldog; It's All Too Much; All You Need Is Love.

This new album compiled them all alongside nine more remixed from the back-catalogue:

From *Rubber Soul* (1965)
    Think For Yourself
    Nowhere Man

From *Revolver* (1966)
    Eleanor Rigby
    Love You To

From *Sgt Pepper* (1967)
    Lucy In The Sky With Diamonds
    Sgt. Pepper's Lonely Hearts Club Band
    With A Little Help From My Friends
    When I'm Sixty-Four

From *Magical Mystery Tour* (1967)
    Baby, You're A Rich Man

There was one curious side issue – in preparing the footage, various bits of the Hey Bulldog sequence had been discovered, that part of the original movie having originally been chopped out of the US cinema cut. The news that Hey Bulldog was now being worked on for release gave rise to the misunderstanding that a Hey Bulldog single was in the pipeline, something EMI did consider before scrapping the idea. It's a shame it didn't happen because the track is one of the group's lesser known and would have been nice to have on single.

Fans didn't really mind – *Yellow Submarine Songtrack* is fondly remembered, and besides impressing with its futuristic remixes, it was housed inside an impressively redesigned sleeve with much better graphics including a selection of artwork from the film. (It's a curiosity that given the strongly visual material available to the designer, the 1969 album had arrived in a disappointingly unremarkable cover.) This new collection also appeared on yellow vinyl – coloured vinyl being a rare thing where the Beatles are concerned (the 1994 Capitol-CEMA singles excepted). But this was more than just dressing – opinion on the album was, and is, of universal approbation, a success story all round, which is unusual when it comes to re-working the Beatles.

Project X

1
★★★★★

UK release:
13 November 2000

US release:
14 November 2000

Love Me Do	Yellow Submarine
From Me To You	Eleanor Rigby
She Loves You	Penny Lane
I Want To Hold Your Hand	All You Need Is Love
Can't Buy Me Love	Hello, Goodbye
A Hard Day's Night	Lady Madonna
I Feel Fine	Hey Jude
Eight Days A Week	Get Back
Ticket To Ride	The Ballad Of John And Yoko
Help!	Something
Yesterday	Come Together
Day Tripper	Let It Be
We Can Work It Out	The Long And Winding Road
Paperback Writer	

EMI had never quite managed to compile the Beatles' hits properly. *A Collection Of Beatles Oldies* had been impressively assembled but concluded in 1966. *Hey Jude* made a decent sequel, but both these albums were only partial in scope and were particular to either the UK or US – neither country had both together. *1962-1966* and *1967-1970* followed in 1973 and were superb, but covered eight expensive sides with multiple album cuts included, and the 1982 *20 Greatest Hits* was OK but fans didn't warm to it, partly due to its association with the rest of the dubious period compilations, and partly due to the fact that its squashing of so many songs onto one vinyl disc smelled a little like a budget throwaway. What EMI really needed was to go back to square one, and work out a truly blockbusting album containing all the big hit singles, which would stand the test of time.

Compiling the Beatles at all was an awkward concept after the run of albums between 1976 and 1982, which were in theory now consigned to history and not to be brought up in polite company. *Past Masters* had been an exception but was purely functional, working as a necessary adjunct to the 1987 studio album CDs. No-one dared broach a collection of Beatles recordings again – until now, when stories started circulating that EMI was working on 'Project X', widely assumed to be an album containing all the group's singles on one CD. (EMI comically denied any knowledge of 'Project X', but of course they knew, and they also knew that we knew they knew.)

The hope was that this hits collection would be out for Christmas 1999, thereby also poignantly marking the start of the new millennium. Once that deadline had passed, there were no pressures of time and it took until the middle of 2000 for EMI to officially show their cards – we could expect a compilation of hits (provisionally titled *The Best Of The Beatles*) by the end of the year. (That meant it would be arriving in the 30th anniversary year of the Beatles' split, although no-one particularly noticed!) There was always a little uncertainty as to what it would contain, the rumoured inclusion of Yesterday leading UK fans to suppose it would add in the post-1970 singles alongside the obvious. But when the final track listing emerged, it instantly sparked the familiar grumbles of objection from fans far and wide.

The premise was simple: all the UK and US number 1 hits, as listed on the official charts, *Record Retailer* in Britain and *Billboard* in the States. That meant the album would essentially be a merging of the UK and US *20 Greatest Hits* albums, which were compiled to the same rules and contained 26 different tracks between them. However there was one difference: the US edition of *20 Greatest Hits* had not included Something, which only got to number 3 on *Billboard*, but this new collection added it in, since, when Come Together was number 1, Something was listed alongside it as its double A-side. What perplexed UK fans more than anything though was that two of the group's most significant British hits, Please Please Me and Strawberry Fields Forever, were missing, and the imaginary arguments with EMI ran and ran, something like this:

Fan: Huh? Where's Please Please Me?

EMI: Sorry, it only got to 2, so it doesn't count.

Fan: But Please Please Me was the Beatles' first number 1!

EMI: True on the *NME* chart, the *Melody Maker* chart and the *Disc* chart, but we're going by the *Record Retailer* chart.

Fan: Well what about America then?

EMI: Number 3.

Fan: So how about Strawberry Fields Forever? You can't leave that out when Penny Lane is included!

EMI: Number 2 UK and 8 in the US – it doesn't qualify. Penny Lane made number 1 on *Billboard* on its own, so it does.

Fan: That's ridiculous. Why then did you include Something? That was only 4 UK and 3 US. If you're bending the rules for Something, bend them for Strawberry Fields!

EMI: Something was listed as joint number 1 on *Billboard*, alongside Come Together.

Fan: Well in that case, you forgot For You Blue, which was also a joint number 1, along with The Long And Winding Road.

EMI: No comment…

Fan: But we want Please Please Me and Strawberry Fields Forever! Surely you can squeeze a couple more tracks on if you want.

EMI: No we can't – it all has to go onto a single CD…

The disgruntlement the track selection aroused has never fully gone away, and you will still find Beatles fans of furrowed brow bemoaning the absence of these two hits, even to the extent of advocating a second album called 2 to round them up.

But 1 is what it is, and on release in November 2000, it dazzled. Apart from the fact that it contained 26 number 1 hits, its packaging was an extravaganza. OK, the front cover was unimaginative, echoing some of the functional 1970s compilation designs, but the vinyl double LP was styled after *The White Album*, but in full colour. It contained Richard Avedon's four psychedelic portraits inside the gatefold then included them again as individual inserts, and also came with a full colour poster. The CD edition squeezed it all down to fit the format of course, but was still warmly welcomed.

As predicted by EMI, who had their disc pressing plants in overdrive, 1 instantly became a major release, topping the album charts around the planet and eventually joined the likes of *Thriller* and *Dark Side Of The Moon* in the lists of all-time best-sellers. 12x platinum in the UK and 11x platinum in the US, this was, finally, the greatest hits package the Beatles deserved all along. And as a sweetener, the full 79 minutes of music, some of the best ever recorded, was issued on a cost-saving single CD – so everyone was finally, completely happy.

Well, apart from certain Beatles fans, that is…

Fan: Wait a minute! From Me To You is only in mono. We want it in stereo for once!

Different fan: Hey – why are the rest of the singles in stereo? We want them in original mono!

…and so on…

As nature intended

Let It Be... Naked
★★★★★

UK release:
17 November 2003

US release:
17 November 2003

Get Back	I've Got A Feeling
Dig A Pony	One After 909
For You Blue	Don't Let Me Down
The Long And Winding Road	I Me Mine
Two Of Us	Across The Universe
	Let It Be

Fly On The Wall disc contains extracts from performances of:

Sun King	Don't Let Me Down
Don't Let Me Down	All Things Must Pass
One After 909	She Came In Through The
Because I Know You Love Me So	Bathroom Window
Don't Pass Me By	Paul's Piano Piece
Taking A Trip To Carolina	Get Back
John's Piano Piece	Two Of Us
Child Of Nature	Maggie Mae
Back In The USSR	Fancy My Chances With You
Every Little Thing	Can You Dig It?
	Get Back

Despite containing three number 1 singles, the Beatles' *Let It Be* has never been a fan favourite. Partly the problem is in the concept – it began as an attempt to record an 'honest' album with few or no post-production effects but ended up with several tracks heavily processed by Phil Spector, presented among some open-air live recordings (the rooftop gig) with spontaneous chatter, and some gentle studio ballads, an indoor-outdoor thing which left proceedings a little disjoined. Then there was the addition to the running order of the 1968 Across The Universe, a year-old single in Get Back, plus the 1970 recording of I Me Mine, edging *Let It Be* oddly towards a compilation album. But it was the Spectorization which most troubled Paul in particular, the story of his Long And Winding Road not something we need go over again.

By all accounts it was Paul who pressed for this album remix. By the time it was released, George had passed away but he reportedly gave his approval at the outset, and Olivia, who then had the power to block it, didn't – and so one presumes all were behind the idea. The main task was to lose Phil Spector's overdubs from The Long And Winding Road, I Me Mine and Across The Universe, exposing the band musicianship underneath – hence the 'naked' concept. And since most of the unadorned studio tracks were recorded 'live' anyway, they meshed well with the four cleaned up rooftop songs, bringing a new sense of cohesion to the set. Work was completed by polishing up the sound, starting and ending tracks with more professional edits, and getting rid of the superfluous sketches which were Dig It and Maggie Mae. The compilers also decided to restore Don't Let Me Down to the album, where it should have been all along.

There's no way of knowing how *Get Back* would have turned out in 1969, had the Beatles completed it then. Glyn Johns' rough-end-ready album prototypes were too raw for release but if the group and George Martin had the requisite enthusiasm, they might have turned out something like this. Certainly there is nothing wrong with the quality of the songs, it was just the way they'd been presented which had put some listeners off. This 'naked' reinvention of *Let It Be* is, we must suppose, close to what the Beatles were hoping for all along, and had it come out in 1969 it may well have earned these sessions a better reputation.

So how does *Let It Be... Naked* differ from *Let It Be*? Track by track, the changes are as follows:

Two Of Us – same version, but with superfluous talking removed.

Dig A Pony – same rooftop version, with chat removed.

Across The Universe – same basic take but correct running speed restored and overdubs removed.

I Me Mine – same version with Phil Spector's time-extending edit re-created, and the various 1970 overdubs stripped off.

Dig It – gone.

Let It Be – same basic take but with a different guitar solo from George edited in.

Maggie Mae – gone.

I've Got A Feeling – part of the same basic rooftop performance (take 1) but edited up with sections of take 2 from the same day.

One After 909 – same basic rooftop performance, with 'Danny Boy' removed.

The Long And Winding Road – different version. *Let It Be* version was taped on 26 January 1969, but this is from 31 January and of course omits the notorious overdubs.

For You Blue – same basic take but with a different lead vocal mixed on along with an extra guitar track. Chit-chat removed.

Get Back – same basic studio take without the originally added top-and-tail chatter.

Don't Let Me Down – new to the album and previously unreleased. This is a mix from both rooftop performances whereas the original release was a studio recording made on 28 January.

Included with *Let It Be… Naked* was a 22-minute disc of seemingly random snippets of conversation and music from the many hours of audio captured in 1969. This was such a vast and valuable stockpile of material the measly amount on the so-called *Fly On The Wall* bonus disc looked very much like Apple were taunting us by giving just a brief glimpse of the treasure we knew they had. The entire *Let It Be* sessions have been extensively documented over the years by Doug Sulpy, who it's fair to say is the expert in the field, and his comments summed up his feelings:

> "For those five of you who have never heard a bootleg in your life, this is your opportunity to hear a few seconds, at least, from Ringo's 'Taking a Trip To Carolina', John's 'On The Road To Marrakesh' and 'I Fancy Me Chances'. Without context, and hopelessly truncated, however, this disc is, for all intents and purposes, worthless."

Well, almost worthless. We should point out that here we can experience a little bit of two early Lennon-McCartney originals, Because I Know You Love Me So and Fancy My Chances With You – which are good to have. And Doug is right to point out Taking A Trip To Carolina (all 19 seconds of it) and the sample from On The Road To Marrakesh (titled here Child Of Nature) as interesting inclusions, to which we might add the minute's worth of Paul's Piano Piece, one of the most impressive session outtakes of all. But it's just not enough, especially given the amount of tapes Apple had to draw on.

There was a missed opportunity to issue the album with the original *Get Back* sleeve art, showing the group looking down over EMI's staircase in 1969, but they didn't. Instead they went for an odd silvery sleeve with photographic negatives of the original cover photos, except where George was concerned: the fact that he was smiling on the cover of *Let It Be* meant that when a negative of his photo was made, it came out with a row of

massive black teeth (left). Hence they changed it for a different shot. Not the best-presented album, and with a frustratingly inadequate set of bonus material, *Let It Be... Naked* was nonetheless a strong proposition which made the top 10 on both sides of the Atlantic and went some way to correcting the history of this troubled set of recordings. (One or two of us prefer it to *Let It Be!*)

George's negative

Dexterity

The Capitol Albums Volume 1
★★★★☆

UK release:
15 November 2004

US release:
15 November 2004

Meet The Beatles!
The Beatles' Second Album
Something New
Beatles '65

It's an odd thing, but after the Beatles' UK album discography became the international standard in 1987, it unwittingly made the Capitol albums of old seem like lost treasures. So by the time CD had become the dominant format, a mixture of loyalty from older fans and curiosity from younger, created a demand for some CD re-issues of the US albums. Negotiations to do just that got underway as early as 1993, but the typical inordinate delays ensured that nothing was made available until late 2004, and when this box set finally arrived, it contained just four of the albums.

Notably, this would ensure these Capitol albums were available in the UK and elsewhere for the first time. So far the UK had only seen releases of two Capitol albums, *Hey Jude* and *Magical Mystery Tour*, as well as an issue of the Vee-Jay album, *Hear The Beatles Tell All* in 1981, with its cover art famously proclaiming, 'George talks about the Paddy Boyd'! But this was new ground for most British buyers, so as in America in 1987, there was transatlantic interest generated.

As we know, the Capitol releases were assembled from the British recordings, piled up with album tracks, singles and anything else they could get hold of to bulk out the song count and squeeze as many LPs as possible from the group. On one level this was looked down on, the Beatles themselves objecting to the idea of putting singles on albums, viewing it as short-changing the fans. On the other hand, a case can be made that so doing makes the album stronger for having the hits on, and fans are not therefore compelled to collect 45s separately, the single-on-album approach gathering up everything in one go. It's a long-standing debate and one which comes into sharp relief when comparing the Capitol Beatles albums of 1964-1966 with the corresponding Parlophone releases. Let it be understood that while the UK discography saw two albums released in 1964 and two more in 1965, Capitol issued twice as many – four per year – although to be fair, they had some catching up to do.

When it comes to Capitol's albums there is one thing which springs to mind, apart from the novel track listings, and that's the alteration of the audio. Capitol, under direction of Dave Dexter Jr, frequently remixed the tapes they obtained from London, so several US tracks are notably different from the UK ones. And things are quite complicated: the UK singles were coming out in mono only, so mono mixes were done and sent to America. Capitol then inserted them onto stereo albums, so duophonic (ie, fake stereo) mixes were created. But Capitol were also issuing mono albums, but in receipt of stereo tapes for album tracks, mixed them down to a single channel. So fake stereo, and also fake mono. And then there was the reverb which capitol often slapped on top for good measure…

The four 1964 Capitol albums appear here, assembled from the original US audio with its unique mixes. And since every CD has the album on twice, once in stereo then again in mono, all the variations are intact. However it must also be noted that in many cases, Capitol did use the original London mixes – stereo tapes for stereo albums and mono tapes for mono albums – and so with the first four UK studio albums still only available on CD in mono, fans were able to get many of the relevant tracks in authentic stereo at last.

Guide to differences

Taking the UK discography as the baseline, this is how Capitol altered the albums for the US market. Note that we are comparing to the original 1960s UK vinyl, not the CD editions of 1987. First some technicalities:

- **Dexterization** is the term often used to describe the addition of reverb and echo by Capitol, to make the recordings sound more dynamic.

- **Duophonic**: fake stereo created by manipulating the mono tapes. Duophonic mixes are often Dexterized as well.

- **Fold-down**: the opposite of the above – mono mixes artificially created by blending both sides of a stereo track into one. Used to create the Capitol mono albums.

Meet The Beatles!

Stereo: I Want To Hold Your Hand and This Boy are duophonic.
Mono: The whole album is a stereo fold-down, excepting I Want To Hold Your Hand and This Boy, which are the original UK single mixes.

The Beatles' Second Album

Stereo: Roll Over Beethoven, You Really Got A Hold On Me, Devil In Her Heart, Money and Please Mister Postman are Dexterized. She Loves You, I'll Get You and You Can't Do That are duophonic.
Mono: Thank You Girl, Roll Over Beethoven, You Really Got A Hold On Me, Devil In Her Heart, Money and Please Mister Postman are fold-downs. Long Tall Sally and I Call Your Name are George Martin mono mixes but different from the later UK versions on the *Long Tall Sally* EP.

Something New

Stereo: all as per the UK mixes.
Mono: I'll Cry Instead, And I Love Her, Any Time At All and When I Get Home are George Martin mixes which differ from the UK versions. (I'll Cry Instead is edited to make it longer.)

Beatles '65

Stereo: I Feel Fine and She's A Woman are duophonic.
Mono: I'll Be Back is a different George Martin mix. I Feel Fine and She's A Woman are also different George Martin mixes and Dexterized from the earlier US single release.

This was expected to be the first part of a series of box sets which would eventually gather up all the Capitol-assembled albums and bring them internationally to CD. And sure enough, a second set would follow…

Reverberations

The Capitol Albums Volume 2
★★★☆☆

UK release:
3 April 2006

US release:
3 April 2006

> *The Early Beatles*
> *Beatles VI*
> *Help!*
> *Rubber Soul*

A year and a half after volume 1, the next batch of Capitol re-issues appeared, this box set gathering up all four of the albums from 1965. As such it contains *The Early Beatles*, Capitol's belated issue of (most of) the *Please Please Me* album, which Vee-Jay had the US rights to first. It also contains *Help!* with its incidental film music, as well as the re-worked, folky *Rubber Soul*. On which subject we should point out that when the UK *Help!* and *Rubber Soul* albums had been issued around the world in 1987, George Martin remixed them, and so the original 1960s mixes were left unavailable on CD. Yet the Capitol albums captured many of these very songs in their original state, filling a Parlophone-shaped hole.

Again, all the CDs here have the albums in both mono and stereo and when this collection first appeared, a production error meant that where *Beatles VI* and *Rubber Soul* were concerned, they carried the wrong mono mixes. The mastering was done at Sterling Sound and for test purposes they created new stereo fold-downs of these two albums, which do not correspond with the 1960s mono mixes, but were somehow put onto disc, meaning early copies are a blundered rarity. The give-away was that Capitol's stereo mix of I'm Looking Through You has a false start, never present in mono, but this 2006 fold-down included a mono mix with the false start intact – so clearly something had gone wrong. You can't really blame Sterling Sound though – it's all ridiculously complicated!

Guide to differences

Again comparing the original UK discography with the Capitol releases:

The Early Beatles

Stereo: all as per the UK mixes.
Mono: all tracks are fold-downs except Love Me Do and PS I Love You, which are the original UK mono mixes.

Beatles VI

Stereo: Yes It Is is duophonic.
Mono: all tracks are fold-downs except Yes It Is, which is the original UK mono mix. Supposedly, Kansas City, Eight Days A Week, I Don't Want To Spoil The Party, Words Of Love, What You're Doing and Every Little Thing are Dexterized, but if so, the audio changes are very slight.

Help!

Stereo: Ticket To Ride is duophonic. (The album also contains non-Beatles instrumental music, not issued in the UK discography, including the 'James Bond intro' to Help!.)
Mono: All are fold-downs, bar Ticket To Ride which is the correct UK mono mix.

Rubber Soul

Stereo: The Word is a different George Martin mix, with double-tracked vocals. I'm Looking Through You has a unique false start but is otherwise the same.
Mono: Michelle is a different George Martin mix.

So this box set meant eight Capitol albums were now available on CD. But there were several more yet to be re-issued, which implied a third box set to finish the project, but things were tricky. The Capitol albums still up for the CD treatment were of varying significance. *A Hard Day's Night* was originally released in the States on United Artists, and Capitol only got hold of it in 1979. It would have had to appear on *Volume 1* with the other 1964 albums, had it been deemed worthy of inclusion. *The Beatles' Story*, with its audio-documentary format was probably never in the running however.

The strongest shout of any must be the famous *Yesterday... And Today* set, and as a consequence, the US *Revolver* from which it pinched three tracks. But how would these two comprise a four-CD box set? There were still *Magical Mystery Tour* and *Hey Jude* to make up the numbers, but *Magical Mystery Tour* was now established in the main album series, and *Hey Jude* was a compilation anyway.

So, the component albums were not really going to stretch to *The Capitol Albums Volume 3*, meaning this was the last, leaving the collection frustratingly incomplete. Maybe they should just have thrown *Yesterday... And Today* in with this box, to make a five-CD edition, and left it there? Few would have complained.

Mr Kite flies through

Love
★★★★★

UK release:
20 November 2006

US release:
20 November 2006

Because

Get Back

Glass Onion

Eleanor Rigby / Julia (Transition)

I Am The Walrus

I Want To Hold Your Hand

Drive My Car / The Word /
    What You're Doing

Gnik Nus

Something / Blue Jay Way
    (Transition)

Being For The Benefit Of Mr Kite! /
    I Want You (She's So
    Heavy) / Helter Skelter

Help!

Blackbird / Yesterday

Strawberry Fields Forever

Within You Without You /
    Tomorrow Never Knows

Lucy In The Sky With Diamonds

Octopus's Garden

Lady Madonna

Here Comes The Sun /
    The Inner Light (Transition)

Come Together / Dear Prudence /
    Cry Baby Cry (Transition)

Revolution

Back In The USSR

While My Guitar Gently Weeps

A Day In The Life

Hey Jude

Sgt Pepper's Lonely Hearts Club
    Band (Reprise)

All You Need Is Love

Later also made available:

The Fool On The Hill

Girl

In some ways, the decision to embark on the *Love* project seemed foolhardy. The initiative was with show producer, Cirque du Soleil, who for some years had been gaining a reputation for staging musical spectaculars, first in Canada and then around the world as the company expanded. Typically their productions would include a couple of hours of live music, but when Cirque owner, Guy Laliberté, originally broached the possibility of creating a Beatles-based show, George Harrison – who one might have thought would have no interest – opened the door to Apple, and years-long negotiations started.

Cirque du Soleil had a concept in mind: the presentation was to be built around the Beatles' story, conceived as a visual extravaganza with flamboyant costume and acrobatics, and featuring fictional characters like Mr Kite, Sgt Pepper and Father McKenzie. Experiences in the late 1970s had left a residual feeling that appropriating the Beatles' music for this sort of project could end in disaster (see our brief discussion on pages 58-59 for examples), which may have played a part in Apple agreeing to something extraordinary: the use of – indeed the preparation of – a custom Beatles soundtrack of original recordings, to be fed to the audience via speakers built into their seats.

In service of the story line, Apple consented to George Martin – now into his 70s and tutoring his son, Giles, in record production – returning to the group's original multi-tracks and creating new mixes and edits. But more than that, there were to be uber-contemporary mash-ups, where elements of two, three or any number of songs, are combined to create new musical concepts which also run into one another continuously, with no breaks – as the hype stickers on the subsequent CD stated, 'the Beatles as you've never heard them before'.

Indeed, nothing like this had ever been attempted, and the Martins approached the task with some trepidation. Their first exploratory work resulted in a mix of Within You Without You, with Ringo's distinctive drum track from Tomorrow Never Knows running beneath the sitars – a striking effect which made it all the way to the final album. Approved by Paul, Ringo and the others, this paved the way for the rest of the music to take shape, and in the end so much was mixed and matched that some had to be left out, such as their re-imaginings of She's Leaving Home and Penny Lane (some of which were played to guests at a 2006 pre-show event).

Partly they were working to a brief – the opening notes of Lucy In The Sky With Diamonds, for example, mixed and vari-speeded to create a shimmering effect to go with the show's LED display of a starry night sky – but their own creativity was very much to the fore throughout, and the song selections seem to be mostly their own.

The strength of *Love* isn't just in the effect of hearing the Beatles' songs in new compounds, but in the sonic quality George and Giles Martin were able to achieve. As had been the case with the *Yellow Submarine Songtrack*, delving into the master tapes showed how poorly the Beatles' catalogue had been reproduced for disc until now, this album in particular revealing a depth and dynamism previously unheard. And in among *Love*'s 26 main tracks were some 130 different components, some of them deviating from the standard versions by being based on alternate takes from *Anthology* and the like. A few of the remix highlights included:

Because – the Beatles' multi-track harmony vocals isolated, against a distant woodland soundscape drawn in part from the effects used on the 'Wildlife' version of Across The Universe

Eleanor Rigby-Julia – a re-arrangement of Paul's song about the death of a lonely woman, juxtaposed with guitar work from John's tribute to his late mother, together with disturbing ambulance siren, in respect of the show's character, Julia

I Want To Hold Your Hand – a necessary nod to the Beatlemania years, mixing in sounds from the 1964 Hollywood Bowl performance, which had been excluded from the 1977 LP

Gnik Nus – the vocals from Sun King, reversed, and re-titled to match the concept

Strawberry Fields Forever – a blend of early versions, weaving in bits and pieces from half a dozen other Beatles songs in its second half.

While My Guitar Gently Weeps – built from George's demo version (see *Anthology 3*), this was the only track for which new music was recorded – namely, an orchestral score by George Martin

As will be apparent from these stand-out examples, *Love* was constructed mostly from latter-period recordings, predominantly the rich and varied sound palettes of their work 1967-1969. Indeed, apart from the Hollywood Bowl mix there are only three other pre-*Pepper* songs among the main tracks, as compared to eight from 1967 alone, another seven from 1968 and seven more from 1969.

And the usual balance of George and Ringo is maintained, the former having four spotlights of his own, including Something with its Blue Jay Way transition and Here Comes The Sun with the Inner Light, while Ringo gets a reinvented Octopus's Garden with a bit of Good Night and Yellow Submarine swirled in.

It was never certain what Beatles fans would make of all this. It was either a stroke of genius or an act of sacrilege, depending how one looked at it, but when it appeared on CD in time for Christmas 2006, it was a hit and Beatle sleuths were able to amuse themselves for hours trying to identify the countless audio samples coming from their speakers.

There was also a special edition with all-engulfing 5.1 surround sound, and for old-time connoisseurs, a vinyl pressing in the new year. Platinum in Britain and America, and bestowed with a couple of Grammy awards, *Love* was one of the more successful dives into the Beatles' back catalogue, working on its own terms as distinct from its purpose as a presentation soundtrack, and has been accepted into the group's wider official discography along with *Anthology* and *Past Masters*.

In 2008 a DVD documentary was released, looking into the making of the *Love* show, oddly titled *All Together Now* after a Beatles song which wasn't in the set. And then in 2011 the album was made available for streaming on iTunes, with the attraction of two of George and Giles Martin's outtakes – The Fool On The Hill and Girl – leading to some additional chart action.

Years since it's been clear

The Beatles (The Original Studio Recordings)
★★★★★

UK release:
9 September 2009

US release:
9 September 2009

Please Please Me
With The Beatles
A Hard Day's Night
Beatles For Sale
Help!
Rubber Soul
Revolver
Sgt Pepper's Lonely Hearts
        Club Band
Magical Mystery Tour
The Beatles
Yellow Submarine
Abbey Road
Let It Be
Past Masters

Despite the endless march of digital technology, and the audio advances obtained as far back as the 1999 *Yellow Submarine Songtrack*, the Beatles' CD catalogue remained stuck in the 1980s. (A reminder again that *Please Please Me*, *With The Beatles*, *A Hard Day's Night* and *Beatles For Sale* were still only available in mono, and for no reason.) What was needed was an overhaul of the whole discography, something EMI-Apple finally got around to addressing in 2004, when the decision was made to remaster the group's entire catalogue.

The plan was to modernise both the mono and stereo releases, with Allan Rouse working as co-ordinator on the project. Rouse's team took to the task with considerable care and over the next four years, spent a great deal of time working to exacting standards. A rule was established at the outset, that this new set of albums would not feature any of the remixing which had characterised *Songtrack*, and would be premised on the basis that authenticity was everything, and so the original mixes would be preserved. That meant returning to the master tapes and using George Martin's 1960s arrangements, which were at once copied onto a digital platform to be worked on. (There was an exception to the 'original mix' rule: The 1987 versions of *Help!* and *Rubber Soul* had become standard, and were kept for this set.) The only intervention into the audio tracks was to fix technical blemishes such as microphone pops or amplifier hum, but the sound created by the Beatles themselves – including the squeak of Ringo's kick pedal – was preserved. A little signal limiting was allowed on the stereo albums, and a touch of EQing, but otherwise these were as close to pure studio audio as was possible.

The listing for this set reinforced what was now universally accepted as the canon: all the studio albums from *Please Please Me* to *Let It Be*, including the original *Yellow Submarine*, plus *Magical Mystery Tour* and *Past Masters*, the latter presented for the first time as a double CD emulating the 1988 double LP. That it took so long prepare the collection for release is testament to the effort which went into it, and this was reflected in the packaging too. From the CD 'labels' which perfectly recreated those of the original vinyl albums (including the gold Parlophone design for *Please Please Me*) to the glossy booklets packed with rare photographs, this set was a great leap forward from the 1987 releases in both sound and appearance. Another nice touch was the inclusion on each CD, of an embedded QuickTime mini-documentary with background details on the making of the relevant album. Those purchasing the whole set in its shiny black box were also given a DVD containing all the mini-documentaries together.

These albums were issued on 9 September, 09/09/09, the date playing up to John's magic number. On the same day, the Beatles' *Rockband* game was released, with its amazing multi-track audio (which hackers extracted for some creative home-remixing fun), as was a novel apple-shaped USB drive containing all the albums as digital files. It really was a triumphant moment for all concerned, definitively setting up the albums for years to come.

In 2012, the collection was remarketed with the digital audio transferred onto pristine vinyl, complete with a deluxe hardback book, which would establish the standard for expensive re-issues of the future.

When the remastered albums hit the racks, they were welcomed with lavish approval. Critics were unanimous in praising the work, and the collection received a Grammy for Best Historical Album.

Fans could purchase each CD album individually too, and as a result, every one of them including *Past Masters*, and the stereo and mono box sets as a whole, were listed in the official UK album chart on 13 September 2009, along with the evergreen *1*, as follows:

5 – *Sgt Pepper's Lonely Hearts Club Band*
6 – *Abbey Road*
9 – *Revolver*
10 – *Rubber Soul*
21 – *The Beatles [The White Album]*
24 – *The Beatles (The Original Studio Recordings)* (stereo box set)
29 – *Help!*
31 – *Past Masters*
33 – *Magical Mystery Tour*
37 – *A Hard Day's Night*
38 – *Please Please Me*
49 – *Let It Be*
51 – *With The Beatles*
54 – *1*
56 – *Beatles For Sale*
57 – *The Beatles In Mono* (mono box set)
89 – *Yellow Submarine*

One could surmise that the relevant positions of these chart entries act as a barometer of each album's popularity. Certainly *Pepper* and *Abbey Road* at the top, and *Beatles For Sale* and *Yellow Submarine* at the bottom, are pretty realistic in that respect.

Back to mono (again)

The Beatles In Mono
★ ★ ★ ★ ★

UK release:
9 September 2009

US release:
9 September 2009

The old argument as to which format is best, stereo or mono, seemed to become more entrenched in the lead up to the release of *The Beatles In Mono*, essentially the single-channel equivalent of *Original Studio Recordings*. Things were stirred up by EMI's temptation to overstate the importance of these antiquated mixes, which was really swung in the faces of unenlightened stereo listeners (most of whom had the temerity to use *two* ears) by those who liked their audio straight down the middle. But whereas a modest, 'I prefer the mono mixes' would have passed along just nicely, arguments like 'the Beatles didn't even *bother* attending the stereo mixing sessions!', with its air of superior knowledge, drew battle lines in the sand, and like a hard-panned copy of *Rubber Soul*, the two extremes would never come together in harmony.

I do have an alternative theory about the mono mixing sessions and why the Beatles attended them, and mono-ists might want to put a finger in their one ear for a second… when the Beatles' albums were being prepped, it was of course necessary to do two different mixes. The Beatles, being the Beatles, wanted to have their say in how the sound was laid out – how loud the drumming should be, where the solo would cut in over the keyboard and so on – so they attended mixing sessions with Mr Martin. Mono mixes being simpler to make, were therefore quicker. The Fabs sat with their producer through the one mixing session and told him what they wanted – and then for the more drawn-out, stereo mixing, they excused themselves. There was no point sitting through the whole process *twice*, was there? It's not that they didn't like stereo – indeed they went to some trouble to *record* Ringo's kit in stereo, and had enjoyed moving the vocals on A Day In The Life or Good Day Sunshine around the spectrum – just that they had expressed their wishes and trusted George Martin to deliver from there. (Never once complained about his stereo mixes, did they?)

So that's my theory, that they didn't think mono more 'important' at all – but am I putting down this historic mono collection? Not a bit of it. It's wonderful and those who prefer the sound of their Beatles in mono can enjoy it to their hearts' content.

The remastering was done in parallel with, and to the same exacting standard as the stereo collection (*better* in a sense, since there was no initial digital transfer), and so sounded magnificent. Mono buyers had not been well served over the years, having an option until now of having just four CD albums, short of tracking down the 1982 vinyl to replace the original LPs which were now four decades past. But here they had the whole lot on CD, including practically all the singles (via the mono-edition of *Past Masters* – see next entry) in one package and in excellent quality. And for traditionalists, each CD in this box set came in a miniature replica of the original LP sleeve, complete with its 'flip-back' construction, an impressive touch adhering to the sense of authenticity about this product.

If there was a drawback to purchasing the mono box over the stereo, it was that simply, not all the Beatles' songs were ever mixed for mono – including their final three albums. That meant *The Beatles In Mono* did not contain *Yellow Submarine*, *Abbey Road* or *Let It Be*, a significant miss.

Could Apple have found a way to include them? *Yellow Submarine* had been released in mono in 1969, and it's quite well known among Beatles collectors that in Brazil, both *Abbey Road* and *Let It Be* were also issued in mono. Less well known, but just as true, is that in the UK there were also mono editions of *Abbey Road* and *Let It Be*, but only on the reel-to-reel format. In all cases these were not true mono mixes, but fold-downs of the stereo mix – but it would have been nice to include them for completeness. A more daring idea would have been to make *real* mono mixes especially for this set, although it would have broken with the true authenticity principle. But still, who would have minded getting something extra inside the box, especially if George and Giles Martin had been asked to supervise the work, as they had with *Love* which was released bang in the middle of work on this new project.

But there were some plusses: so as not to lose the 1965 stereo mixes of *Help!* and *Rubber Soul*, which were omitted from the stereo collection, these were added onto their mono CDs as a bonus – and we should also call out *Magical Mystery Tour*, which had not been in the 1982 mono box set by virtue of not then being considered canon, but was included here in true mono.

The Beatles In Mono was delivered in a gloss-finish white box, short and square where the stereo one was tall, and was similarly followed by a vinyl edition a few years down the line.

The one after 9-9-9

Mono Masters
★★★★☆

UK release:
9 September 2009

US release:
9 September 2009

Love Me Do (Original	Day Tripper
Single Version)	We Can Work It Out
From Me To You	Paperback Writer
Thank You Girl	Rain
She Loves You	Lady Madonna
I'll Get You	The Inner Light
I Want To Hold Your Hand	Hey Jude
This Boy	Revolution
Komm, Gib Mir Deine Hand	Only A Northern Song
Sie Liebt Dich	All Together Now
Long Tall Sally	Hey Bulldog
I Call Your Name	It's All Too Much
Slow Down	Get Back
Matchbox	Don't Let Me Down
I Feel Fine	Across The Universe
She's A Woman	You Know My Name (Look
Bad Boy	Up The Number)
Yes It Is	
I'm Down	

The singles and other non-studio-album tracks had been rounded up in 1988 for *Past Masters*, which in those days was seen as comprehensive. However the new box sets made a firm distinction between stereo and mono, and so *Past Masters*, which was to be included in both, needed to be reshaped into two versions to take into account the different formats.

The stereo box included much the same edition as previously, since most of it was in stereo anyway, but they did cheat a little in that four of the tracks *only* existed in mono, and rather than take them out, or swap in fake stereo versions, Apple opted to keep these mono selections intact, the rogue quartet being: Love Me Do (version 1); She Loves You; I'll Get You; and You Know My Name (Look Up The Number). Fair enough, *Past Masters* was the mass-market edition so they wanted one authentic version of every song (they could hardly have removed She Loves You!) – but the mono equivalent, *Mono Masters*, was for more discerning listeners and so no such liberties were taken.

This was mono-only, and if a track didn't exist in a true mono mix, it wasn't going in. This meant three songs which qualified for *Past Masters* were not included in *Mono Masters* at all, each dating from the period 1969-

1970, after the original singles started being issued in stereo. It so happened that The Ballad Of John And Yoko, Old Brown Shoe and the 45 version of Let It Be had never been mixed for mono, and so they could not be featured here – and as with the missing *Abbey Road* and *Let It Be*, the mono collection was consequently left somewhat short. There was also no *Yellow Submarine* in the mono box, although genuine, unused mono mixes had been done when the tracks were pencilled in for an unreleased 1969 EP. Therefore, they were available for *Mono Masters* and so the set includes, for the first time, the mono mixes of Only A Northern Song, All Together Now, Hey Bulldog and It's All Too Much – which also goes some way to making up for the lost singles. Fans would still have to do without George Martin's original film score tracks, but that's no great loss.

Mono Masters was only available inside the mono box, none of the individual albums being sold separately. However in 2014, when *The Beatles In Mono* was re-issued on vinyl, a triple-LP edition of *Mono Masters* was made available on its own terms, so should be considered a separate release, as was *Rarities* back in 1979.

Counter culture

The Singles
★★☆☆☆

**US release:
25 November 2011**

Ticket To Ride / Yes It Is
Yellow Submarine / Eleanor Rigby
Hey Jude / Revolution
Something / Come Together

Record Store Day began in 2008 as an initiative to give a boost to independent record shops, acting as a publicity event to pull in customers. It rapidly became a diary date for labels, bands and collectors, and special products were manufactured by record companies in limited numbers, for sale in participating stores. In addition to the regular April Record Store Day, there is also an annual Black Friday event, which on 25 November 2011 saw the arrival of a white vinyl *Imagine* LP with bonus disc of six sessions outtakes, and alongside it, this box set of four re-pressed US Beatles 45s.

The box was fashioned as a red flip-top with the familiar dropped T logo on the front, and contained the following:

Ticket To Ride / Yes It Is (Capitol 5407)

Yellow Submarine / Eleanor Rigby (Capitol 5715)

Hey Jude / Revolution (Apple 2276)

Something / Come Together (Apple 2654)

The set was visually appealing, using reproductions of the Capitol swirl labels on the first two, and all of the singles had large play holes. However they all use the 2009 remastered audio, and all bar the last one are the mono mixes, so from a musical point of view there's nothing too noteworthy, but it's nice to see that George and Ringo were allowed a vocal spot each. (Another neat touch, given that Hey Jude and Something were on large-hole Apple, was the inclusion of a 'spider' adapter, printed up in the Apple pattern so it appears almost part of the label.)

There were, apparently, only 15,700 of these made for the world and as is so often the case with these RSD specials, the number is much too small to satisfy demand and many true fans missed out as dealers swooped in on stocks. Consequently the box sets were typically sold on at a profit and still maintain their high market value. It's an ironic twist that the RSD event, designed to bring fans out of their homes and into shops, equally ends up encouraging online sales platforms, servicing those with little chance of getting scarce products like this new over the counter.

There have been numerous solo Beatles releases for Record Store Day over the years, but only three others from the group as a whole, each of them re-issuing an existing disc:

April 2010: Paperback Writer / Rain

Stereo pressing (!) on an unusual blue Parlophone label with large play hole, and a new Parlophone catalogue number. Limited to 1,000 copies.

December 2014: *Long Tall Sally* EP

Intended for the November event but delayed until December for marketing reasons. Nicely reproduces the 1964 disc, but with tell-tale changes to the company small-print.

April 2017: Penny Lane / Strawberry Fields Forever

Looking like the original UK 45 but containing new remixes by Giles Martin, and issued a few weeks ahead of the *Sgt Pepper* anniversary album, giving a sneak peek at what was to come.

Part Three – The Digital Age

Yes, we know. CD is a digital format too – but that's not what we mean by the digital age. What we are defining here is the steady move in the music market, away from physical media and over to online streaming and downloads, which now predominate. The move didn't happen as rapidly as the change from vinyl to CD had, but by the end of the noughties, streaming had become a very big deal indeed.

In this section, starting with *Tomorrow Never Knows*, there are a good number of Beatles collections which *only* exist as digital files. And as when CD usurped vinyl, the older formats still exist and the albums are still usually released that way too, but just about everything from here on was made available on Spotify, iTunes and the like, with the physical disc editions pitched somewhat to the connoisseur.

Where next for music consumption? Time will tell, but it's hard to imagine anything taking the place of streaming platforms, which apart from anything else, allow record companies and retailers to market product in limitless quantity and with the minimum of overheads. We should welcome the increased access we now enjoy, but not lose sight of what an album is and isn't, in this brave new world where music buyers can and do obtain whatever they want, one song at a time.

Tomorrow Never Knows (2012)
On Air – Live at the BBC Volume 2 (2013)
The Beatles Bootleg Recordings 1963 (2013)
The US Albums (2014)
The Japan Box (2014)
Live At The Hollywood Bowl (2016)
Sgt Pepper's Lonely Hearts Club Band 50th Anniversary Edition (2017)
The Christmas Records (2017)
The Beatles [The White Album] Anniversary Edition (2018)
Abbey Road Anniversary Edition (2019)
The Singles Collection (2019)

Free As A Bird / Real Love (2019)
1969 Recordings (2019)
The 'lockdown' EPs (2020-2021)
Let It Be 6-Disc Edition (2021)
Get Back: The Rooftop Performance (2022)
Revolver Super Deluxe Edition (2022)

Relax and stream

Tomorrow Never Knows
★★☆☆☆

UK release:
24 July 2012

US release:
24 July 2012

Revolution
Paperback Writer
And Your Bird Can Sing
Helter Skelter
Savoy Truffle
I'm Down
I've Got A Feeling (*Let It Be...
Naked* Version)
Back In The USSR
You Can't Do That
It's All Too Much
She Said, She Said
Hey Bulldog
Tomorrow Never Knows
The End (*Anthology 3* Version)

If the Beatles' transition to the CD format was behind the curve, their absence from the streaming service, iTunes, was positively baffling and gave the public the impression they were dragging their feet again. Streaming was capturing such a large market share through the noughties that by the start of 2008 iTunes had become the biggest music seller in America, eclipsing physical formats. But where the Beatles were concerned, matters were complicated. The problem had its roots in Paul's Magritte paining which in 1967, inspired the Beatles to name their new business structure Apple. There was no issue until the rise of the home computer in the 1980s, which brought the Apple Computer Company to the fore, who'd derived their name when Steve Jobs visited an apple farm – or so the story goes. In any case, the chance correspondence with the Beatles' brand and logo meant legal battles, and it was agreed that there was no technical breach if Apple Computers stayed out of the Beatles' way – ie, did not get involved in music. They could peacefully co-exist: computers were one thing; music was another thing.

Then streaming happened.

Apple Records, which had reactivated as an ongoing label in the 1990s, saw Apple Computers' launch of iTunes as a breach of the agreement and so another lengthy round of legal disputes arose, putting the two Apples at loggerheads until 2007 when a fresh settlement was found. And that's the real reason why there were no Beatles recordings on iTunes until 2010, three more years elapsing before the streaming door was finally opened, and all the Beatles' albums were uploaded to the service.

As one would expect, the availability of the Beatles' music for download was a big success, satisfying all sides. Meanwhile in other business news, corporate giant Universal Music Group paid more than £1bn for EMI's recorded music division, meaning they now owned the Beatles' sound recordings. Universal then created Calderstone Productions to administer the catalogue, and if you're keeping up with all this, Calderstone-Universal and Apple Computers joined forces in 2012 to release *Tomorrow Never Knows* – the Beatles' first download-only compilation, exclusive to iTunes and pitched to big-up the group's credentials in helping develop the art of rock music itself. (Perhaps displaying a sense of humour, the package could be bought in the States for $9.99 – recalling the release of the Beatles' remastered CDs on 09/09/09.)

Futuristic though it was to see a Beatles album on the digital highway, *Tomorrow Never Knows* was in some ways a throwback to the 1970s with its themed selection of tracks, based here on the rock genre. The only interesting variations are the versions of I've Got A Feeling, as heard on the more recent *Let It Be... Naked*, and the *Anthology 3* take of The End with its extra guitar licks near the start, and the A Day In the Life chord at the finish. Otherwise it's standard stuff, though with an odd distribution: there's nothing, for example, from 1967, but six tracks are from 1968, three of them from *The White Album*. Another four are from 1966, including the title track – speaking of which, although the collection is named after a John song, he only gets two of the first eight, while tracks 2, 4, 6, 7 and 8 are all given to Paul – then John gets three in a row near the end. It's a little strange, but overall the album is a fair set of rockier numbers, giving only a vague hint of side 4 of *Rock 'N' Roll Music* from 1976.

The album would have remained a virtual thing, except that Apple Computers noted they had just streamed $50 million worth of Beatles through iTunes, and to celebrate the milestone and throw some crumbs from the table, they rewarded the staff involved with a physical vinyl copy of *Tomorrow Never Knows* as a keepsake. Housed in a white paper cover, it was strictly for personal use and was not to be sold on – but of course it was, and so a lucky few collectors now have the record in their hands. There's only 1000 of them in existence, making this one of the rarest and least known Beatles albums. If you are lucky enough to find one, be prepared to part with hundreds, if not thousands – but as ever, beware of counterfeits!

BBC 2

On Air – Live at the BBC Volume 2
★★★☆☆

UK release:
11 November 2013

US release:
11 November 2013

Words Of Love	I Saw Her Standing There
Do You Want To Know A Secret	Glad All Over
Lucille	I'll Get You
Anna (Go To Him)	She Loves You
Please Please Me	Memphis, Tennessee
Misery	Happy Birthday Dear Saturday Club
I'm Talking About You	From Me To You
Boys	Money (That's What I Want)
Chains	I Want To Hold Your Hand
Ask Me Why	This Boy
Till There Was You	I Got A Woman
Lend Me Your Comb	Long Tall Sally
The Hippy Hippy Shake	If I Fell

Roll Over Beethoven	And I Love Her
There's A Place	You Can't Do That
PS I Love You	Honey Don't
Please Mister Postman	I'll Follow The Sun
Beautiful Dreamer	Kansas City
Devil In Her Heart	I Feel Fine (Studio Outtake Sequence)
Sure To Fall (In Love With You)	
Twist And Shout	

It had been 17 years since the *Anthology* releases had come to and end, in which time there was nothing really new for the fans. *Love* had been a fine release and there was *Let It Be... Naked*, bonus disc included, but really these were meagre pickings given what Apple-EMI were sitting on. Apart from extensive stocks of Abbey Road recordings as yet unheard, there were the old BBC tracks left on the shelf when *Live At The BBC* appeared in 1994, and plenty of them. That was now nearly two decades ago, during which the bootleg market had continued to benefit from Apple's reticence. The Beatles were not the only artists to have recorded extensively for BBC radio, and meantime other labels seemed to have little trouble issuing out packages like *Electric Light Orchestra – Live At The BBC* (1999), *The Jam At The BBC* (2002), *Blondie At The BBC* (2010), *The Kinks At The BBC* (2012) and so on. It was all very frustrating to Beatles fans, many of whom were ready with their hard-earned cash, if only Apple would release something.

On Air – Live At The BBC Volume 2 plugged that gap with another 40 songs from the BBC archives, 36 of which were previously unreleased. (Lend Me Your Comb had appeared on *Anthology*, while three more tracks had featured alongside *Baby It's You* on the 1995 EP: I'll Follow The Sun; Devil In Her Heart; and Boys.) The overall format was based on that of its predecessor album, random songs interspersed with bits of studio chat and larking about, the music this time presented in a generally chronological way, although not strictly so.

The main difference was that the earlier album had rounded up a version of nearly every non-EMI *song* in the vaults, leaving a much smaller number of 'new' options here, and six of those chosen had also been featured on volume 1 in different performances. Thus, with Lend Me Your Comb already on *Anthology*, there were only two *songs* on this album which had not been previously released in some version or other:

Beautiful Dreamer

Recorded: 22 January 1963

Broadcast: *Saturday Club*, 26 January 1963

> The only BBC recording of a very old song, as re-written by
> Gerry Goffin and Jack Keller in 1962, for singer, Tony Orlando.

I'm Talking About You

Recorded: 16 March 1963

Broadcast: *Saturday Club*, 16 March 1963

> The only BBC recording of an old Chuck Berry B-side. An earlier
> Beatles version had been taped live at the Star Club, Hamburg,
> in December 1962.

Much of the rest then, treads old ground and the album therefore has more familiarity than volume 1, but less importance. One track included in the listing is Happy Birthday Dear Saturday Club, basically the Beatles performing Happy Birthday To You a couple of times through, which you can count as another unreleased track if you so desire.

It's interesting to note that if one were to compile the two BBC albums together, they would have all the tracks from three different episodes of *Pop Go The Beatles*, as broadcast on 23 July, 30 July and 6 August 1963, and the whole of *Saturday Club*, as broadcast 5 October 1963. It would be rather nice to have them presented that way, as whole shows.

And after this, what was left on the BBC cutting-room floor? Very little, really. There were recordings of three non-EMI songs yet to be released: A Picture Of You; Besame Mucho; Dream Baby (How Long Must I Dream?). All were taped just once, in 1962 with Pete Best on drums, and surviving copies are in low fidelity, unsuitable for an official issue. And there were four of the group's standard EMI songs taped for the BBC but never selected for disc: I Call Your Name; I Should Have Known Better; I'm Happy Just To Dance With You; The Night Before. All are Lennon-McCartney compositions and we have them in their proper versions on the original records of course. The rest of the unissued recordings were merely alternative performances of songs which were taped on more than one occasion. But for completeness we should mention Sheila and Three Cool Cats, both of which were recorded at the BBC but never broadcast, the tapes now lost, presumed wiped.

In short, the two BBC albums just about cover it. If you really want all nine BBC versions of She Loves You, all six versions of Till There Was You, and so on, they circulate freely on bootlegs. The two albums, *Live At The BBC* and *On Air*, make a solid pair, and when *On Air* came out, *Live At The BBC* was simultaneously re-issued in remastered form, and it was possible to buy both together in a double pack. Sadly there was no EP this time around.

50 years adrift...

*The Beatles Bootleg
Recordings 1963*
★★★☆☆

**UK release:
17 December 2013**

**US release:
17 December 2013**

There's A Place (Takes 5 & 6)
There's A Place (Take 8)
There's A Place (Take 9)
Do You Want To Know A Secret (Take 7)
A Taste Of Honey (Take 6)
I Saw Her Standing There (Take 2)
Misery (Take 1)
Misery (Take 7)
From Me To You (Takes 1 & 2)
From Me To You (Take 5)
Thank You Girl (Take 1)
Thank You Girl (Take 5)
One After 909 (Takes 1 & 2)
Hold Me Tight (Take 21)
Money (That's What I Want) (RM 7 Undubbed)

Some Other Guy (BBC *Saturday Club*, 26 January 1963)

Love Me Do (BBC *Saturday Club*, 26 January 1963)

Too Much Monkey Business (BBC *Pop Go The Beatles*, 11 June 1963)

I Saw Her Standing There (BBC *Saturday Club*, 16 March 1963)

Do You Want To Know A Secret (BBC *Saturday Club*, 25 May 1963)

From Me To You (BBC *Saturday Club*, 25 May 1963)

I Got To Find My Baby (BBC *Saturday Club*, 29 June 1963)

Roll Over Beethoven (BBC *Saturday Club*, 29 June 1963)

A Taste Of Honey (BBC *Easy Beat*, 23 June 1963)

Love Me Do (BBC *Easy Beat*, 20 October 1963)

Please Please Me (BBC *Easy Beat*, 20 October 1963)

She Loves You (BBC *Easy Beat*, 20 October 1963)

I Want To Hold Your Hand (BBC *Saturday Club*, 21 December 1963)

Till There Was You (BBC *Saturday Club*, 21 December 1963)

Roll Over Beethoven (BBC *Saturday Club*, 21 December 1963)

You Really Got A Hold On Me (BBC *Pop Go The Beatles*, 4 June 1963)

The Hippy Hippy Shake (BBC *Pop Go The Beatles*, 4 June 1963)

Till There Was You (BBC *Pop Go The Beatles*, 11 June 1963)

A Shot Of Rhythm And Blues (BBC *Pop Go The Beatles*, 18 June 1963)

A Taste Of Honey (BBC *Pop Go The Beatles*, 18 June 1963)

Money (That's What I Want) (BBC *Pop Go The Beatles*, 18 June 1963)

Anna (Go To Him) (BBC *Pop Go The Beatles*, 25 June 1963)

Love Me Do (BBC *Pop Go The Beatles*, 10 September 1963)

She Loves You (BBC *Pop Go The Beatles*, 24 September 1963)

I'll Get You (BBC *Pop Go The Beatles*, 10 September 1963)

A Taste Of Honey (BBC *Pop Go The Beatles*, 10 September 1963)

Boys (BBC *Pop Go The Beatles*, 17 September 1963)

Chains (BBC *Pop Go The Beatles*, 17 September 1963)

You Really Got A Hold On Me (BBC *Pop Go The Beatles*, 17 September 1963)

I Saw Her Standing There (BBC *Pop Go The Beatles*, 24 September 1963)

She Loves You (BBC *Pop Go The Beatles*, 10 September 1963)

Twist And Shout (BBC *Pop Go The Beatles*, 24 September 1963)

Do You Want To Know A Secret (BBC *Here We Go*, 12 March 1963)

Please Please Me (BBC *Here We Go*, 12 March 1963)

Long Tall Sally (BBC *Side By Side*, 13 May 1963)

Chains (BBC *Side By Side*, 13 May 1963)

Boys (BBC *Side By Side*, 13 May 1963)

A Taste Of Honey (BBC *Side By Side*, 13 May 1963)

Roll Over Beethoven (BBC *From Us To You*, 26 December 1963)

All My Loving (BBC *From Us To You*, 26 December 1963)

She Loves You (BBC *From Us To You*, 26 December 1963)

Till There Was You (BBC *From Us To You*, 26 December 1963)

Bad To Me (Demo)

I'm In Love (Demo)

Following the patching up between the Beatles and Apple Computers, this second iTunes-only collection appeared – very different to *Tomorrow Never Knows* and the product of more legal concerns. In this case the issue boiled down to European copyright law, which held that unreleased recordings automatically transfer into the public domain if not officially issued within 50 years. What did that mean? Simply that at the end of 2013, all the unreleased Beatles recordings from 1963 would become public property, and since many were circulating via bootleggers, and increasingly, on-line file sharing, they could be legitimately packaged up and sold in shops by all and sundry.

The solution was for Universal Music to formally release them before 1 January, thereby setting the clock at day one on a 50-year period, through which they would remain protected. Clever idea, and one which other record companies were also pursuing at the time – but in the case of the Beatles they weren't going for an all-out album release with its attendant publicity; this was a download-only operation, which could and did slip under the radar of all but the most attentive fans.

Loaded onto iTunes on 17 December 2013, *The Beatles Bootleg Recordings 1963* was taken down after a matter of hours, but had served its purpose and delivered the recordings to the public, however briefly. The irony is that the law was suddenly changed to extend the period of protection to 70 years for all released recordings – so the original classic 1963 tracks won't now expire until 2033, but these ones, consisting mainly of studio outtakes and BBC sessions, will be under control until 2083. So, for example, the famous take of From Me To You is set to fall into the public domain decades before the unfavoured attempts 1 and 5 as included here, which will thereafter remain protected!

There was no hype around this discreet package, which is perhaps unfortunate since it contains the most important audio to emerge since *Anthology* – particularly, the 15 EMI studio outtakes. (Technically there are 18, since three of the tracks here contain a double attempt at the given song, one of which breaks down.) Of course they are all from 1963 and all are alternative versions of tracks which were issued at the time, so the scope is somewhat limited. In addition, Universal opted to include essentially complete performances only (bar those three breakdowns), overlooking a still considerable stockpile of 1963 tapes which are yet to see light of day – including the fabled second go at Twist And Shout, from the *Please Please*

Me sessions – assuming there's enough of it worth hearing, since John was famously unable to muster his vocal chords one more time.

In addition to the studio offerings, this bundle includes another 42 BBC radio recordings from shows such as *Saturday Club*, *Easy Beat* and *Pop Go The Beatles*, to add to the material on the two earlier BBC albums. Here, the selections consist of repeat songs in different takes, so there's nothing significantly new and in the case of some of the earlier ones the fidelity is wanting. Nonetheless we do have alternative versions of five non-EMI songs, namely Some Other Guy, Too Much Monkey Business, I Got To Find My Baby, The Hippy Hippy Shake and A Shot Of Rhythm And Blues. Additionally, it should be noted that half a dozen of the BBC tracks were taped in front of a concert audience, adding to the amount of live material which has been officially released, and bringing the total number of 1963 Beatlemania recordings to 11 (see next page).

There are two little gems here though, kept to the very end of the track listing: John's demos of two Lennon-McCartney originals which the Beatles never recorded. The first is a guitar rendition of Bad To Me, which they donated to Billy J Kramer with the Dakotas for a UK number 1 hit; the second is I'm In Love, a more modest hit for the Fourmost, which John here plays on piano. A nice ending to an ephemeral download collection, which stopped unwanted labels issuing the stuff but which is, quite ironically, the only fully sanctioned Beatles product calling itself a bootleg.

Footnote: a shout-out to Margaret Ashworth, a Beatles fan who over the summer of 1963, taped a dozen or more BBC shows featuring the Beatles, on a good-quality tape recorder hooked to the wireless by cable. Thus her superior tapes were acquired by EMI in the 1990s and used for the two BBC albums. More of her recordings appear here, and although a definitive list has not been published, it seems likely that all the September recordings, including versions of She Loves You, Twist And Shout, Love Me Do and I Saw Her Standing There, are from her copies.

1963, live for the BBC

This collection includes six BBC recordings from 1963 made in a theatre setting in front of audiences, therefore qualifying as live gigs. These sit alongside five such tracks on the two BBC albums, to make 11 performances in total. (Add them to the 2016 *Hollywood Bowl* album and the live recordings listed under *Anthology 2*, and this covers every concert performance so far released through official channels.)

Key:

[A] = *Live At The BBC*
[B] = *On Air – Live At The BBC Volume 2*
[C] = *The Beatles Bootleg Recordings 1963*

6 March 1963: Playhouse Theatre, Manchester
(*Here We Go*, broadcast on BBC radio on 12 March 1963)

- **Misery** [B]
- **Do You Want To Know A Secret** [C]
- **Please Please Me** [C]

19 June 1963: Playhouse Theatre, London
(*Easy Beat*, broadcast on BBC radio on 23 June 1963)

- **Some Other Guy** [A]
- **Thank You Girl** [A]
- **A Taste Of Honey** [C]

16 October 1963: Playhouse Theatre, London
(*Easy Beat*, broadcast on BBC radio on 20 October 1963)

- **I Saw Her Standing There** [A]
- **From Me To You** [B]
- **Love Me Do** [C]
- **Please Please Me** [C]
- **She Loves You** [C]

Simulations

The US Albums
★★★★☆

UK release:
17 January 2014

US release:
21 January 2014

Meet the Beatles!
The Beatles' Second Album
A Hard Day's Night
Something New
The Beatles' Story
Beatles '65
The Early Beatles
Beatles VI
Help!
Rubber Soul
Yesterday and Today
Revolver
Hey Jude

The spectacular success of the 2009 British album repackagings had demonstrated that Beatles fans were willing to pay for the bigger ticket items and were generally welcoming of them, despite the fact that they contained no new songs. For commercial reasons alone, it made sense to explore this further, and it won't have escaped Universal Music's notice that 2014 was the 50th anniversary of the Beatles' arrival in America. Neither would they have missed the fact that the two box sets, *The Capitol Albums Volumes 1* and *2* from 2004 and 2006, left matters hanging, since a third volume was always required to finish the project. So what they decided to do was not merely issue out the 'missing' albums, but mark the anniversary by assembling a new box with *all* the US Capitol originals in one place. What's more, each CD had the album in stereo *and* mono on a single disc, stealing a march on the UK equivalents and making this pretty comprehensive, so it was hoped.

As ever there was debate as to whether they really succeeded, since this collection of 13 Capitol titles did not include *Magical Mystery Tour*, which they had put together in 1967 – presumably because it had been adopted into the UK catalogue and was therefore no longer uniquely American. The set did include the essential and long-awaited CDs of the US *A Hard Day's Night* plus *Yesterday… And Today* and Capitol's take on *Revolver*, but while it was pleasing to see the non-standard *The Beatles Story* also added in, less sure was the decision to feature *Hey Jude* which was, after all, a comp. Still, it was great for fans to finally have them all on CD, but don't assume everyone was happy…

Beatles fans being highly knowledgeable recognised that what they were getting here wasn't the same deal as with *The Capitol Albums*. Instead of the original audio tapes, nearly all the tracks were the newer mixes from 2009, essentially making each album a modern playlist matching the track listing on the vinyl of old. This meant that things like mono fold-downs from the 1960s were gone, replaced by the 2009 true mono versions, which arguably represents improvement, but is not authentic.

Things were further complicated by inconsistency, While it's perhaps not fair to call a fold-down (or, for that matter fake-stereo) a unique US mix, Capitol *had* introduced its own mixes on several album tracks in the 1960s, and here, those Capitol versions were re-created from scratch – and thus, although they mimic the originals, they are technically new and unique. But for some reason, the 1960s Capitol mixes of a few songs were ignored, and the 2009 remasters dropped in instead. This is not true of the mono versions, where new Capitol remixes were always done where needed, but stereo versions of the following tracks were not re-made and so we only have the existing 2009 stereo remasters for:

- **Long Tall Sally**
- **I Call Your Name**
- **I'm Only Sleeping**
- **Doctor Robert**

There's also some disagreement whether the original Capitol albums had included their own stereo remixes of two other songs in the first place (it's hard to be sure by listening), but if they did, then these too had been swapped out:

- **Komm, Gib Mir Deine Hand**
- **And Your Bird Can Sing**

Complicated enough? Let's add in one more factor: recall that when the UK albums were issued on CD in 1987, George Martin did new mixes of *Help!* and *Rubber Soul*, and these 1987 mixes were the ones used for the 2009 remasters. So in this US set, where the relevant tracks were replaced with the 2009 versions, we were of course given the stereo 1987 mixes. That applies to 26 of the 28 tracks pulled from those two UK albums, but since Capitol had done their own thing with The Word and I'm Looking Through You in 1965, those were *not* 2009 remasters of the 1987 remixes but were 2014 remixes done in the States, modelled on the 1965 mixes on stereo Capitol. (In the case of Help!, by the way, the 2009 remaster was used with the 'James Bond intro' edited back on, a bit of a trick.)

You may need a stiff drink after reading all this, but I did warn you that Beatles fans were obsessive.

These albums, like the UK mono set, came packaged as miniature replicas of the original vinyl, right down to using the correct inner sleeves. This was a superb touch, and the box itself was much more striking outwardly than the 2009 sets, featuring a colour shot of the group in front of a US flag, a photograph sometimes credited to Dezo Hoffman but possibly taken by someone else at some uncertain location. Anyway it fitted the bill and put a handsome finish on the product. I wonder what Universal would think of next?

East to West

The Japan Box
★★★★☆

UK release:
25 June 2014

US release:
25 June 2014

Meet the Beatles!
The Beatles' Second Album
A Hard Day's Night
The Beatles No 5
Help!

2014 was also the 50th anniversary of the Beatles' breakthrough in Japan, and with the UK and US album re-issues having caused a bit of a stir, it seemed like a good idea to give the Japanese catalogue the same box-set treatment. This book does not generally explore releases from outside the UK and US, but in this case, *The Japan Box* was marketed in these countries as well, so it qualifies. Which is a good thing, since it's well worth a look at this under-discussed package. Western-based collectors don't always know the finer details of the original Japan discography, so here follows a quick overview.

The first Japanese Beatles album appeared in April 1964, three months after the USA, the host being EMI's Odeon label. Titled *Meet The Beatles!*, it *looked* like the Capitol album, with the same title and cover art, but the contents were different – it had 14 tracks as against 12, and only six of them were in common. It was followed by *The Beatles' Second Album*, looking outwardly like the US release, but this time there were only four matching songs. Then something odd happened: Odeon released the UK albums *A Hard Day's Night* and *Beatles For Sale*. After that it was back to the US as a point of reference with *The Beatles No 5*, whose artwork matched up with *Beatles '65*, although the contents didn't, and then *Help!*, which was again a pressing of the UK album.

Despite the apparent flip-flopping between the US and the UK, it will be noted that the Japanese albums, *Meet The Beatles!*, *The Beatles' Second Album* and *The Beatles No 5* were all Odeon compilations, unique to the Japanese market. There were three, and only three, such albums in existence, since after *Help!*, Japan conformed to the UK releases, two years ahead of the US which only fell into line with *Sgt Pepper*.

Three unique albums wasn't much to turn into a CD box set, but that's what was done – with the Japanese incarnation of *A Hard Day's Night* and *Help!* included too – but not *Beatles For Sale*, for some reason, whose omission had the unfortunate effect of making *The Beatles No 5* the fourth album in the set.

The original Japanese releases, in their standard red vinyl editions, are widely seen as top-notch by audiophiles, and photos of those LPs were included in the accompanying booklet. However the audio on these discs is, in fact, as per the 2009 remasters again – but there's some interesting variety: the original Japan LPs were only issued in mono, except for the two UK-sourced movie soundtracks, *A Hard Day's Night* and *Help!*, which were stereo. That is reflected here in the choice of audio format, but in the case of *Help!*, Japan did not use the standard stereo 2009 version with its 1987 remixes as its source, but deferred to the original 1965 mix, as was included in the UK only as a bonus on the 2009 mono disc.

Somewhat confusingly the outer box carried a picture of Odeon's *Meet The Beatles* on it, making it look at a glance like just that album, in some kind of deluxe package. The CDs inside are once again designed as mini-LP replicas complete with reproductions of the 1960s lyric sheets – which is also notable since the 1967 release of *Sgt Pepper* is recognised in the West as ground-breaking for the fact that the song lyrics were included on the cover. Japan was at it years earlier, another way in which these albums are unfairly overlooked.

This five-CD box serves to remind UK and US listeners that the Beatles were a worldwide phenomenon and that other countries too had some important and compelling albums of their own, which are at least worth knowing about.

Encore

Live At The Hollywood Bowl
★★★☆☆

UK release:
9 September 2016

US release:
9 September 2016

216

Twist And Shout
She's A Woman
Dizzy Miss Lizzy
Ticket To Ride
Can't Buy Me Love
Things We Said Today
Roll Over Beethoven
Boys
A Hard Day's Night
Help!
All My Loving
She Loves You
Long Tall Sally
You Can't Do That
I Want To Hold Your Hand
Everybody's Trying To
        Be My Baby
Baby's In Black

In 2015, stories started percolating that Universal Music was planning a new Beatles project, going by the title *The Beatles Live*, which was described as a film covering the group's performing career from Liverpool and Hamburg right through to Candlestick Park. The stats they put out in support of the project claimed it would encompass 166 performances in 90 different cities across 15 countries, which in concept and scale seemed pretty promising since there had been nothing focussing on this specific angle of the Beatles' career before. Then in May 2016 the somewhat deflating news came that it was being re-shaped not as a film about live touring but as a general overview of the group's goings on *during* those years – in other words, half the same old story which we'd seen and heard many times including in the supposed last-word *Anthology*. And to further miff the dedicated fan, it was to be titled *Eight Days A Week*, after a song the Beatles never performed on stage – and a promotional video was issued with clips of footage from the Shea Stadium concert running behind the studio recording, in an unwanted attempt to bluff it.

Directed by Ron Howard, the film had its London premiere on 12 September, and was a decent piece of work for the mainstream audience but stuck to the familiar lines, even where at variance with the facts. The Hamburg years were scarcely covered, with two of the Beatles, Pete Best and Stu Sutcliffe not mentioned, while the storyline hurried to get to 1964 and America as quickly as possible. (But as Mark Lewisohn has pointed out, 1964 was Beatle year seven.) The odd bit of audio fakery and the occasional continuity error proved irksome to those who knew enough to notice, and after Candlestick Park it moved to EMI Studios with the group, where we got a few tiny fragments of previously unheard recording tapes – nothing much, but enough to further distract from the original premise.

Released in parallel was this album, not really new so much as a reinvention of the 1977 set, *The Beatles At The Hollywood Bowl*, with its mishmash of tracks from three different shows. What marked this as an improvement wasn't just that a CD edition was in the offing, but that extra audio was to be included – four additional songs tacked onto the end after the original album sequence is complete. The quartet of newbies was:

- **You Can't Do That** – from 23 August 1964

- **I Want To Hold Your Hand** – from 23 August 1964

- **Everybody's Trying To Be My Baby** – from 30 August 1965

- **Baby's In Black** – from 30 August 1965

Not all of these were completely unknown. Part of the audio of I Want To Hold Your Hand had been included on *Love* (2007) in a mix with the studio recording. In addition, this performance of Baby's In Black can be heard in full on the B-side of Real Love (1996), albeit with the correct spoken intro missing, which is reinstated here.

In short, there's something about *Live At The Hollywood Bowl* which is hard to get excited about. It's not that there's anything wrong – a movie release with colourised live footage and A1 sound, and an expanded CD of some famous gigs – but we Beatles fans are a demanding lot and if something falls short in any way, it matters. There really wasn't much to twist and shout about, although the album cover created a strong identity, with its shot of the Beatles in Seattle in August 1964. (But somebody should have told them, the Hollywood Bowl isn't in Seattle, it's in… Hollywood.)

Sadly, while this album was in preparation, we lost George Martin who died on 8 March 2016. *Live At The Hollywood Bowl* was remixed from the same tapes he'd worked on in 1977 and remastered under the supervising eye of his son, Giles, who is credited as the album's producer. Thus, exactly 50 years after Beatlemania officially ended, the baton was symbolically passed for a new generation to hear and appreciate the Beatles as a live outfit.

Pepper box

Sgt Pepper's Lonely Hearts Club
Band 50th Anniversary Edition
★★★★★

UK release:
26 May 2017

US release:
26 May 2017

Including the following outtakes and extras:

Strawberry Fields Forever (Take 1)
Strawberry Fields Forever (Take 4)
Strawberry Fields Forever (Take 7)
Strawberry Fields Forever (Take 26)
Strawberry Fields Forever (Stereo Mix 2015)
When I'm Sixty-Four (Take 2)
Penny Lane (Take 6 – Instrumental)
Penny Lane (Vocal Overdubs and Speech)
Penny Lane (Stereo Mix – 2017)
A Day In The Life (Take 1)
A Day In The Life (Take 2)
A Day In The Life (Orchestra Overdubs)
A Day In The Life (Hummed Last Chorus) (Takes 8, 9, 10 And 11)
A Day In The Life (The Last Chord)
Sgt Pepper's Lonely Hearts Club Band (Take 1 – Instrumental)
Sgt Pepper's Lonely Hearts Club Band (Take 9 And Speech)
Good Morning Good Morning (Take 1 – Instrumental Breakdown)
Good Morning Good Morning (Take 8)
Fixing A Hole (Take 1)
Fixing A Hole (Speech And Take 3)
Being For The Benefit Of Mr Kite! (Speech From Before Take 1;
        Take 4 And Speech At End)
Being For The Benefit Of Mr Kite! (Take 7)
Lovely Rita (Speech And Take 9)

Lucy In The Sky With Diamonds (Take 1 And Speech At End)
Lucy In The Sky With Diamonds (Speech, False Start And Take 5)
Getting Better (Take 1 – Instrumental And Speech At End)
Getting Better (Take 12)
Within You Without You (Take 1 – Indian Instruments)
Within You Without You (George Coaching The Musicians)
She's Leaving Home (Take 1 – Instrumental)
She's Leaving Home (Take 6 – Instrumental)
With A Little Help From My Friends (Take 1 – False Start
      And Take 2 – Instrumental)
Sgt Pepper's Lonely Hearts Club Band (Reprise) (Speech And Take 8)
A Day In The Life (First Mono Mix)
Lucy In The Sky With Diamonds (Original Mono Mix – No 11)
She's Leaving Home (First Mono Mix)
Penny Lane (Capitol Records Mono US Promo Mix)

Beatles fans love their anniversaries, giving them an excuse to delve into Beatledom once more, with EMI/Apple/Universal seldom failing to supply some new goodies. *Sgt Pepper* has a special place in the catalogue and tends to be afforded more attention than anything else, so when *Pepper* turned 20 it had its own CD release in a relatively plush package. The 25th anniversary was marked by George Martin's special television show, *The Making of Sgt Pepper* featuring Paul, George and Ringo, while the 30th saw a planned special edition with CD and extras – which unfortunately never came out. And when the UK hosted the Olympic Games in 2012, *Pepper*-suited athletes paraded around a celebration of all things British in the opening ceremony, underlining the cultural significance of the album to the world as a whole, and in another five years, *Pepper* was set to turn 50.

This anniversary above all others needed something special, and left hanging from the 1999 *Yellow Submarine Songtrack* was the exceptional improvement in sound which could be achieved not just by remastering, as was done in 2009, but by going back to the source tapes and preparing fresh mixes. (*Songtrack*, incidentally, had included four remixed *Pepper* songs: Sgt Pepper itself plus With A Little Help From My Friends, Lucy In The Sky With Diamonds and When I'm Sixty-Four.)

And so the idea of remixing the entire album suggested itself, Giles Martin tasked with the job, having earned his stripes on *Love* and *Eight Days A Week*, and several others including Paul's album, *New* in 2013. He was, therefore, the perfect candidate for this daring project, keeping things in the family while also bringing a modern producer's ear to proceedings.

Giles finished his work in early 2017 and sent out copies to the remaining Beatles for approval, which was readily granted, so all systems were 'go'. Meanwhile news of this admittedly risky move started to trickle out in the spring, fans experiencing a mix of trepidation balanced by excitement for what could be in the offing. A taster was had when, on Record Store Day in April, a new pressing of Penny Lane / Strawberry Fields Forever was released, containing Giles's new mixes (these two songs having originally been recorded for *Pepper* but released separately). Strawberry Fields Forever was dated 2015, which was presumably when the work was done, Penny Lane 2017, and the reception was cautiously positive, whetting the appetite for the full *Pepper* release, scheduled for 26 May. (The original album is routinely said to have first appeared on 1 June 1967, but it's now widely understood that the correct release date was 26 May 1967 – a Friday – so this was its true anniversary date.)

But there was bigger news: this remixed album was to come as part of a deluxe package which contained what, for many, was the holy grail: a pile of EMI studio outtakes from the vaults. Although fans had lapped up *Anthology* 20 years earlier, and had some more 1963 outtakes meantime, this was new ground in that these 31 selections all belonged to the same set of sessions – a behind-the-scenes look at the Beatles as they worked through an album. News spread quickly and no sooner was a track listing leaked than Beatles fans started to pore over what was new and what had been booted before. In fact there turned out to be quite a bit of new, more than half of the outtakes having been thus far unheard, and although a few were repeated from *Anthology*, they were always presented here differently – either with more pre-chat or with mix variants. For some, Giles may have gone a tad too far in creating his own occasional edits to showcase the audio scraps, but in the end, this was a brand new listening experience, and it's difficult to fault. (If there is a criticism, it might have contained fewer instrumental backing tracks.)

There was one thing conspicuous by its absence, and that's the long-lost Carnival Of Light, which was recorded on 5 January 1967, right in the middle of the Penny Lane sessions. It would have fit the general idea, given *Pepper*'s carnival overtones, but the fact that it was not envisaged as part of the album in the first place probably led to its exclusion, again.

So far as the CD format was concerned, this was delivered as a multi-disc package, sized as if it were an LP box set but actually containing some six CD-sized discs. There was the newly remastered album, of course, and two full discs of outtakes, plus a direct transfer of the old mono mix, and a DVD with high-res audio and videos for Strawberry Fields Forever, Penny Lane and A Day In The Life plus *The Making Of Sgt Pepper* documentary. And there was even more – a Blu-Ray disc mirroring the DVD contents in the best quality possible. Never had Beatles fans been so indulged.

Packaging all this up was another feat, and the box itself had a striking 3D lenticular rendering of the album photo on the front, while inside was a 144-page book containing all sorts of photos, notes and lyrics, which was a piece of art on its own. And it was inside the back of the book that the music lived – each disc slipped into a little pocket and wrapped in an outtake image from the original cover photo session, to make a superb series of mini alternates.

This was, of course, an expensive proposition but for once the fan mood was judged exactly right, with a parallel and much cheaper two-disc edition also available, containing just the new remaster plus one alternative version of each song compiled in the correct playing order to match the album proper. That standard-price edition was also available on vinyl, so practically everyone had what they wanted – not to mention the fact that the remix itself, the heart of this latest project, was brilliant to hear. From the crooning backing vocals of Fixing A Hole, unburied at last, to the cascading calliopes of Mr Kite and the cymbal smashes in A Day In The Life, which somehow seem to *whisper* at you, this was an audio tour-de-force. *Sgt Pepper Anniversary Edition* was one of those landmark releases, which set the standard for similar projects to come.

Available formats:

- Single album containing new album remix. Available CD or LP.
- Double album containing new album mix plus a selection from the outtakes. Available CD or LP.
- Super Deluxe, six-disc set (not released on vinyl) comprising stereo album remix; two CDs containing all the studio outtakes; the 1967 mono mix (plus extras) on CD; Blu-Ray disc and DVD, both with 5.1 mixes, hi-res album files and videos.

Highlights From The Outtakes Discs

- **Strawberry Fields Forever (Take 1)**
  Beautiful, delicate rendition which had been included on *Anthology* but without the backing vocals, which are restored here.

- **When I'm Sixty-Four (Take 2)**
  The album take, before all the overdubs were applied, revealing just the skeletal Beatles musicianship beneath.

- **Penny Lane (Take 6 – Instrumental)**
  A bit of a revelation, this instrumental run-through centres on Paul's piano and displays a myriad of ideas and instrumentation not heard in the more dense final arrangement.

- **A Day In The Life (Take 1)**
  This version is deceptively familiar, since John's spoken introduction was used on *Anthology*, but this is the full recording, and a quite hypnotic listen. Paul handles the 'orchestral' sweep on his piano keyboard!

- **Good Morning Good Morning (Take 1 – Instrumental Breakdown)**
  Less than a minute long, this rough and ready take reveals a genuine immediacy – the Beatles as a tight, rocking band.

- **Within You Without You (Take 1 – Indian Instruments)**
  Off the wall, and not really the Beatles, this recording is fascinating in style and texture, lending an exotic mood to proceedings. This isolates the Indian instruments (no orchestra involved), and the melodic strengths of the composition are suddenly to the fore.

- **Sgt Pepper's Lonely Hearts Club Band (Reprise) (Speech And Take 8)**
  Good, punchy version of the song, with Paul displaying some attitude in his informal vocal. Nice to hear more unadulterated live playing on an album usually renowned for its studio trickery.

Happy returns

The Christmas Records
★★★☆☆

UK release:
15 December 2017

1963: The Beatles Christmas Record
1964: Another Beatles Christmas Record
1965: The Beatles Third Christmas Record
1966: Pantomime: Everywhere It's Christmas
1967: Christmas Time Is Here Again!
1968: The Beatles 1968 Christmas Record
1969: The Beatles Seventh Christmas Record

It's a mystery why, in spite of all the commercial exploitation of the Beatles' recordings over the years, including BBC tapes and rehearsal scraps, their fondly recalled Christmas recordings had never been available to buy. The only time they were officially repackaged (in 1970 – see page 24), the compilation was given out to fan-club members, as had been the original flexis, so they were never on sale in shops. That was finally put right in 2017 with this latest product.

The seven Christmas recordings, with their erratic content and scattergun humour, were never really a mainstream proposition and in the commercial vacuum, they had been bootlegged countless times meaning most fans had them, or at least, knew what they were about. Therefore, Universal Music had to go the extra mile to make this release attractive enough to sell, and a standard CD compilation would have fallen well short.

What they came up with was a box set containing seven individual discs, each replicating the original flexis, in faithful reproduction sleeves. However these were not flexi-discs but hard vinyl, each one pressed up in a different colour – in order, starting with 1963: white, red, blue, yellow, green, clear, and finally orange. The labels were as per the originals, and the collection was housed in a red box, whose artwork replicated the cover of the 1963 sleeve, but with pictures of the Beatles Santa-hatted and smiling. It was a well-designed package, down to the booklet reproducing the original fan club newsletters, and the attention to detail extended to having the discs run at 33, bar the 1967 disc at 45, and the fact that they were all one-sided records until 1968 and 1969.

Apparently, Apple had misplaced some of the original tapes, so when mastering this new collection they had to resort to dubbing from disc (most likely, using the 1970 vinyl LP with its superior fidelity). As for the contents, it's all standard and as one would expect. There was scope for adding some outtake material, snippets of which circulate, and there was a missed opportunity to re-issue Christmas Time (Is Here Again) on its own disc – but in the interests of reproducing the originals, the records were presented as they had first appeared.

As thebeatles.com proclaimed at the time, 'Happy Christmas, Beatle People!'.

It's been a long, long, long time

The Beatles [The White Album]
Anniversary Edition
★★★★★

UK release:
9 November 2018

US release:
9 November 2018

Including the following outtakes and extras:

Esher demos:

Back In The USSR
Dear Prudence
Glass Onion
Ob-La-Di, Ob-La-Da
The Continuing Story Of
      Bungalow Bill
While My Guitar Gently Weeps
Happiness Is A Warm Gun
I'm So Tired
Blackbird
Piggies
Rocky Raccoon
Julia
Yer Blues
Mother Nature's Son

Everybody's Got Something To
      Hide Except Me And
      My Monkey
Sexy Sadie
Revolution
Honey Pie
Cry Baby Cry
Sour Milk Sea
Junk
Child Of Nature
Circles
Mean Mr Mustard
Polythene Pam
Not Guilty
What's The New Mary Jane

Studio outtakes:

Revolution 1 (Take 18)
A Beginning (Take 4) / Don't Pass Me By (Take 7)
Blackbird (Take 28)
Everybody's Got Something To Hide Except Me And My
      Monkey (Unnumbered Rehearsal)
Good Night (Unnumbered Rehearsal)
Good Night (Take 10 With A Guitar Part From Take 5)
Good Night (Take 22)
Ob-La-Di, Ob-La-Da (Take 3)
Revolution (Unnumbered Rehearsal)
Revolution (Take 14 – Instrumental Backing Track)
Cry Baby Cry (Unnumbered Rehearsal)
Helter Skelter (First Version – Take 2)
Sexy Sadie (Take 3)
While My Guitar Gently Weeps (Acoustic Version – Take 2)
Hey Jude (Take 1)
St Louis Blues (Studio Jam)
Not Guilty (Take 102)
Mother Nature's Son (Take 15)
Yer Blues (Take 5 With Guide Vocal)
What's The New Mary Jane (Take 1)
Rocky Raccoon (Take 8)
Back In The USSR (Take 5 – Instrumental Backing Track)
Dear Prudence (Vocal, Guitar And Drums)
Let It Be (Unnumbered Rehearsal)
While My Guitar Gently Weeps (Third Version – Take 27)
(You're So Square) Baby, I Don't Care (Studio Jam)
Helter Skelter (Second Version – Take 17)
Glass Onion (Take 10)
I Will (Take 13)
Blue Moon (Studio Jam)
I Will (Take 29)
Step Inside Love (Studio Jam)
Los Paranoias (Studio Jam)
Can You Take Me Back? (Take 1)
Birthday (Take 2 – Instrumental Backing Track)
Piggies (Take 12 – Instrumental Backing Track)
Happiness Is A Warm Gun (Take 19)
Honey Pie (Instrumental Backing Track)
Savoy Truffle (Instrumental Backing Track)
Martha My Dear (Without Brass And Strings)

Long, Long, Long (Take 44)
I'm So Tired (Take 7)
I'm So Tired (Take 14)
The Continuing Story Of Bungalow Bill (Take 2)
Why Don't We Do It In The Road? (Take 5)
Julia (Two Rehearsals)
The Inner Light (Take 6 – Instrumental Backing Track)
Lady Madonna (Take 2 – Piano And Drums)
Lady Madonna (Backing Vocals From Take 3)
Across The Universe (Take 6)

As the dust settled on the *Sgt Pepper* anniversary release, a question was buzzing around Beatles circles: was the box set to be a one-off, or would *The White Album* receive a similar package when its own anniversary came around? Speculation as to what might be in the pipeline was rife, the Esher demos (AKA the Kinfauns demos – early acoustic run-throughs of many of the album tracks) top of most people's wants list. The rumours intensified in June when none other than Paul McCartney casually mentioned an anniversary package was virtually complete – so we knew *something* was coming. The official announcement followed towards the end of September: *The Beatles* was indeed getting the *Pepper* deluxe treatment.

Principally the project revolved around the hoped-for Giles Martin remix, and fans were not disappointed as he came up with the goods in spectacular fashion once again. Although in general not as sonically adventurous as *Sgt Pepper*, this album still benefits immensely from superb soundscaping on unlikely numbers such as Piggies, which reveals musical details hitherto buried. We can clearly now hear the 'yeah' in the vocals running into the instrumental break of While My Guitar Gently Weeps, and the definition and separation of vocal tracks on Revolution 1. Also raised is possibly Giles's finest moment on the album – Long, Long, Long – which is now fuller, stronger, yet at the same time more seductive, and there's definitely much more going on in Revolution 9. There was the odd compromise of course, and due to the general idea of centralising the sound, the arch panning on Dear Prudence is lost, but the bass now dances around, preserving the sense of panorama in the stereo stage.

The Beatles is, apart from anything else, a much larger proposition than *Pepper* and accordingly there would be no problem filling a multi-disc edition. The Esher demos themselves were arguably the most important of the unreleased recordings, and although seven of them had been included on *Anthology 3*, there were another 20 circulating on bootlegs, all with potential for a full release here, in the best sound quality available – and that's exactly what was delivered. And in presenting them, the powers that be sequenced the tracks to match the main album, starting with Back In The USSR and ending with Cry Baby Cry, and apart from those familiar numbers, we also now have first-ever Beatles releases of Sour Milk Sea, Child Of Nature and Circles. In short, a really excellent addition to the group's catalogue, which served as disc 3 of the reduced format edition.

There were another three CDs worth of studio outtakes here, encompassing no fewer than 50 recordings of various sorts, with some new gems among them, the most surprising of which was an early run-through of Let It Be, never known to have been written so early on. There's also a provisional attempt at nailing While My Guitar Gently Weeps, as well as curios such as Blue Moon and (You're So Square) Baby I Don't Care.

There are, inevitably, omissions from the mountain of tapes left behind in 1968, and for practical reasons it was never likely we'd get the 27-minute take of Helter Skelter, or the extraordinary take 20 of Revolution (although we do get the full 10 minutes of take 18), but given that three whole discs were given to session recordings, we can't complain. The remainder of the package followed the format of the *Pepper* release, with no videos but an audio-only Blu-Ray disc of high-res files, a transfer of the original mono album, and for those with the hardware to enjoy it, a 5.1 surround sound mix of the album proper. And once again there was a substantial book included, detailing the sessions and making the full £140 septuple-disc box set possibly the most action-packed piece of Beatles repackaging ever.

Available formats:

- Double album containing new album remix. Available on LP only.
- Package containing new album mix plus the Esher demos, available as 3CD or 4LP.
- Super Deluxe, seven-disc set (not released on vinyl) comprising stereo album remix; one CD containing the Esher demos; three CDs containing all the studio outtakes; Blu-Ray disc with hi-res album, two different 5.1 mixes, and a transfer of the original mono album.

Highlights From The Outtakes Discs

The Esher demos need no further note. Collectively they make a *White Album Unplugged* and as such, stand alone as an 'album' in their own right. These are the picks of the EMI sessions:

- **Everybody's Got Something To Hide Except Me And My Monkey (Unnumbered Rehearsal)**
  Impressive musical track which is looser and more enjoyable than the uncompromising album version.

- **Good Night (Take 10 With A Guitar Part From Take 5)**
  Presented as a mix from two different performances, this endearing, guitar-picked arrangement benefits from some sensitive lullaby backing vocals from the other three Beatles.

- **Cry Baby Cry (Unnumbered Rehearsal)**
  Ushered in by John reciting the old 'green slop pie' poem, this remarkable version of Cry Baby Cry is almost soulful, slow and with George's lead guitar licks behind the vocal lines.

- **Helter Skelter (First Version – Take 2)**
  A mammoth 12:53 track consisting of the 'slow' version of the song which was previously picked up for *Anthology* where it was edited down to a third of the length. If you can get into this grooving long version, it's worth the time.

- **While My Guitar Gently Weeps (Acoustic Version – Take 2)**
  Intimate acoustic version performed by just George and Paul, with keyboard backing. There's an interruption in the first verse as George calls up to the control room – might it have been allowable to edit over the break for a continuous track? No matter – what we have is superb.

- **Let It Be (Unnumbered Rehearsal)**
  A headline-grabber. This informal version doesn't have the structured chords of the 1969 arrangement, and Paul sings Brother Malcolm in place of Mother Mary (in respect of Mal Evans). Only a minute's worth but a real find.

- **While My Guitar Gently Weeps (Third Version – Take 27)**
  Eric's in the room now, as George goes for a take. Interesting
  largely for the alternative guitar lines, a result of Eric improvising
  his way through the track. Breaks down as George complains
  about his singing not coming off as good as Smokey Robinson's:
  "I just aren't Smokey".

- **Can You Take Me Back? (Take 1)**
  Hypnotically, seemingly endless version which circulates around
  for a couple of minutes. From this jam, we got the fragment on the
  1968 album.

- **Martha My Dear (Without Brass And Strings)**
  As it says, this is the song minus the overdub arrangement, and it's
  arguably the better for it, Paul's performance coming over as pure
  and honest, especially in the middle 8 sections.

- **Across The Universe (Take 6)**
  John singing, accompanied only by his acoustic guitar, and with
  Ringo keeping time on a drum. There are several versions of this
  non-*White Album* track available, this one being previously
  unknown.

Love is old, love is new

Abbey Road Anniversary Edition
★★★★★

UK release:
27 September 2019

US release:
27 September 2019

Including the following outtakes and extras:

I Want You (She's So Heavy) (Trident Recording Session
        And Reduction Mix)
Goodbye (Home Demo)
Something (Studio Demo)
The Ballad Of John And Yoko (Take 7)
Old Brown Shoe (Take 2)
Oh! Darling (Take 4)
Octopus's Garden (Take 9)
You Never Give Me Your Money (Take 36)
Her Majesty (Takes 1-3)
Golden Slumbers / Carry That Weight (Takes 1-3)
Here Comes The Sun (Take 9)
Maxwell's Silver Hammer (Take 12)
Come Together (Take 5)
The End (Take 3)
Come And Get It (Studio Demo)
Sun King (Take 20)
Mean Mr Mustard (Take 20)
Polythene Pam (Take 27)
She Came In Through The Bathroom Window (Take 27)
Because (Take 1 – Instrumental)
The Long One (Trial Edit And Mix – 30 July 1969)
Something (Take 39 – Strings Only)
Golden Slumbers / Carry That Weight (Take 17 – Instrumental
        – Strings And Brass Only)

This time, it was expected. *Pepper* and *White* had started the ball rolling on an annual series of deluxe remix collections marking the 50th anniversary of the Beatles' albums. *Abbey Road* was next in line, its half-centenary due on 26 September 2019. (This box set was released one day after, on 27 September.) Unfortunately, for *Abbey Road* the pickings are slim compared to the stocks of *White Album* outtakes, although there was still enough to fill a couple of discs to supplement Giles's new album mix, which thereby matches the scale of the *Pepper* box set before it.

Abbey Road was always the best recorded and best produced Beatles album, with a sound quality superior to the rest. Consequently Giles had a bit of a head start when it came to making it sound great, and brought his magic to bear as expected. Overall the sound palette is refreshed and sparkling –

tracks like Something benefit from Giles bringing out of the previously subdued orchestral parts. She Came In Through The Bathroom Window is another winner, with exciting dynamics and depth, while the resonant brass underscore toward the end of Golden Slumbers is a joy. It was also a great idea to separate out George, Paul and John's guitar leads in The End, sending them to different parts of the stereo spectrum, emphasising the roundhouse nature of the recording.

Following the other album packages, the remaster was accompanied by an audio Blu-Ray with both Dolby Atmos and 5.1 surround sound album mixes and a hi-res version of Giles's standard new version. There was no mono this time, since *Abbey Road* was not mixed that way in the first place, but it might have been a legitimate option to create an authentic mono version for this release.

The 100-page hardback book contained pockets housing the other CDs, and as with *Pepper* there were alternate cover photos available, which were used to make novel new sleeve designs. And again following the earlier release as its example, one outtake version of each album track was deployed for an alternative *Abbey Road*, included as the second part of the much cheaper two-CD edition. Then to top it off, although not really part of this set, a new picture disc of the album also went on sale on its own this day, inundating fans with all things *Abbey Road*.

Available formats:

- Single album containing new album remix. Available on CD or LP.
- Double CD containing new album remix plus selections from the studio outtakes. Available on CD only.
- Triple LP containing new album mix plus two LPs with all the studio outtakes.
- Super Deluxe, four-disc set (not released on vinyl) comprising stereo album remix; two CDs of studio outtakes; and Blu-Ray containing Dolby Atmos mix, 5.1 mix, and hi-res files of the whole album.

Highlights From The Outtakes Discs

- **Goodbye (Home Demo)**
  Paul's charming 1969 recording for Mary Hopkin, as preserved all
  these years on acetate disc. It was already known to collectors, but
  here was its official debut.

- **The Ballad Of John And Yoko (Take 7)**
  John on guitar and Paul on drums, simply playing it through
  together, before the dense layering which turned the song into a
  rocker.

- **You Never Give Me Your Money (Take 36)**
  After some unnecessary chatter which could have been chopped
  out, Paul launches into the song and we get to appreciate the band
  musicianship in a 'live' run-through. Paul's vocal is soft, while the
  extended coda rocks with bluesy guitar licks.

- **Mean Mr Mustard (Take 20)**
  Slow, subdued version which is interesting to imagine as part of
  the medley. Mr Mustard's sister is still called Shirley at this stage.

- **Because (Take 1 – Instrumental)**
  On *Love* we were given the Beatles' vocal track less the
  Moog/harpsichord backing. Here we have the inverse – just the
  instrumentation, to which Ringo adds a softly tapping percussion.

- **The Long One (Trial Edit And Mix – 30 July 1969)**
  The side 2 medley, in its early form with different spots of music
  here and there (oohs and ahhs behind the 'out of college' section of
  You Never Give Me Your Money; keyboard notes in the transition
  to Sun King; Paul's uncertain vocals in Golden Slumbers (which
  also lacks the orchestral parts); the completely missing lead vocals
  in the final section of The End – and so on.) Most noticeably, Her
  Majesty is still included in the sequence, moving over from right to
  left, which we now understand facilitates the bold guitar chords at
  the start of Polythene Pam also exclusively in the left channel.

Brits abroad

The Singles Collection
★★★★☆

UK release:
22 November 2019

Love Me Do / PS I Love You
Please Please Me / Ask Me Why
From Me To You / Thank You Girl
She Loves You / I'll Get You
I Want To Hold Your Hand / This Boy
Can't Buy Me Love / You Can't Do That
A Hard Day's Night / Things We Said Today
I Feel Fine / She's A Woman
Ticket To Ride / Yes It Is
Help! / I'm Down
We Can Work It Out / Day Tripper
Paperback Writer / Rain
Eleanor Rigby / Yellow Submarine
Strawberry Fields Forever / Penny Lane
All You Need Is Love / Baby, You're A Rich Man
Hello, Goodbye / I Am The Walrus
Lady Madonna / The Inner Light
Hey Jude / Revolution
Get Back / Don't Let Me Down
The Ballad Of John And Yoko / Old Brown Shoe
Something / Come Together
Let It Be / You Know My Name (Look Up The Number)
Free As A Bird / Real Love

The Beatles' UK singles had not been issued on vinyl since the 1980s, when the picture sleeve editions came out, followed one at a time by the picture discs. It was assumed that after the CD format came along, vinyl would gradually shrink and disappear, and to some extent that was true. But in recent years a resurgence in vinyl was seen, LP records started being stocked in supermarkets and bands began making 45s available again for new releases. Where the Beatles were concerned, their sales were usually high enough to justify vinyl pressings alongside CD anyway (although at the time of writing, some of the full anniversary box sets remain unavailable on record) – and so in 2019 the British 45s were revamped and reinvented, almost four decades after the previous set.

This new collection breaks with the tradition of attempting to faithfully reproduce the original records, and as a result ends up with something of a split personality. On the one hand it is the UK catalogue of 1962-1970 (plus the two 1990s reunion tracks), but on the other it takes an international slant, and each of the UK couplings is re-styled to match an original release from another country. This brings much new artwork and indeed several new labels to the UK for the first time (each label and country is given in the table overleaf), with the sleeves themselves made of strong card rather than paper, and with spines. In fact, as communications technology had progressed in the previous 20 years, knowledge and interest in the overseas catalogues had increased, and Apple had to some extent primed fans with the poster included with 1, which carried illustrations of many of the global singles sleeves. The decision to issue these new 45s this way certainly adds an attractive element to the collection, especially as compared to the UK original paper bags which would have been repetitive and fairly bland – but just for completeness, there were colour photos of the old UK singles in the enclosed booklet.

As for the music, these were not merely a rehash of the 2009 versions; each track was remastered afresh, directly from the original analogue studio tapes, and effort was expended to make them sound as close to the original 45 releases as possible. As such they are unique, and since there was no CD edition, collectors need this box set to have their Beatles fully up to date.

The set was housed in an unfussy blue outer box, styled to match the 2009 mono and stereo album box sets.

The country the sleeves originate from and the names of the individual labels are given in brackets:

- **Love Me Do / PS I Love You** (Tollie, USA)
- **Please Please Me / Ask Me Why** (Parlophon, Italy)
- **From Me To You / Thank You Girl** (Parlophone, Norway)
- **She Loves You / I'll Get You** (Parlophone, Greece)
- **I Want To Hold Your Hand / This Boy** (Odeon, Chile)
- **Can't Buy Me Love / You Can't Do That** (Parlophon, Austria)
- **A Hard Day's Night / Things We Said Today**
  (Parlophone, Netherlands)
- **I Feel Fine / She's A Woman** (Parlophone, Sweden)
- **Ticket To Ride / Yes It Is** (Odeon, Spain)
- **Help! / I'm Down** (Parlophone, Belgium)
- **We Can Work It Out / Day Tripper** (Odeon, France)
- **Paperback Writer / Rain** (Odeon, Turkey)
- **Eleanor Rigby / Yellow Submarine** (Odeon 'Pops', Argentina)
- **Strawberry Fields Forever / Penny Lane** (Parlophone, Australia)
- **All You Need Is Love / Baby, You're A Rich Man**
  (Odeon, West Germany)
- **Hello, Goodbye / I Am The Walrus** (Capitol, Mexico)
- **Lady Madonna / The Inner Light** (Odeon, Japan)
- **Hey Jude / Revolution** (Parlophone, South Africa)
- **Get Back / Don't Let Me Down** (Apple, Denmark)
- **The Ballad Of John And Yoko / Old Brown Shoe**
  (Parlophone, Portugal)
- **Something / Come Together** (Apple, Israel)
- **Let It Be / You Know My Name (Look Up The Number)**
  (Apple, UK)
- **Free As A Bird / Real Love** (new)

Second flight

**Free As A Bird /
Real Love**
★★★☆☆

**UK release:
22 November 2019**

The two reunion singles of the 1990s were never truly embraced by the group's fan-base, sometimes seen as artificial and seldom appreciated from a musical point of view. George Martin refused to produce them, and neither topped the charts anywhere, while Ian Macdonald, writing in 2005, asserted, 'Free As A Bird stands no comparison with the Beatles' Sixties music'. However, in 2014, a cover version of Real Love was included in television adverts by John Lewis, bringing it to the attention of millions of appreciative listeners, many of whom didn't realise it was a Beatles track, and the following year, both Real Love and Free As A Bird were remixed for a revamp of the *1* album on DVD, the latter having some noticeable changes in the vocal. It's conceivable that these two underrated songs will eventually gain more credence as the years progress.

When the 2019 *Singles Collection* was assembled, Universal decided to include these two in their original mixes sequentially after Let It Be, despite ignoring the intervening singles (including the 1976 chart hit, Yesterday, as well as Baby It's You and the long-disowned Movie Medley). However instead of simply inserting the two 45s of old, they opted to put the A-sides back-to-back on one disc, thereby creating a brand new coupling, either side of which had a different catalogue number, as per the original singles.

Both tracks had a new remaster done especially for this release.

Fly tipping

1969 Recordings
☆ ☆ ☆ ☆ ☆

UK release: 23 December 2019
US release: 23 December 2019

Glyn Johns mixes:

One After 909 – Glyn Johns Mix
I'm Ready – Glyn Johns Mix
Save The Last Dance For Me / Don't Let Me Down – Glyn Johns Mix
Don't Let Me Down – Glyn Johns Mix
Dig A Pony – Glyn Johns Mix
I've Got A Feeling – Glyn Johns Mix
Get Back – Glyn Johns Mix
For You Blue – Glyn Johns Mix
Teddy Boy – Glyn Johns Mix
Two Of Us – Glyn Johns Mix
Maggie Mae – Glyn Johns Mix
Dig It – Glyn Johns Mix
Let It Be – Glyn Johns Mix
The Long And Winding Road – Glyn Johns Mix
Get Back – Reprise – Glyn Johns Mix

All Things Must Pass – Rehearsal 3 January 1969
I Me Mine – 8 January 1969
Suzy Parker (AKA Suzy's Parlour) – 9 January 1969
Oh! Darling – Paul's solo performance

Don't Let Me Down – 22 January 1969
Two Of Us – 24 January 1969
I Lost My Little Girl – 24 January 1969
For You Blue – Take 1 – 25 January 1969
For You Blue – Take 3 – 25 January 1969
For You Blue – Take 4 – 25 January 1969
For You Blue – Take 11 – 25 January 1969
For You Blue – Take 13 – 25 January 1969
Let It Be – 26 January 1969
Medley: Rip It Up / Shake, Rattle and Roll – 26 January 1969
Medley: Kansas City / Miss Ann / Lawdy Miss Clawdy – 26 January 1969
Blue Suede Shoes – 26 January 1969
I Told You Before – 26 January 1969
The Walk – 27 January 1969
I've Got A Feeling – 27 January 1969
Get Back – 27 January 1969
Dig A Pony – 28 January 1969
Something – 28 January 1969
One After 909 – 29 January 1969
Medley: Cannonball / Not Fade Away / Hey Little Girl / Bo Diddley
          – 30 January 1969
Mailman, Bring Me No More Blues – 29 January 1969
Get Back – First Roof Performance – 30 January 1969
Get Back – Second Roof Performance – 30 January 1969
Don't Let Me Down – First Roof Performance – 30 January 1969
God Save The Queen – Roof Performance – 30 January 1969
I've Got A Feeling – Second Roof Performance – 30 January 1969
Don't Let Me Down – Second Roof Performance – 30 January 1969
The Long And Winding Road – 31 January 1969
All Things Must Pass – George's Demo
Something – Take 37

The 2013 *Bootleg Recordings* download was assumed to be a one-off so far as the Beatles were concerned, there having been none of the expected annual equivalents in the years which followed. Meantime other acts and labels continued to issue their outtakes in similar fashion, the so-called 'copyright dump', the Beach Boys' *Keep An Eye On Summer*, for example, followed by sets from the Stones, Dylan and so on – but no Beatles. Or, so we thought, until someone discovered a collection called *1969 Recordings* discreetly tucked away on streaming platform, Spotify.

What was it? No-one was sure. The tracks were listed but wouldn't play. There was no official explanation or mention of it anywhere, and the existence of the virtual album prompted speculation that Calderstone may have issued a corresponding set every year – but no-one noticed. That seems unlikely, not least because Beatles fans are all over the internet and surely someone would have spotted such things, and besides, there was something exceptional about the 1969 tracks which might explain why this was the only one: recall that unreleased recordings went out of copyright after 50 years. Recall that the *Pepper* outtakes were released in their anniversary box *before* the end of 2017, and ditto *The White Album* in 2018 then *Abbey Road* in 2019 – so they were caught in time. But the *Let It Be* box set, which was in the planning stage, would contain 1969 recordings but was not scheduled to appear until 2020 – too late for the outtakes to earn protection. Thus, the planned session recordings had to be released in advance, before the close of 2019, or they would already be public property when the box set came out.

Regardless, the very act of uploading this collection to Spotify is surely enough to show the tracks were released there, if only for a millisecond. This was presumably a result of Calderstone's legal team taking the minimum moves to protect their rights, and on that basis we must assume they succeeded. Just to be clear, European Parliament Directive 2011/77/EU states, "if a fixation of the performance in a phonogram [they mean a record] is lawfully published or lawfully communicated to the public [they mean released] within this period, the rights shall expire 70 years from the date of the first such publication". So even if no-one downloaded it, the fact that it could in theory be listened to just once would appear to satisfy the law – it had momentarily been 'lawfully communicated to the public' and so the rights were fixed for the next 70 years.

Of course, once word of this copyright dump got out, it was assumed we were seeing a preview of the anticipated *Let It Be* box set – however if we fast-forward to the eventual release, there is not a complete cross-over. 11 of the fully released outtakes had not been included in this Spotify list, and may therefore have missed their copyright deadline completely, while conversely, the streamed *1969 Recordings* contained the following studio outtakes which were missing from the eventual *Let It Be 6-Disc Edition*:

Suzy Parker – 9 January 1969
Oh! Darling – Paul's solo performance
I Lost My Little Girl – 24 January 1969
For You Blue – Take 1 – 25 January 1969
For You Blue – Take 3 – 25 January 1969
For You Blue – Take 11 – 25 January 1969
For You Blue – Take 13 – 25 January 1969
Medley: Rip It Up / Shake, Rattle and Roll – 26 January 1969
Medley: Kansas City / Miss Ann / Lawdy Miss Clawdy
     – 26 January 1969
Blue Suede Shoes – 26 January 1969
I Told You Before – 26. January 1969
Medley: Cannonball / Not Fade Away / Hey Little Girl /
     Bo Diddley – 30 January 1969
Mailman, Bring Me No More Blues – 29 January 1969
All Things Must Pass – George's Demo
Something – Take 37

Note: the Cannonball / Not Fade Away / Hey Little Girl / Bo Diddley medley was truly recorded on 29 January, not 30, which was the day of the rooftop gig.

The above might read like a typical old vinyl boot from the *Get Back* files, but of course these will have been prepared officially, in best-quality audio. (The first two, due to their dates, must have been copied from the mono Nagra tapes, which is to say, the sound picked up by the 1969 camera crew, as opposed to their being proper studio recordings, which were not being made in the early part of the *Get Back* project.)

These tracks are of varying interest. Suzy Parker was already widely known from the *Let It Be* movie, while *Anthology 3* had secured the medley, Rip It Up / Shake Rattle And Roll, plus Blue Suede Shoes and Mailman, Bring Me No More Blues – meaning they did not actually need to be included here as copyright on them was already established. Ditto the final two tracks, presumably the same George demos as on the 1996 CDs. On the other hand, there is a stand-out title: I Lost My Little Girl, one of the very earliest of Paul's compositions, written before he even joined the Quarry Men. There is in circulation a Beatles performance from the *Get Back* sessions, with John singing. However it was recorded on 25 January and is more than five minutes long; what is (supposedly) included here is a much shorter version, hitherto unknown if, as claimed, it was recorded the day before. Since no-one got to hear this download, we can only wonder, but if anyone tells you the Beatles never officially released I Lost My Little Girl, you can at least correct them.

Additionally the track listing shows the entire Glyn Johns *Get Back* album, and the remaining rooftop recordings which had not been used on *Let It Be* in 1970 (also omitting the third performance of Get Back, which was on *Anthology*). As we now know, the rooftop gig audio was at this stage intended for the *Let It Be* box set, as was Glyn Johns' *Get Back*, but we have to ask why, in the middle of all these leftovers and oddities, are there four versions of For You Blue, all recorded on 25 January? We might speculate that when the box set was in the planning, it was to contain a newly edited up version, made from parts of these recordings. A guess it is, and a guess it will have to remain, for unless Calderstone ever re-publish this download set, it remains nothing more than a track list, drawn up, dumped and deleted in the blink of an eye.

The rock and roll oldies

The list of tracks unique to this collection hints at something particularly interesting to *Get Back* aficionados, due to the presence of a run of old rock and roll favourites. What we have here is:

> **Rip It Up / Shake, Rattle and Roll**
> **Kansas City / Miss Ann / Lawdy Miss Clawdy**
> **Blue Suede Shoes**
> **Cannonball / Not Fade Away / Hey Little Girl / Bo Diddley**
> **Mailman, Bring Me No More Blues**

To recognise the significance of this, we need to return to 1969 and see what was in the air at the time. Let's start with Glyn Johns, who while he was preparing a provisional mix of *Get Back* in the spring, also put together a separate acetate containing old rock and roll tracks. The words 'Beatles Sunday' were written on the label, since virtually all of them had been recorded on Sunday 26 January, and the full acetate contained these tracks:

I've Got A Feeling
Dig It
Rip It Up / Shake, Rattle and Roll
Kansas City / Miss Ann / Lawdy Miss Clawdy
Blue Suede Shoes
You Really Got A Hold On Me

Why would he do that? The answer seems to be because *Get Back* was possibly going to be issued as a double album – the standard songs on one disc and these and other rockers on another. It seems to have been a serious idea at the time and was being openly discussed, but it wasn't until July 1969 that Mal Evans attempted to dampen down fan expectations: "The Beatles didn't want to repeat the 'double disc' idea and make everyone buy a pair of LP records together. Instead all the other tracks are held 'in the can' so that they can be used later. Amongst the stuff that 'stays on file' so to speak is enough material for a special rock 'n' roll LP – including famous American rock hits like Shake Rattle And Roll and Blue Suede Shoes."

And so it never happened, the songs remaining 'on file' until they were added to this Spotify album playlist. We could speculate (we often do) that the Beatles were now considering putting the fabled oldies disc together at long last and including it when the *Let It Be* box came out. They knew what fans knew, and in plotting to release Glyn Johns' aborted *Get Back* LP as part of the project, they may well have considered the second disc which was being explored back in '69. It would have been a superb inclusion, and those who have heard copies of the old acetate will attest that it sounds a lot better than it looks on paper.

Play time

The 'lockdown' EPs
★★☆☆☆

UK release: 31 October 2020 - 12 March 2021
US release: 31 October 2020 - 12 March 2021

The Beatles' relationship with online music streaming services (or rather, Calderstone's relationship with them) had gone from strength to strength through the 2010s, practically all of the group's output including recent repackagings, made available on iTunes, Spotify and the like. And by all accounts the availability of digital Beatles was a good move, bringing in considerable revenues for all concerned. In fact the streaming platforms were to some extent now leading the way, with exclusive and innovative releases such as the *1963 Bootleg Recordings* and the *Tomorrow Never Knows* compilation unavailable as conventional product. In 2014, iTunes had even put out a free download EP containing one solo track from each of the boys, and with corresponding Beatley artwork as well – stepping into territory unheard of in discworld.*

Meanwhile back on the physical plane, as 2020 kicked in the world was rocked by the Covid pandemic which saw many retail outlets across the Western world closed up, families instructed to stay indoors and where possible, work from home. One of countless consequences was that 2020, and as the situation endured, early 2021, were bad times to be trying to sell hard goods like CD and vinyl box sets, and so in the case of the Beatles, the 2020 *Let It Be* anniversary collection was suspended. But business is business, and to keep the bucks rolling in Calderstone assembled and released a whole series of download-only EPs, which could be bought and enjoyed from the comfort of one's armchair.

These EPs were really just playlists of already available tracks, but in being officially planned out, and with artwork drawn up, could also be counted as new. The collected tracks are themed (songs about animals, love, cover

---

* The EP was called, simply, *4* – presumably a play on *1*. The contents were: Love (John, 1970); Call Me Back Again (Paul/Wings, 1975); Let It Down (George, 1970); Walk With You (Ringo, 2009).

versions etc) in sets of six. The first of them, *Spooky Songs*, appeared on Halloween, although it didn't really fit the description, containing half a dozen psychedelic rock songs like Tomorrow Never Knows and It's All Too Much. A fortnight later a kids' collection was released, with fare such as Yellow Submarine and Good Night, and so it went on with a new set at regular intervals until the spring when the 15th and final one appeared.

The compilers of these would-be EPs were fairly creative in scouting around for relatively obscure cuts, taking the opportunity to shine a light on some of the Beatles' lesser-heard gems like You Can't Do That (on *New Year's Workout*) or Old Brown Shoe (on *The Beatles For Kids – Colours*). One novelty was the inclusion of George Martin's *Yellow Submarine* track, Sea Of Time (on *Meditation Mix*) but despite stretching their imagination to fill the sets, there were 14 tracks which were repeated as the underlying themes crossed over – for example And I Love Her was on two different romantically-tinged EPs, *All About The Girl* and *Love Me Do*. Now and then the compilers seemed to loose the plot a little, the EP, *For Kids – Animals*, including Martha My Dear (OK, it's supposedly named after Paul's pet dog although not many kids will have known that) and Here Comes The Sun (eh??). *For Kids – Colours* was also a bit weird, including oblique tracks like Yes It Is ('if you wear red tonight'?) and Lucy In The Sky With Diamonds ('cellophane flowers of yellow and green'?), but not for example, All Together Now ('pink, brown, yellow, orange, and blue, I love you').

For audio sources, the playlists were usually made up of the most recent updates of each song, generally the 2009 remasters, but some of the tracks from a special 2015 remastering of *1* were also included, and in the case of songs from *Pepper*, *The White Album* and *Abbey Road*, Giles Martin's new mixes were available and were used. Which gave rise to the most interesting EPs of the lot, the two volumes of *Study Songs* from December 2020. It's not entirely clear why they were called that – they would hardly help someone revising for their exams. What they were likely getting at was that these could be listened to for study of the music itself, for all 12 tracks across these two EPs were instrumental versions and vocal-less backing tracks pulled from *Anthology* and the anniversary boxes. Not new audio, but newly assembled and worth hearing in this unusual context.

By the time the last of these EPs was released, *Inspirations* in March 2021, the sun was coming back out and *Let It Be* was in preparation again, ready for its belated anniversary edition later in the year.

Spooky Songs
(31 October 2020)

Tomorrow Never Knows
I Am The Walrus
Lucy In The Sky With Diamonds
It's All Too Much
Long, Long, Long
I'm Only Sleeping

*For Kids – Morning, Afternoon
& Night*
(13 November 2020)

Ob-La-Di, Ob-La-Da
Yellow Submarine
Good Day Sunshine
Rock And Roll Music
Your Mother Should Know
Good Night

Got To Get You Into My Life
(27 November 2020)

Got To Get You Into My Life
It Won't Be Long
When I Get Home
Two Of Us
With A Little Help From
        My Friends
Hey Jude

Meditation Mix
(4 December 2020)

Across The Universe
Mother Nature's Son
While My Guitar Gently Weeps
            (*Love* Version)
Sea Of Time
Sun King
In My Life

Study Songs Vol 1
(11 December 2020)

Because (Take 1)
Penny Lane (Take 6)
Within You, Without You (Instr)
She's Leaving Home (Take 1)
Something (Take 39)
Golden Slumbers / Carry That
            Weight (Take 17)

Study Songs Vol 2
(18 December 2020)

I'm Only Sleeping (Rehearsal)
Honey Pie (Backing Track)
Piggies (Take 12)
Savoy Truffle (Backing Track)
The Inner Light (Take 6)
With A Little Help From
            My Friends (Takes 1/2)

At Home With The Beatles
(25 December 2020)

Here, There And Everywhere
There's A Place
Let It Be
All You Need Is Love
Here Comes The Sun
Hello, Goodbye

Getting Better All The Time
(1 January 2021)

Getting Better
I'll Follow The Sun
I Feel Fine
Good Morning Good Morning
Ob-La-Di, Ob-La-Da
Good Day Sunshine

We Can Work It Out
(8 January 2021)

We Can Work It Out
Ticket To Ride
Day Tripper
I've Just Seen A Face
I'm Down
It Won't Be Long

New Year's Workout
(22 January 2021)

Get Back
You Can't Do That
I Saw Her Standing There
Eight Days A Week
Slow Down
Got To Get You Into My Life

For Kids – Colours
(29 January 2021)

For You Blue
Yes It Is
Yellow Submarine
Baby's In Black
Old Brown Shoe
Lucy In The Sky With Diamonds

All About The Girl
(5 February 2021)

Anna (Go To Him)
Oh! Darling
And I Love Her
Martha My Dear
Something
Julia

Love Me Do
(12 February 2021)

Love Me Do
I Feel Fine
I Need You
Here, There, And Everywhere
And I Love Her

For Kids – Animals
(19 February 2021)

Blackbird
I Am The Walrus
Octopus's Garden
Martha My Dear
Hey Bulldog
Here Comes The Sun

Inspirations
(12 March 2021)

Long Tall Sally
Boys
Soldier Of Love
Money (That's What I Want)
Slow Down
Rock And Roll Music

Getting back

Let It Be 6-Disc Edition
★★★★★

UK release:
15 October 2021

US release:
15 October 2021

Including the following outtakes and extras:

Morning Camera (Speech – Mono) / Two Of Us (Take 4)
Maggie Mae / Fancy My Chances With You
Can You Dig It?
For You Blue (Take 4)
Let It Be / Please Please Me / Let It Be (Take 10)
I've Got A Feeling (Take 10)
Dig A Pony (Take 14)
Get Back (Take 19)
One After 909 (Take 3)
Don't Let Me Down (First Rooftop Performance)
The Long And Winding Road (Take 19)
Wake Up Little Suzie / I Me Mine (Take 11)
On The Day Shift Now (Speech – Mono) / All Things Must
        Pass (Rehearsals)
Concentrate On The Sound
Gimme Some Truth (Rehearsal)
I Me Mine (Rehearsal)
She Came In Through The Bathroom Window (Rehearsal)
Polythene Pam (Rehearsal)
Octopus's Garden (Rehearsal)
Oh! Darling (Jam)
Get Back (Take 8)
The Walk (Jam)

Without A Song (Jam) – Billy Preston With John And Ringo
Something (Rehearsal)
Let It Be (Take 28)
Across The Universe (Unreleased Glyn Johns 1970 Mix)
I Me Mine (Unreleased Glyn Johns 1970 Mix)
Don't Let Me Down (New Mix Of Original Single Version)
Let It Be (New Mix Of Original Single Version)

Get Back LP:

One After 909
I'm Ready (AKA Rocker) / Save The Last Dance For Me /
     Don't Let Me Down
Don't Let Me Down
Dig A Pony
I've Got A Feeling
Get Back
For You Blue
Teddy Boy
Two Of Us
Maggie Mae
Dig It
Let It Be
The Long And Winding Road
Get Back (Reprise)

The world started coming out of the Covid crisis in early 2021 as retailers opened for business and millions went back to work. What this meant for the Beatles was commercial opportunity once again, for products such as the ongoing series of Super Deluxe Edition albums, next on the list, *Let It Be* which was by now a year past its golden anniversary.

The creation of the *Let It Be* package was part of a multi-media campaign which included these CDs and records, and also a separate, official hardback book about the sessions, and most eagerly awaited of all, a sensational documentary series directed by Peter Jackson, and featuring a sumptuous near eight hours of impressively restored video and audio. The documentary, entitled *Get Back*, did what many of us suspected needed doing, and re-framed the 1969 sessions without bias, which is to say, it did not repeat the sad portrait of the group as seen in *Let It Be* in 1970, and showed the four-piece jamming, laughing and working together as they had all along. It didn't re-write history; it finally overturned the earlier re-writing, and made things good.

The *Let It Be 6-Disc Edition* beat *Get Back* to the general public by a few weeks, and fans with deep enough pockets might have guessed what they would find when they unboxed it. It was assembled much like its predecessors, with a parallel vinyl box edition this time, slotting neatly into the series: the original album remixed by Giles, a couple of discs of session outtakes, and… something else, something special.

In this case the something special was *really* special: it was the unreleased *Get Back* LP *a-la* Glyn Johns, here mixing up individual tracks from his various attempts to present a finished album in 1969-1970 to make a best version. This release is, therefore, not strictly a Glyn Johns' original, but close enough that it didn't matter – and, it had the correct stairwell cover photo, which had been passed by when *Let It Be… Naked* was released in 2003. This landmark item was unfortunately only available in the entire box set, but stands next to the Esher Demos of 1968/2018 as a key Beatles release – and it's not a bad listen, some even tipping it the nod over Phil Spector's final LP. (Beatles experts will also know that in Japan, a different mix of this album was used in this box set – for reasons unknown, but presumably in error.)

The session outtakes were mostly taken from the second half of the 1969 sessions, which were recorded at Apple on a professional console. It will be remembered that the earlier Twickenham sessions were only captured on film, with its less defined audio (the mono 'Nagra tapes'), although a couple of particularly worthy Twickenham tracks still made it. There is plenty to get engrossed in here, with all manner of additional scraps, from rehearsals of songs like Gimme Some Truth and All Things Must Pass to snatches of Please Please Me and Wake Up Little Susie, and bits of conversational narrative to help the music along. It's a pity that when it comes to the alternative versions of album tracks, most don't differ substantially from what we already had, and many of them had already turned up in the *Let It Be* film, or *Anthology* or *Let It Be… Naked* anyway – which is a pretty poor show considering how much material there was to select from – but they fit the idea and give us some session performances to enjoy.

One item was conspicuously missing though: when the set was in development it was supposed to include audio of the full rooftop concert on its own disc. Calderstone had shielded it from lapsing into the public domain by including what they needed to in *1969 Recordings*, but it wasn't in the box here. It seems likely that the rooftop show was sidelined when Disney secured rights to Peter Jackson's documentary, for which it made a superb final 40 minutes' viewing, so fans would have to wait for an audio edition – but not for long (see next item).

There was one little thing included though, which gave Beatle-ists a reason to grumble. Inside the pack was an EP. A new EP, on 12-inch vinyl, on the Apple label, in an old-style company sleeve. It included four tracks: the original Glyn Johns mixes of Across The Universe and I Me Mine from 1970, and brand new mixes of Don't Let Me Down and Let It Be. What's not to like? Well, ask someone who bought the CD edition and they will tell you they shelled out for a full-sized disc, capable of holding 80 minutes of music, but carrying just a quartet of songs. They had a point, but it is what it is – an EP, conceived for vinyl all along. The CD version was just a bonus. (If Apple had *really* wanted to treat fans, they could have released a 10-inch disc of *Beatles Sunday*, the rock and roll jams compilation which we discussed under *1969 Recordings*, but you can't have everything – especially where the gargantuan *Get Back* sessions are concerned.)

What purchasers of the CD set did get was a Dolby Atmos mix of the main album, and a 5.1 mix, and a high-res mix – enough to satisfy any hardened audiophile. Which brings us back to the main event, Giles Martin's *Let It Be* remix, which follows its predecessors in buffing up the sound and presenting the music on a balanced panoramic stage. Billy's organ work on the title track, for example, is brought up and contrasts nicely with the fuzz tone of George's lead guitar, while I've Got A Feeling sounds more alive and immediate than before. Surprisingly, one of the best remixes turns out to be The Long And Winding Road, which in having its strings pushed back behind Paul and the band, while the brass parts are emphasised, comes through as more classically assured than ever. This track more than any shows what a challenge Giles had on his hands, trying to re-shape a set consisting of a mix of studio ballads, live rockers and heavily produced arrangements while keeping things consistent. He did a good job on it.

Available formats:

- Single album containing new album remix. Available on CD or LP.
- Double CD containing new album remix plus selections from the studio outtakes.
- Five-record set comprising stereo album remix; two LPs of studio outtakes; the Glyn Johns *Get Back* album; and a four-track EP.
- Super Deluxe, six-disc set comprising stereo album remix; two CDs of studio outtakes; the Glyn Johns *Get Back* album; four-track EP; and Blu-Ray containing Dolby Atmos mix, 5.1 mix, and hi-res files of the whole album.

Highlights From The Outtakes Discs

This list omits outtakes which had been made commercially available before.

- **Let It Be (Take 10)**
  Gentle, stripped back version, fully formed but lacking the later lush overdubs. Features a unique solo from George and some nice keys from Billy.

- **One After 909 (Take 3)**
  Fun, rocking version with Billy giving it some at the piano.

- **I Me Mine (Take 11)**
  Mostly instrumental, this open performance of what became the finished track shows the song in a raw state, before the vocal was added and Phil Spector worked his magic on it.

- **All Things Must Pass (Rehearsals)**
  A fairly lengthy collage of performance bits and dialogue, this captures a sense of the song being worked out, and includes some of the lovely harmonies we were denied when it was dropped back in 1969. This is the closest we have to a full group performance, on any official release.

- **Without A Song**
  Billy's moment to shine, he leads the Beatles through a ragged but soulful version of this oldie.

Above us only sky

Get Back: The Rooftop Performance
★★★★☆

UK release:
28 January 2022

US release:
28 January 2022

Get Back (Take 1)	Dig A Pony
Get Back (Take 2)	God Save The Queen
Don't Let Me Down (Take 1)	I've Got A Feeling (Take 2)
I've Got A Feeling (Take 1)	Don't Let Me Down (Take 2)
One After 909	Get Back (Take 3)

The fact that the famous 1969 rooftop concert audio was *not* included in the *Let It Be* box set hints that Apple/Calderstone had plans for it above and beyond. The performance itself was rivetingly covered in the *Get Back* movie, so much so that it was extracted and released to cinema as a stand-alone film, remarkable given that the full footage had laid at the bottom of a proverbial drawer for more than half a century.

Long-since booted in its entirety, the rooftop soundtrack was compromised by the documentary format which included several cut-aways to street interviews and up-close exchanges with the police, interrupting the flow of the music. But it was clear there was interest in the concert recording as an audio event, and so on 28 January 2022 it was made available for streaming audiences – a new Beatles album, in a way, timed as close as possible to the correct anniversary (30 January) but one which went scarcely noticed.

The audio is not technically complete as there are bits of between-song recording which do not feature – but leaving them out tends to improve the listening experience anyway. All the musical performances are there, in superb quality and in a different mix to that heard in the documentary film. The nine tracks are well-known of course, and there's no need for any explanation from us. We note that the *ad-hoc* doodle on God Save The Queen is listed as a track in its own right, but otherwise these are all well-travelled songs, seven of which have been released previously, some place, somehow:

- **Don't Let Me Down (Take 1)**
  Included on *Let It Be… Naked* in 2003, as an edit along with Take 2, and by itself on *Let It Be 6-Disc Edition* in 2021

- **I've Got A Feeling (Take 1)**
  Included on *Let It Be* in 1970 and *Let It Be… Naked* in 2003, as an edit along with Take 2

- **One After 909**
  Included on *Let It Be* in 1970 and *Let It Be… Naked* in 2003

- **Dig A Pony**
  Included on *Let It Be* in 1970 and *Let It Be… Naked* in 2003

- **I've Got A Feeling (Take 2)**
  Included on *Let It Be… Naked* in 2003, as an edit along with Take 1

- **Don't Let Me Down (Take 2)**
  Included on *Let It Be… Naked* in 2003, as an edit along with Take 1

- **Get Back (Take 3)**
  Included on *Anthology 3* in 1996

The rooftop concert is a legendary event in popular music and it's a fine thing that it was recognised as such for this streaming-only package. It's not impossible that a hard disc version will appear one day through official channels, its quality as an uninterrupted live show giving it a slight edge over the documentary sequence with its interruptions, but until then, enjoy it 'live' on Spotify, iTunes, Apple Music and the like.

Abracadabra!

Revolver Super Deluxe Edition
★★★★★

UK release:
28 October 2022

US release:
28 October 2022

Including the following outtakes and extras:

Tomorrow Never Knows (Take 1)
Tomorrow Never Knows (Mono Mix)
Got To Get You Into My Life (First Version – Take 5)
Got To Get You Into My Life (Second Version – Unnumbered Mix)
Got To Get You Into My Life (Second Version – Take 8)
Love You To (Take 1)
Love You To (Unnumbered Rehearsal)
Love You To (Take 7)
Paperback Writer (Takes 1 And 2 – Backing Track)
Rain (Take 5 – Actual Speed)
Rain (Take 5 – Slowed Down For Master Tape)
Doctor Robert (Take 7)
And Your Bird Can Sing (First Version – Take 2)
And Your Bird Can Sing (First Version – Take 2 – Giggling)
And Your Bird Can Sing (Second Version – Take 5)
Taxman (Take 11)
I'm Only Sleeping (Rehearsal Fragment)
I'm Only Sleeping (Take 2)
I'm Only Sleeping (Take 5)
I'm Only Sleeping (Mono Mix RM1)
Eleanor Rigby (Take 2)
For No One (Take 10 – Backing Track)
Yellow Submarine (Songwriting Work Tape Part 1)
Yellow Submarine (Songwriting Work Tape Part 2)

Yellow Submarine (Take 4 Before Sound Effects)
Yellow Submarine (Highlighted Sound Effects)
I Want To Tell You (Speech And Take 4)
Here, There And Everywhere (Take 6)
She Said She Said (John's Demo)
She Said She Said (Take 15 – Backing Track Rehearsal)

Over the span of five years, Beatles collectors had lapped up the Super Deluxe albums in order, *Pepper* through to *Let It Be*. But where next? It seemed possible that the Giles Martin remixes would continue until the whole catalogue was covered, but what could follow *Let It Be*? One idea debated on the forums was that Apple would go back to the start and release *Please Please Me*, continuing from there. Another was that there simply wouldn't be enough archive material to keep going, and so *Let It Be* would prove to be the last. The best guess was that they would start working backwards from *Pepper*, and with the albums no longer locked to their 50th anniversaries, this became the most popular theory. It was proved correct when, in August 2022, *Revolver* was officially announced.

Giles Martin's remixes, sonically accomplished though they are, have split Beatles collectors in recent years, not everyone warm to his altering the way the albums sound. Against this is the argument that many Beatles tracks, particularly mid-period, had overly severe panning applied on the original mixes, hence why George Martin re-did *Help!* and *Rubber Soul* for the 1987 CDs. So even some of those not keen on Giles's approach must have been pleased to hear track 1 of *Revolver*, where the usual split channels of Taxman are blended back to a centrally focused sound, guitars and percussion *surrounding* the vocal, instead of being way off at the sides. Similarly, track 2, Eleanor Rigby, had lead vocals held in the centre, overcoming the ungainly jump to the left which had always occurred at the start of verse 1.

And so the album progresses, with a renewed sense of purpose as we have come to expect, bass guitars resonant and focused, while higher frequencies shine and vocal textures enjoy a sense of realism. In this mix Paul's songs seem to benefit most, with their more open arrangements, the harmonies in Here, There And Everywhere smooth and bright, the punchy brass of Got To Get You Into My Life energetic and clear. That said, John's She Said She Said is quite radically different, drums muted and the two lead guitars panned opposite each other, leaving John's centrally exposed voice sounding gentler than ever – and this particular listener had never noticed the keyboards we now hear subtly in the left channel. Love it or hate it, this kind of thing is what makes *Revolver* 2022 so distinct from *Revolver* 1966. (Giles's critics would have been less than impressed with the ending to Good Day Sunshine, however, where a poor edit chops the drum track off while the cymbal is still ringing.)

Giles was able to work these changes in part because of the ground which was prepared by Peter Jackson's *Get Back* movie. To untangle the ambient noises and cross-conversations in those 1969 tapes, his collaborators in New Zealand-based production company, WingNut Films, developed advanced de-mixing technology so that individual sounds could be isolated from one another. That meant background chatter could simply be removed, when, for example, John was strumming a guitar – and the brainwave was to deploy the same wizardry on the *Revolver* tapes. Since *Revolver* was originally made using four-track equipment, once a bounce-down was done (merging two of the tracks together to free up space), the parts were forever mixed up and could not be separated again – except now they could. (As Giles described it, "It's like I'm giving them a cake, and they're giving me [back] flour, eggs, and milk and some sugar".) So Giles could effectively now generate a set of multi-track tapes to use, one for each instrument, and thus bass and guitars could be pulled apart then processed and positioned separately from one another – the key leap forward in getting *Revolver* to sound as good as it now did.

In terms of what came inside the expensive multi-disc box, there was the remix, of course, plus a new transfer of the mono album, and a (now standard) pair of outtake discs, condensed to just one on the cheaper package. There's another EP too, following on from that in the *Let It Be* set, this time containing new stereo and original mono mixes of both Paperback Writer and Rain, the single recorded during the same sessions. What's *not* there is a hi-res disc with Dolby Atmos – for that, listeners needed streaming service, Apple Music, which came as a surprise but also meant it was possible for the deluxe box set to be exactly mirrored, for once, by an equivalent vinyl edition.

Superbly packaged, *Revolver* came with a 100-page book to which Paul contributed, and extensive session notes and information, photos and in the case of the outtakes discs, the unused album cover art as designed in 1966 by Robert Freeman.

Available formats:

- Single album containing new album remix. Available on CD or LP.
- Double CD containing new album remix plus selections from the studio outtakes.
- Super Deluxe, five-disc set comprising stereo album remix; two discs of studio outtakes; original mono mix album; and four-track EP. Available on CD or vinyl.

Highlights From The Outtakes Discs

- **Tomorrow Never Known (Mono Mix)**
  Not radically different, but this is the legendary alternative mono mix RM11, which slipped out on a tiny number of original 1966 LP pressings. The instrumental section has noticeably different elements in.

- **Got To Get You Into My Life (Second Version – Unnumbered Mix)**
  This alternative take has some fascinating pitching in the 'oooh' backing vocals, and where the brass is normally heard, George is playing the riffs on lead guitar, to make it more of a band version.

- **Love You To (Take 1)**
  Another legendary outtake, AKA Granny Smith, and not heard until now – this is George's acoustic guitar demo of the song, and it's an amazing listen.

- **Love You To (Take 7)**
  A fantastic take, differentiated from the *Revolver* version by some harmonies from Paul, tracking George at an interval of a sixth, as opposed to the drone effect on the original album.

- **And Your Bird Can Sing (First Version – Take 2)**
  This is the superb guitar-riffed arrangement we had on *Anthology*,
  but whereas that release carried a superimposed 'laughing' vocal,
  this has a 'straight' vocal, actually only a guide but effectively
  presenting the song as it was originally conceived. (The 'laughing'
  version immediately follows it, so we have both!) This is arguably
  the best alternate take ever.

- **Yellow Submarine (Songwriting Work Tape Part 1)**
  If finding Let It Be on *The White Album* tapes was a revelation, this
  is no less so – everyone thought Yellow Submarine was Paul's
  baby until this appeared. It's John sketching out *his* song on
  acoustic guitar, 'In the place where I was born, no-one cared, no-
  one cared'.

- **Here, There And Everywhere (Take 6)**
  Simple, honest version in an uncluttered take. This was previously
  heard on the Real Love single (where it was described as take 7,
  incidentally), but 'there' it was artificially decorated with backing
  vocals whereas 'here' it is in its original, unadorned state.

And so, at least for now, we end this survey. At the time of writing,
Revolver was the last thing issued, but there is little doubt there will be
more Beatles repackagings to come, and we look forward to them. This
book will, therefore, suffer the inevitable fate of continually going out of
date. There's nothing much we can do about that, except maybe an
updated edition will appear one of these days...

Listings

A few of the releases discussed in this book fall into more than one category, eg the 1980 *Beatles Box* which is both a box set and a compilation. Where box sets are concerned, there is a persistent habit of repeatedly giving them bland names like *Singles Collection*, so here and there we have added some explanatory pointers in square brackets. Numbers to the left indicate page numbers in this book.

Compilation albums

Album box sets

EP box sets

Singles box sets

'New' singles

Studio outtakes collections

Remix albums

Live recordings

*These releases only include a limited number of live recordings

Download/streaming-only

Others

Appendix: Worldwide

This book focuses on releases in the UK and US, but there were several compilation albums put out in other countries too. Most overseas territories released the albums coming out of Britain on their own local labels. However since Beatlemania only spread worldwide in 1964, many of them were playing catch-up and assembled belated albums of their own, made up of 1962-1964 tracks which they'd not yet issued. We won't count these as compilations in the usual sense, and restrict the following to LPs consisting of material already released in that country.

The albums included here are not exhaustive, but do include practically all those of note. Sometimes these sorts of compilations were re-issued with different titles in different countries, in some cases with the odd track change, and we need not be obsessive about documenting every known variation of them all. These are the main ones, and they cover the period which in this book, we called the Vinyl Age – which is to say, those released on record prior to 1987 when the Beatles' international catalogue was standardised.

The Beatles Beat (West Germany, April 1964)
The Big Beat Of The Beatles (South Africa, 1964)
The Beatles' Hottest Hits (Denmark, April 1965)
The Beatles' Greatest (West Germany, July 1965)
The Beatles Greatest Hits Volume 1 (Australia, June 1966)
The Beatles Greatest Hits Volume 2 (Australia, February 1967)
The Beatles (West Germany, 1967)
Por Siempre Beatles (Spain, October 1971)
The Essential Beatles (Australia/New Zealand, 1972)
Golden Greatest Hits (West Germany, 1978)
20 Golden Hits (Europe, 1979)
62-65 (Czechoslovakia, 1981)
Expedice R'n'R (Czechoslovakia, 1983)
A Taste Of Honey (USSR, 1986)

The Beatles Beat (West Germany, April 1964)

She Loves You	Can't Buy Me Love
Thank You Girl	You Can't Do That
From Me To You	Roll Over Beethoven
I'll Get You	Till There Was You
I Want To Hold Your Hand	Money
Hold Me Tight	Please Mr Postman

Likely the world's first true Beatles compilation album, containing 11 tracks which had already been issued on West German singles as either A- or B-sides. There is one odd man out, Till There Was You, which wasn't on seven-inch. This collection was re-released a number of times in different sleeves, with titles like *And Now: The Beatles* and, simply, *The Beatles*.

The Big Beat Of The Beatles (South Africa, 1964)

Can't Buy Me Love	I Want To Hold Your Hand
She Loves You	From Me To You
Love Me Do	Ask Me Why
This Boy	I'll Get You
You Can't Do That	Thank You Girl
I Wanna Be Your Man	

Competing with the West German album as the first of its kind, this is not a typical catch-up collection but a compilation of already-released singles. (I Wanna Be Your Man was the only track not on an existing South Africa 45.) It shares seven track choices with its West German equivalent, since the hit singles were generally the same in each country. The album cover is, of course, based on the US *Second Album* of April 1964.

The Beatles' Hottest Hits (Denmark, April 1965)

I Feel Fine
I Call Your Name
I'll Get You
From Me To You
This Boy
She Loves You
Long Tall Sally
Thank You Girl
Matchbox
She's A Woman
Slow Down
I Want To Hold Your Hand

A survey of the Danish discography as of April 1965 reveals exactly one dozen tracks released on singles and EPs, but not on album. (These included the four tracks on *Long Tall Sally*, which Denmark had also issued.) This compiles them all and thus forms a complement to the studio albums, tailored to the Danish market. This set was also issued in Sweden as *The Beatles' Greatest Hits* and was then picked up in Italy and issued in July as *The Beatles In Italy* – a record sometimes mistaken for a live album due to its cover photo of the group on stage. In Italy, She Loves You / I'll Get You were swapped out and replaced by the new single, Ticket To Ride / Yes It Is. Later in the year the album was issued again in Argentina, who called it *Los Beatles* and removed I Call Your Name in favour of, again, Ticket To Ride.

The Beatles' Greatest (West Germany, July 1965)

I Want To Hold Your Hand	I Feel Fine
Twist And Shout	Rock And Roll Music
A Hard Day's Night	Ticket To Ride
Eight Days A Week	Please Please Me
I Should Have Known Better	It Won't Be Long
Long Tall Sally	From Me To You
She Loves You	Can't Buy Me Love
Please Mr Postman	All My Loving

This album seems to have been a commercial success since it was issued out in multiple countries over the following couple of years, sometimes in a different sleeve. It serves as a sequel to West Germany's *The Beatles Beat*, but repeats five of the tracks including the hits, From Me To You, She Loves You, I Want To Hold Your Hand and A Hard Day's Night, and together with the new selections better constitutes a best-of. West Germany themselves kept it in production until into the 1980s, with an attractive sleeve change along the way (above). It's probably the most successful of the overseas compilations to come out of the 1960s.

The Beatles Greatest Hits Volumes 1 and 2

(Australia, June 1966; February 1967)

Please Please Me	A Hard Day's Night
From Me To You	Boys
She Loves You	I Should Have Known Better
I'll Get You	I Feel Fine
I Want To Hold Your Hand	She's A Woman
Love Me Do	Till There Was You
I Saw Her Standing There	Rock And Roll Music
Twist And Shout	Anna (Go To Him)
Roll Over Beethoven	Ticket To Ride
All My Loving	Eight Days A Week
Hold Me Tight	Help!
Can't Buy Me Love	Yesterday
You Can't Do That	We Can Work It Out
Long Tall Sally	Day Tripper

The first of these albums compiled tracks released on Australian 45s, some of them B-sides, with a few more from the EPs. As a collection, it is not fully comprehensive for its time, only going up to 1964, and so *volume 2* appeared in 1967 and ran through the best singles and EP tracks from 1964 and 1965. It's interesting to note that between these two volumes, Australia also issued *A Collection Of Beatles Oldies*, meaning three new compilations in nine months. They were piling up the comps again in 1973, when both volumes of this release were put out as a double album, just ahead of *1962-1966* and *1967-1970*.

The Beatles (West Germany, 1967)

Eight Days A Week	Girl
Rock And Roll Music	Eleanor Rigby
No Reply	Things We Said Today
And Your Bird Can Sing	Yellow Submarine
Good Day Sunshine	Michelle
All My Loving	If I Fell
And I Love Her	I Should Have Known Better
A Hard Day's Night	Dr Robert

This compilation, yet another from West Germany, has a convoluted history, initially appearing on the book club label, Deutscher Schallplattenclub, and then being re-issued on Fono-Ring as *Great Hits*, in a different cover and with a few track switches. S*R International put a third version out in 1968 in another new cover, this time calling it *The World's Best* and reinstating the original track listing. (The Netherlands also put it out in yet another new sleeve, on the Dutch Parlophone label.)

It was never taken up by the West German EMI-Odeon label, who kept going with *The Beatles' Greatest* throughout.

Por Siempre Beatles (Spain, October 1971)

Day Tripper	Your Mother Should Know
Yes It Is	Penny Lane
I'm Down	Baby, You're A Rich Man
The Fool On The Hill	I Call Your Name
Strawberry Fields Forever	The Inner Light
We Can Work It Out	Blue Jay Way

The first notable compilation after the Beatles' official split, this Spanish creation used the *White Album* photos for its cover. Capturing many of the group's non-album singles from 1965 onwards it makes a decent complement to *Hey Jude*, and in its day was the only album anywhere to include The Inner Light or I'm Down. However it wasn't sizable enough to capture *all* the singles, and so tracks like You Know My Name (Look Up The Number) and the 45 versions of Get Back and Let It Be slipped between the cracks. (It might have been better to include those at the expense of the *Magical Mystery Tour* tracks, which were not complete anyway.)

When issued in Argentina, it acted as a sequel to their *Los Beatles*, the Argentinian edition of the 1965 Danish album, *The Beatles' Hottest Hits* (see page 270), and it also scooped up I Call Your Name which had been shunted off *Los Beatles*. The album was re-issued in other South American countries in 1972, with its title translated to *Beatles Forever*.

The Essential Beatles (Australia/New Zealand, 1972)

Love Me Do	Penny Lane
Boys	Magical Mystery Tour
Long Tall Sally	Norwegian Wood
Honey Don't	With A Little Help From My Friends
PS I Love You	All You Need Is Love
Baby, You're A Rich Man	Something
All My Loving	Ob-La-Di, Ob-La-Da
Yesterday	Let It Be

This compilation was issued simultaneously in Australia and New Zealand, and has the added attraction of being on the Apple label. (Those with an interest in technical variations will note that it contains a unique edit of With A Little Help From My Friends, which fades in at the start.) As an overview of the group's career, it's somewhat lopsided, containing both Love Me Do and PS I Love You from 1962, but equally only two tracks from the whole of 1963, and no fewer than five from 1967. In among it all are three Ringo lead vocals, an unusually high tally, but only one from George.

The album went top 10 on the Australian charts.

Golden Greatest Hits (West Germany, 1978)

Twist And Shout	Help!
Ob-La-Di, Ob-La-Da	Lady Madonna
Ticket To Ride	Yesterday
Let It Be	We Can Work It Out
Paperback Writer	Hey Jude
Penny Lane	Sgt Pepper's Lonely Hearts Club
Day Tripper	Band-With A Little Help
All You Need Is Love	From My Friends

Despite its odd title, this album was another major hit which was created in West Germany but also issued in other countries. There's no rhyme nor reason to the track listing which, for example, sandwiches Ob-La-Di, Ob-La-Da between Twist And Shout and Ticket To Ride, but it includes a good selection of major hits.

20 Golden Hits (Europe, 1979)

She Loves You	All You Need Is Love
I Want To Hold Your Hand	Penny Lane
Can't Buy Me Love	Sgt Pepper's Lonely Hearts Club
A Hard Day's Night	Band-With A Little Help
Ticket To Ride	From My Friends
Help!	Lady Madonna
Something	Paperback Writer
We Can Work It Out	Ob-La-Di, Ob-La-Da
Michelle	Yesterday
Hey Jude	Get Back
	Here Comes The Sun
	Let It Be

The West German *Golden Greatest Hits* seems to have spawned a second album the following year – *20 Golden Hits* being essentially an expanded version of same. There were a few changes, the LP losing Day Tripper, Lucy In The Sky With Diamonds and Twist And Shout, but gaining eight additional tracks, including Something and She Loves You. The West German pressing of this reinvention exists on Apple, unusually so for 1979, since the label was supposedly in mothballs by then. It was released in several European countries in different sleeves, and later made its way across the continents. It may also have served as a template for the London-sanctioned *20 Greatest Hits* album of 1982.

62-65 (Czechoslovakia, 1981)

Love Me Do	I Want To Hold Your Hand
Please Please Me	Can't Buy Me Love
Ask Me Why	You Can't Do That
From Me To You	A Hard Day's Night
She Loves You	Things We Said Today
I'll Get You	I Feel Fine
All My Loving	Eight Days A Week
This Boy	Yes It Is
	Ticket To Ride

Czechoslovakia released only one Beatles record in the 1960s: *A Collection Of Beatles Oldies* which appeared in 1969. It was followed in 1972 by *Abbey Road* and a couple of singles, so come the 1980s they had plenty of catching up to do. This Czech-only compilation focuses on the Beatlemania era, and whoever compiled it knew which tracks to go for, the LP containing all the major hits from the period and often their B-sides too – although Yesterday is curiously overlooked. It appeared on the Supraphon label. (The cover photo, incidentally, is from the same shoot as that used on the cassette, *Their Greatest Hits*, in 1984 – see page 102.)

Expedice R'n'R (Czechoslovakia, 1983)

Rock And Roll Music	Twist And Shout
Long Tall Sally	Kansas City
Dizzy Miss Lizzy	Honey Don't
Slow Down	A Taste Of Honey
Chains	Mr. Moonlight
Baby It's You	Money
Boys	Please Mr Postman
Everybody's Trying To Be My Baby	Words Of Love

This has to be one of the most surprising Beatles compilations, issued again in Czechoslovakia where the group was apparently catching on 20 years too late.

Beatles experts will recognise the theme at once: this consists solely of cover versions recorded by the Beatles for EMI. However it's not simply a reinvention of *Rock 'N' Roll Music*, since it contains seven tracks not on that earlier album, including slower material such as Baby It's You and Words Of Love. For its source material it scours *Please Please Me*, *With The Beatles*, *Beatles For Sale* and *Help!* as well as grabbing two tracks from the *Long Tall Sally* EP. Expedice, incidentally, means 'expedition' in Czech, so the album title is (roughly) *Rock And Roll Expedition* – or maybe, *Journey Into Rock And Roll*.

A Taste Of Honey (USSR, 1986)

PS I Love You	I Don't Want To Spoil The Party
Do You Want To Know A Secret	Rock And Roll Music
A Taste Of Honey	Please Mr Postman
I Saw Her Standing There	It Won't Be Long
Baby's In Black	Till There Was You
No Reply	Little Child
I'll Follow The Sun	Devil In Her Heart
Eight Days A Week	I Wanna Be Your Man

Beatles compilations come to the Soviet Union! Perhaps following the Czech lead, this assemblage of 16 tracks dating from 1963-1964 was issued on the Melodiya label. It is of course a compilation not of hit singles, but of selections from the studio albums, *Please Please Me*, *With The Beatles* and *Beatles For Sale*. (There was no need to include anything from *A Hard Day's Night* since that album was simultaneously issued in USSR on its own.) Although a few Beatles tracks had been released there previously on single or flexi-disc, these were the first Soviet Beatles albums.

By the same author

An in-depth discussion of the Beatles' 'second phase', taking a look into all the individual studio recordings by John, Paul, George and Ringo before the group's legal dissolution at the end of 1974.

Covering every track from the first 18 solo albums including:
John Lennon/Plastic Ono Band, All Things Must Pass, RAM, Imagine, Ringo, Living In The Material World, Band On The Run, Walls And Bridges
… and many more!

Printed in Great Britain
by Amazon